Castle. Warm summer ...

...enged to HE Wire Spid... ...

blue den spider and missed...

... shrimps tumbled off the...

...she nest tunnel in use - b...

Hemp agrimony growing on ban...

...table morning. Dead badger...

Process reel very good combine...

...old. Arrived at 9:30 with Clive. ...

I caught 4 - actually 3 since ...

...hackle. A really good morning.

... + adequate lunch on farm...

...corner - upstream + stripping a...

...ck Spider. Visible fis...

ANGLING WITH THE FLY

ANGLING WITH THE FLY

Flies & Anglers of Derbyshire and Staffordshire

J N WATSON

First published in 2008 by
Ken Smith Publishing Limited

UK Smith Settle, Gateway Drive, Yeadon, West Yorkshire LS19 7XY
France Chavagnac, 16260 Cellefrouin, Charente

ISBN 978 1 906159 02 3

Design : Ken Smith
Typesetting, repro : Ron Farnworth
Ronset, Blackburn, Lancashire

Printed in China by
1010 Printing International Ltd

FOR ANNE

CONTENTS

LIST OF ILLUSTRATIONS

LIST OF FLY PLATES

NOTE TO THE ILLUSTRATIONS

The author and publishers offer their thanks to those who have allowed reproduction of items in their collections or who have supplied photographs for reproduction. All photographs and reproductions from original books have been taken from the author's own collection with the exception of those noted hereunder:

Ashley Bryant, watercolours and vignettes: frontispiece and pages 2, 34, 41, 82, 194, 197, 280; K. Smith, loan of original copies for reproduction: Aldam's *Quaint Treatise*, Ronalds' *The Fly Fishers Entomology*, Terry Griffiths, photography of flies: pages 138, 187, 252 and 16 fly plates: pages 49, 106, 108, 114-115, 118-119, 124-125, 128-129, 132-133, 158-173; Margaret Gilbert, fly vignettes: pages 139, 143, 146; John Neville, loan of Heywood's *Charles Cotton and His River* and photo, page 231; Colleen and Vic Benson, photo of Roger Woolley, page 224, and Woolley's dressing notes page 252; A K Bridgett, photo page 233; Steve Trigg, Steve Woolley, Tim Thorpe, Peter Arfield and Peak Forest Angling Club for photography by John Watson pages 234, 236, 238 and 301; Noel Smith, photo of Donald Mackenzie, page 245, and loan of letter, page 246; the Duke of Devonshire, copy of Chatsworth Fishery Report, page 287.

ACKNOWLEDGEMENTS

The transition of this work from an idea to a reality has only been made possible through the help of a number of organisations and individuals. All have been generous in their valued contributions. My thanks and appreciation go to:

The British Library at Thorpe Arch, whose staff have been both helpful and courteous in accessing research material; The Cromford Fly Fisher's Club, Derby County Angling Club, Leek and District Fly Fishing Association and Peak Forest Angling Club for information about the rivers and to their officials who gave advice, access to waters and encouragement; The Devonshire Collection, especially Stuart Band and Andrew Peppit, for their efforts in accessing material and permission to reproduce items; Haddon Estate for permission to photograph stretches of the Wye and Lathkill, also for advice and research regarding the portrait of the Marquess of Granby; the Environment Agency, via Mavis Atkin and Alan Brown, for resources and maps; the staff of Matlock Local Studies and Archive departments for their expert assistance in locating information; the Peacock Hotel at Rowsley for permission to reproduce a selection of fly patterns purchased there by the author.

I particularly thank those who have trusted a complete stranger with their valuable books, artefacts, family papers, photographs, flies, dressings and experience, but above all for their enthusiasm, goodwill and time. Allowing their material to be researched, quoted or used has been immensely helpful for without it this would have been a very slim volume indeed: Peter Arfield, Bakewell Fly Fishing Shop; John Austin; Colleen and Victor Benson; Tony Bridgett, Leek and District Fly Fishing Association; Julie Bunting, Peak Advertising; Michael Collins; Terry Griffiths; Vernon Hall; Paul Hughes, Vinovium Books; Colin Jones, Peak Forest Angling Club; Ian Kilgour; Paul MacCormaic; Barbara Myatt; Mike Nash; John Neville; John Pass, The Cromford Fly Fisher's Club; Paul Procter; Warren Slaney, Haddon Estate; Noel Smith; David Stretton, The Cromford Fly Fisher's Club; Tim Thorpe, Derbyshire Fishing Flies; Walter Thorpe; Steve Trigg; Richard Ward; Stephen Woolley, rodmaker, Ashbourne.

Graham Walker and John Pattison for their technical help in the wonderland of word processing; Gordon Evans for gifts of books and tackle over many years which otherwise would have been practically unobtainable, also for the bankside hours sipping Mulligatawny and sometimes catching fish.

Margaret Gilbert for rising admirably to my request to paint some fly patterns and for being tolerant, appearing attentive, even interested, when the author discussed them.

Ashley Bryant, with whom I have shared so many adventures, for painting the lovely watercolours of the Manifold, Dove, Derwent, Fishing House and the natural insects. His advice, enthusiasm and friendship have been invaluable in the preparation and completion of this work.

Clive Harris, my angling partner, whose on-coming old age initially inspired this project. He has provided critical appraisal, encouragement, good humour and delicious angling picnics. His roll casts are a delight to behold and he is awfully good at falling in.

Ken Smith, my publisher, for expertise, guidance and patience in the face of my naivety and incompetence in matters literary; in addition for the loan of books and permission to quote material.

To those I have been unable to locate, and those I have omitted to mention, I offer my apologies and will remedy such omissions should the opportunity arise in the future.

My wife, Anne, has been my constant support and without her encouragement I would never have begun to write.

FOREWORD

'It just goes to show! You learn something new every day…….'

In the context of *Angling With The Fly*, this old saying is a not very ambitious one. The years of painstaking research and detective work that John Watson has invested, on your behalf, has resulted in a veritable treasury of fascinating and extraordinarily useful information!

Gathering together a personal library of all the works referred to herein would take decades of searching, and require an outlay of many thousands of pounds, just for the published works alone. You are holding in your hands a lot more than a simple collection, or mere compendium. John's work has uncovered much that would have been lost forever, had he not searched out living relatives and friends of Staffordshire and Derbyshire fly fishers; skilful and creative anglers, whose names have already passed into legend.

Samples from angling notebooks, recollections from memory, even fly boxes still filled with delightful artificials, as if they were about to be slipped into a pocket for a day's sport on some Peakland river, have been retrieved from obscurity. John marshals them before us to bear witness on behalf of their previous, influential owners.

Seekers of truth will enjoy themselves within these pages; John does a lot of setting the record straight. Did you know, for instance, that an angler from Derbyshire was probably the first angler to tie flies deliberately intended to float? Or that, in the seventeenth century, Charles Cotton and his contemporaries caught fish with flies that were floating, two hundred years before F M Halford popularised the 'dry fly'? You may be amazed to learn that one of our greatest fly fishing forebears once built himself a fish observatory over the river Blythe. In the pursuit of his observations, he went so far as to set off firearms in an effort to determine whether fish might hear anglers if they chatted together on the bank! These and many other surprises await you within……..

Regular Rod

Bakewell 2008

Away to the brook
All your tackle outlook
Here's a day that is worth a year's wishing;
See that all things be right,
For 'tis very a spite
To want tools when a man goes a-fishing

The Angler's Ballad   *Charles Cotton*

INTRODUCTION

Water has always attracted my attention. I have been drawn to brooks, rivers, lakes, even large puddles, as long as I can remember. Each time the question recurs. What is in there?

Early in my childhood my father built a pond in our garden, no doubt as a result of my prompting. Once filled, it was stocked with the results of expeditions to the local canal. The plants acquired brought with them aquatic travellers, such that, as the water cleared, strange creatures could be seen on and beneath the surface. With my mother's supervision and encouragement I was allowed to dip the pond, though not too frequently. The net was made from a brush handle, wire rim and linen flour bag; our examination tray, a white enamel pie dish. My interest and knowledge grew and, thanks to one incident, so did respect. A large dragonfly nymph attached to a tender finger is an effective teacher. A neighbour provided some very small goldfish and my regular daily visit wore out the lawn by the pool edge.

New birds were attracted to the garden along with frogs and a variety of insects. The first dragonfly hawking above the water created great excitement and fascination. I remembered the nymph and it seemed incredible to a young mind that the ferocious nymph became the rustling helicopter.

Further investigations followed. Accompanied by my mother, as tutor and security system, I was allowed to visit the canal. Here the net brought up larger numbers of fauna, including some new species. The small fish, shoaled up in the margins, were very difficult to catch, despite considerable efforts and the odd bootfull. Larger fish swirled and dimpled the surface by the far bank and were very interesting. An angler we had passed on previous visits actually caught a fish as we watched. He will be fishing greater waters now, but that day he not only landed a lovely roach, but also caught a small boy's imagination and made an angler for life.

My father was persuaded to make a fishing rod. He was a shooter, and had never fished, but he produced a valiant effort. It was made from the longest cane we could find, with copper wire rings bound on with adhesive tape. A small tackle shop on Nottingham Road, near the canal, supplied an alloy centre pin, silk line, float and hooks to gut. I like to think I still have the porcupine float bought that day but it is almost certainly wishful thinking. With my new tackle the canal was visited once, twice, thrice but without success. While I fished, one or other of my parents patiently sat and read, awaiting the next tangle.

Throughout this angling apprenticeship, my walks to and from school usually followed the course of the brook through the local park. Small though it was, stoneloach, bullheads and a few sticklebacks inhabited its pools and bends. These were successfully netted at weekends but the weekday results of the daily journey were too often wet feet. A serious

The Derwent, Ford Lane Bridge, Allestree.

matter on the way to school. Waterskaters and whirlygig beetles cruised the surface in quiet places, and beneath the waterfall by the road bridge big fish were alleged to reside.

One Saturday my father took me to Allestree Park and the rod went with us, sticking out of the car window. It was a warm summer afternoon and my worm-baited tackle was cast from the first of the wooden footbridges, which then crossed the top lake. It settled close to some low overhanging alder branches. The float cocked and almost immediately bobbed and slid away. The throb of the fish was transmitted through the stiff rod and it was safely landed. Two other perch followed the first that day.

Eventually we moved to Allestree, the lakes and then the river Derwent at Home Farm becoming regular and favourite haunts. My first trout was caught in the Derwent below Ford Lane bridge while fishing for minnows. These were used for perch or pike bait. Some little time later, on a visit to an uncle in Sheffield, I was taken to Dam Flask reservoir. Here I caught several rainbows on bait but saw fish caught on fly.

By now proper tackle had gradually been accumulated, but pocket money was scarce and more tackle desired. Together with a close friend, I began to make as much tackle as possible at home. We spent many winter evenings in shed or garage constructing rods, boxes, floats, nets and even trying to tie flies. It was cold but very enjoyable activity and, when fish were caught on 'our' tackle, very rewarding. And so it remains today. We still make time to fish the Derwent a couple of times a year. Now a professional artist, Ashley contributed the paintings in this book, along with encouragement and advice.

Angling took me out into the countryside and created two further interests; botany and ornithology. The three activities are now inseparable, complementing one another on each visit to river, lake or loch. The momentary distraction caused by a passing dipper or kingfisher has cost the chance of many fish, but delights as it always has, and always will. Visits to the rivers in the limestone dales are still enhanced by rediscovering sites of Jacob's Ladder and Nottingham Catchfly.

Preoccupation with tench and pike gave way to one of grayling and trout. Strangely, the first grayling I caught was below Ford Lane bridge on the Derwent, the same place I caught my first trout. The two events were separated by teens of years. In that same stretch of water my daughter caught minnows and crayfish, though there were none of the latter when I fished there as a boy.

As with others, fly fishing came to me first through still waters. Ladybower beckoned for many years and still has its attractions. Scottish lochs and Welsh lakes yielded their wild fish and inspiring scenery. Finally the mysteries of upstream wet, across and down began to unravel and become familiar. Different materials and much smaller hooks appeared on my fly dressing bench. Small hackles, nymphs and dry flies filled the fly case and my journeys took me to the Derwent, Manifold, Wharfe and Nidd.

Oncoming old age was the genesis of this book. It began as a collection of local fly patterns for my fishing partner's sixtieth birthday. I would simply collect a dozen or fifteen dressings used in the Derwent and Dove watersheds. These would then be described regarding their origin and dressing, the flies dressed and all presented in a wooden case.

I began the research with my own books. One of these, *Fishing in Derbyshire and Around* (1905) by W M Gallichan, should, I thought, provide sufficient material and advice. Having re-read the book I found difficulty in determining, 'What is a local pattern?'. I decided the criteria would be those patterns tied by local anglers, keepers or dealers for Derbyshire and Staffordshire waters. This, of course, entailed much more research. The more I sought simplicity, the more complex the project became. The inventors of dressings were inseparable from their products and so the anglers themselves were to be included. By now it had become a reference document for our own use, but others suggested that it may be of interest to a wider audience.

Research had revealed a number of authors, much of whose work was based in Derbyshire or Staffordshire. These books had been written over a time scale of about 250 years. The extraction of traditional and local patterns provoked both thought and discussion, but eventually six authors were selected. All had considerable experience of the Derwent and Dove watersheds. They also lived near or had spent a great deal of time on the respective rivers.

From the fly lists given by these anglers I selected the patterns common to them all. These form the group of patterns I have called 'Traditional' flies and include the Derbyshire Bumbles. A second group were collected; these being patterns tied by local anglers, waterkeepers, fly dressers and regular visitors. These are referred to as 'Specialities'. Being local patterns, they would not have survived had they not been useful and successful flies. Where relevant, information about their originators has been included in the text. Some of these are the personal local patterns of those who have contributed to the 'Flybox' section of this project. A third list, Standard and Modern Flies, consists of those nationwide, even worldwide, patterns used by regulars on the region's rivers. Along with the flies, a wealth of information about tackle, fly dressing styles, rivers and angling accommodation has emerged. Where these are complementary they have been included.

The first clear record of angling in Derbyshire and Staffordshire is that of Charles Cotton in Part II of the fifth edition of *The Compleat Angler,* printed in 1676 and the last edition published in Izaak Walton's lifetime. The dialogue and action of Viator and Piscator takes place in the localities of Ashbourne and Beresford Dale, but specifically on the Dove. Largely as a result of the publicity afforded by the many editions of *The Compleat Angler*, Ashbourne and its nearby rivers became, for nearly two centuries, one of the main angling centres of the country.

The giants of the piscatorial art visited Dovedale, Beresford Dale and the Manifold. Izaak Walton, Sir John Hawkins, Sir Humphrey Davy, Charles Bowlker, John Turton, T C Hofland; all travelled far on horseback or by coach to fish the rivers. Later came W H Aldam, Sir Edward Grey, F M Halford, John Bickerdyke (C H Cook), G E M Skues and R B Marston. Along with them were the 'locals', Cotton, Ronalds, Shipley, Foster, Granby and Gallichan.

Matlock, too, became a place for anglers to gather, along with artists, tourists and those 'taking the waters.' The Derwent, whilst very different from the Dove, was a productive and interesting river in which to fish. In addition its tributaries, the Wye, Lathkill and Bradford provided most attractive alternatives. Parts of the Dove and Derwent tributaries were, over many years, altered by their owners and leasees to create a better environment for angling. Low weirs and dams were built which slowed the flow, made pools with runs between them and provided cover for fish. With them also came some alteration, in aquatic and marginal plants along with new habitats for insect life. On the Dove, lack of maintenance is now resulting in the river reverting to its more natural form, as the weirs begin to deteriorate. In one way a good idea, but it does seem a pity to allow what is long term 'angling architecture' on an historic piece of water to gradually collapse and disappear. Flora and fauna have adapted to the 'new' conditions and created a stable, if man made, environment.

There are other changes. Anglers who have fished the Dove and Manifold for over forty years report a noticeable fall in the numbers of insects. Tony Bridgett gives a telling example. A fly which anglers did not really bother with years ago, the Hawthorn, is now eagerly anticipated by anglers, in the absence of other species such as the Iron Dun. On the other hand, migratory fish have been seen in the lower Derwent, even as high as Belper, and also in the Dove.

Transport improved with the coming of the railways and Derbyshire towns provided all manner of accommodation, from the palatial to boarding houses with 'clean linen'. Access to water was often offered to resident anglers of these establishments free of charge or at reduced rates. Both the Dove and Derwent valleys had their keepers and professional fishermen who acted as guides and tackle suppliers to visiting anglers. These were the men, and at least one lady, who also provided speciality fly patterns for their clients.

The upland rough water streams gave rise, as in Yorkshire, to a style of fly dressing which is rather thin and sparse in body, hackle and wing. Patterns were handed on by word of mouth or by written manuscript at first. In the early to mid-nineteenth century, there appeared a number of publications allowing those able to afford and read them, access to a wider range of patterns and methods. This may well have contributed to the formalisation of local patterns and specialities some of which undoubtedly became standard flies.

Until the latter half of the 1850s, fishing a dry fly meant allowing a fly to fish on the surface before it became wet and sank. Some anglers, having noticed that these flies caught trout, began to develop the idea. James Ogden was one of the first and tied floating mayfly patterns. These created quite a stir on the Wye at Bakewell when first used. Over the next thirty years, others became interested in 'dry fly angling'. The work of H S Hall, G S Marryat and F M Halford on the southern chalk streams eventually led to the decline in influence of northern rivers, methods and anglers. The method of using an imitative fly, cast upstream, to a specific feeding fish became, for many, the only way to fish.

Dry flies, which could be expected to float reliably, filled a gap in the angler's calendar. Wet fly was fished very successfully until the end of May on most rivers. With the mayfly hatch fish became disinterested in subsurface aquatic food, to partake in the Drake feast. At this time anglers traditionally fished live mayfly on special hooks by dibbling or dapping. There was an influx into the angling centres at Bakewell, Ashbourne and Matlock at mayfly time to partake in the sport. After the mayfly through July, fish are difficult to catch in the daytime. Reasons have long been proposed for this phenomenon. High light levels result in increased awareness by fish of bank-side activity, coupled with reluctance to leave shady lies. Low water levels and reduced hatching and emerging of insects compound the problem.

Worm, minnow and caddis fishing would no doubt be held irresponsible on many waters today, but as far back as Cotton, and probably before, these were the methods used to catch fish over this period of inactivity. The dry fly largely filled this gap, being very successful in early morning and evening. Many older books have illustrations of anglers waiting for the rise as they would not, or were not allowed, to fish the hackle or wet fly. Dry fly found its adherents on the Derbyshire and Staffordshire rivers too, this being the period when much of the weir or dam building took place. In addition, hatcheries and model fisheries were created to supplement depleted wild stocks, as most fish caught were killed. Some waters were very highly stocked to ensure sport for the owners and their guests.

The fly pattern used by anglers also altered to accommodate the dry fly method. To a large extent, this eclipsed further development of traditional patterns where dry fly was used. There would be little need for local specialities on rivers which became 'Dry'. On rough water streams the wet fly and hackles were, and still are, fished but the success of dry fly was often at the expense of more traditional local methods of angling.

There is still a vital place in the methods used by fly fishers for these traditional flies and styles. It is arguable that there is as much skill in upstream wet fly fishing as upstream dry, nor does across and down have to be an affair of 'chuck it and chance it'. Most experienced fly anglers agree that presentation usually comes before either size or colour of fly. As will be seen, there is no shortage of suitable traditional and speciality local patterns to try in their 'home' waters.

CHAPTER ONE

ANGLER-AUTHORS OF DERBYSHIRE AND STAFFORDSHIRE 1676 - 1882

CHARLES COTTON

Charles Cotton was born at Beresford Hall near Hartington on the Derbyshire-Staffordshire border in April 1630. His father Charles Cotton senior was the squire of Beresford and Bentley, having acquired the estate by marriage to Olive Stanhope, daughter of Sir John Stanhope of Elvaston.

Cotton fished the Dove from childhood. He received a classical education spending some time at Cambridge University in the footsteps of his father. During his youth he had a considerable reputation as both spendthrift and rake, also writing poetry which many considered obscene. It should be added that others thought it a delight. He was a Royalist courtier and after the Restoration received a commission from Charles the Second for services rendered to the King in exile.

In 1658 the elder Charles died. With the inheritance of the Beresford and Bentley estates, came associated debts for which Cotton was pursued. In this period he spent his time between Beresford and London. Eventually he deserted the capital and settled in Derbyshire, allegedly hiding in Cotton's Cave from time to time in order to avoid the attentions of his creditors. No doubt he fished a good deal, catching large numbers of trout.

In 1656 he married Isabella, daughter of his 'kinsman' Sir Thomas Hutchinson. They had five children, a son Beresford, and four daughters. Sadly, his wife died in 1670. Cotton married a second time to Mary, dowager Countess of Ardglass, and daughter of his neighbour.

Cotton's contact with Izaak Walton was probably begun early in his life. Walton and the elder Charles Cotton were known to one another. The younger man and Walton spent time together in London but despite the difference in their ages and attitudes to angling (Walton was a bait fishing coarse angler), they were good friends. The entwined initials over the portal of the Fishing House at Beresford testify to this. The house was built in 1674 and Cotton was most anxious for Izaak Walton to see the building, despite his advancing years and the arduous journey from southern England. In 1676 Charles Cotton received word from Walton that a further edition of *The Compleat Angler* was to

Charles Cotton
Portrait from *The Compleat Angler* (1853 edition)

Charles Cotton's Fishing House
built in Beresford Dale, 1674.
The initials of Cotton and Walton
are entwined as a cipher in the
keystone of the arch.

be produced. This reminded Cotton of his promise to write a second part to the book, about angling with the fly. The printing date had been set for April and the letter with the news arrived in late February or March. Cotton completed *Being Directions how to Angle for Trout and Grayling in a Clear Stream* in something like ten days. His work is often compared to that of Walton as being of poorer literary quality. Small wonder in terms of the speed of its creation!

As a document for anglers it is full of sound instruction, advice and interest, particularly so if the reader dresses flies. It is written in dialogue and narrative form. The journey of Viator and Piscator takes place in March; the descriptions of the weather, daylight and angling conditions reflect this clearly. No doubt in the haste of writing, it would be easier to describe the current time of year. Piscator is portrayed as a most competent angler and fly dresser. The latter he labours to the point of boredom. In *Charles Cotton and His River* (1928), Gerald Heywood admires the patience and tolerance of Viator in this respect. Another comment of Heywood gives an insight into Cotton's importance as an angler:

> (Cotton's work)...*remains to this day the best ever penned for fishing the clear and narrow waters of the upper Dove. Cotton too is the first of the Dove valley school of fly fishers and fly tyers which includes Ronalds, Shipley and David Foster, pioneers who cleared the way for the modern Hampshire school of dry fly entomologists.*

Little wonder that many Derwent and Dove anglers carry at least one fly pattern of Cotton's with them. His 'Black Flie' still regularly swims in both rivers.

The days of angling described with Viator and Piscator are full of incident. Disappointment at lost fish, delight at those caught and amazement at expertise and the scenic setting of Dovedale. Woven into the dialogue are hard advice and sympathetic instruction. There is clear direction on fly dressing including the specifics of tying a good wing.

The 65 patterns are arranged in calendar order with recommendations on how and when to fish them. Cotton evidently collected patterns from others. It is very unlikely he used all the flies he lists. Much time has been spent relating his patterns to modern dressings and natural flies. Some seem very obvious; 'Thorn Tree Fly' and 'Cow Turd Fly,' others obscure 'Dun Cut' or 'Peacock Fly'. Many are well known naturals in a thin disguise. Cotton would have tried to copy from life, as would those who invented the patterns he acquired. I like to think of him as an open-minded naturalist who brought his observations to bear in the dressings of his flies. Heywood highlights Cotton's accuracy in describing the Green Drake.

Viator is instructed that the dressings of the flies should be slim and with appropriate proportions. Cotton wickedly mocks the southern bulky style of dressing. Colours of silk, dubbing and wax are discussed, as is the importance of viewing hackles in the hand and against the light, to check the correct colour and sparkle in the feather.

At the riverside, Charles Cotton was a cautious angler. He made a quiet and stealthy approach and fished with as much bank between himself and the fish as possible. 'Fine and far off', the oft-quoted advice, is still good on clear water streams. Some of this caution was demanded by the limitations of the tackle used. Eighteen-foot rods with fixed lines gave limited range and were unwieldy in use. Cotton was very aware of how easily trout can be put down.

His remarks about lines indicate considerable experiment and trial: three strands of horsehair, it had to be white and glassy, were much too thick. One strand was of insufficient strength. Two, untwisted, led to the fly tangling in the resultant loop. It had to be two strands twisted together. I wonder if he joined the lengths with a 'Water knot' or maybe a 'Staffordshire knot'?

Whilst he liked fishing for trout, he was not complimentary about the sporting qualities of grayling. He considered them 'dead-hearted'. This did not prevent him recommending certain flies for grayling, nor eating them. Preparation and cooking of the catch are detailed, but I have my doubts as to whether Charles, as squire, would have done much of either activity.

The methods of fishing at the 'middle' and 'bottom' are given a brief airing, as are worm, minnow and caddis as bait. Cotton defers to Izaak Walton for those who require more information about these methods, though he obviously was an experienced bait angler.

In 1681 Beresford Hall had to be sold, and was bought by Charles Cotton's cousin, John Beresford of Newton Grange. Little more is known of Cotton. Charles Cotton was a man who enjoyed life. In youth boisterous, perhaps feckless, but in later life a generous man who enjoyed his home, family and environs. He died in 1687 and was buried in St James' church in Piccadilly.

Herewith are his fly patterns in total. These must be considered the basis of the traditional patterns of two counties. Cotton's advised dates of fishing need to be considered. In 1752 the calendar was adjusted eleven days forward. 6th March became 17th March. It has a surprising effect!

JANUARY

1. A red brown, with wings of the male of a mallard almost white: the dubbing of the tail of a black long-coated cur, such as they commonly make muffs of; for the hair on such a dog dies and turns to a red-brown, but the hair of a smooth-coated dog of the same colour will not do, because it will not die, but retains its natural colour, and this fly is taken in a warm sun, this whole month through.

2. There is also a very little bright dun gnat, as little as can possible be made, so little as never to be fished with, with above one hair next the hook; and this is to be made of a mixed dubbing of marten's fur, and the white of a hare's scut; with a very white and small wing; ...

FEBRUARY

1. Where the red-brown of the last month ends, another almost of the same colour begins, with this saving, that the dubbing of this must be of something a blacker colour, and both of them wrapped on with red silk. The dubbing that should make this fly, and that is the truest colour, is to be got off the black spot off a hog's ear; not that a black spot in any part of the hog will not afford the same colour but that the hair in that place is, by many degrees, softer, and more fit for the purpose. His wing must be as the other; and this kills all this month, and is called the lesser red-brown.

2. This month also, a plain hackle, or palmer-fly, made with a rough black body, either of black spaniel's fur, or the whirl of an ostrich feather, and the red hackle of a capon over all, will kill, and, if the weather be right, make very good sport.

3. Also, a lesser hackle, with a black body, also silver twist over that, and a red feather over all, will fill your panier, if the month be open, and not bound up in ice and snow, with very good fish; but, in case of a frost and snow, you are to angle only with the smallest gnats, browns and duns you can make; and with those are only to expect graylings no bigger than sprats.

4. In this month, upon a whirling round water, we have a great hackle, the body black, and wrapped with a red feather of a capon untrimmed; that is, the whole length of the hackle staring out (for we sometimes barb the hackle-feather short all over; sometimes barb it only a little and sometimes barb it close underneath), leaving the whole length of the feather on the top or back of the fly, which makes it swim better, and, as occasion serves, kills very great fish.

5. We make use also, in this month, of another great hackle, the body black, and ribbed over with gold twist, and a red feather over all; which also does great execution.

6. Also a great dun, made with dun bear's hair and the wings of the grey feather of a mallard near unto his tail; which is absolutely the best fly can be thrown upon a river this month, and with which an angler shall have admirable sport.

7. We have also this month the great blue dun, the dubbing of the bottom of a bear's hair next to the roots, mixed with a little blue camlet, the wings of a dark grey feather of a mallard.

8. We have also this month a dark-brown, the dubbing of the brown hair off the flank of a brended cow, and the wings of the grey drake's feather.

For making of a hackle, or palmer-fly, my father Walton has already given you sufficient direction.

MARCH

For this month you are to use all the same hackles and flies with the other; but you are to make them less.

1. We have besides, for this month, a little dun, called a whirling dun (though it is not the whirling dun, indeed, which is one of the best flies we have); and for this the dubbing must be of the bottom fur of a squirrel's tail; and the wing of the grey feather of a drake.

2. Also a bright brown; the dubbing either of the brown of a spaniel, or that of a red cow's flank, with a grey wing.

3. Also a whitish dun; made of the roots of camel's hair; and the wings of the grey feather of a mallard.

4. There is also for this month a fly called the thorn-tree fly: the dubbing an absolute black, mixed with eight or ten hairs of Isabella-coloured mohair; the body as little as can be made; and the wings of a bright mallard's feather. An admirable fly, and in great repute amongst us for a killer.

5. There is, besides this, another blue dun, the dubbing of which it is made being thus to be got. Take a small tooth-comb, and with it comb the neck of a black greyhound, and the down that sticks in the teeth will be the finest blue that ever you saw. The wings of this fly can hardly be too white, and he is taken about the tenth of this month, and lasteth till the four-and-twentieth.

6. From the tenth of this month, also till towards the end, is taken a little black gnat; the dubbing either of the fur of a black water-dog, or the down of a young black water-coot, the wing of the male of a mallard as white as may be, the body as little as you can possibly make it, and the wings as short as his body.

7. From the sixteenth of this month also to the end of it, we use a bright brown; the dubbing for which is to be had out of a skinner's lime-pits, and of the hair of an abortive calf, which the lime will turn to be so bright as to shine like gold; for the wings of this fly, the feather of a brown hen is best; which fly is also taken to the tenth of April.

APRIL

All the same hackles and flies that were taken in March will be taken in this month also, with this distinction only concerning the flies, that all the browns will be lapped with red silk, and the duns with yellow.

1. To these a small bright brown, made of spaniel's fur, with a light grey wing; in a bright day, and a clear water, is very well taken.

2. We have too a little dark brown, the dubbing of that colour, and some violet camlet mixed, and the wing of the grey feather of a mallard.

3. From the sixth of this month to the tenth, we have also a fly called the violet fly, made of a dark violet stuff, with the wing of the grey feather of a mallard.

6

4. About the twelfth of this month comes in the fly called the whirling dun, which is taken every day, about the mid-time of day, all this month through and, by fits, from thence to the end of June, and is commonly made of the down of the fox-cub, which is of an ash colour at the roots next the skin, and ribbed about with yellow silk; the wings of the pale grey feather of a mallard.

5. There is a yellow dun, the dubbing of camel's hair, and yellow camlet or wool, mixed, and a white-grey wing.

6. There is also this month another little brown, besides that mentioned before, made with a very slender body, the dubbing of dark brown and violet camlet mixed, and a grey wing, which, though the direction for the making be near the other, is yet another fly, and will take when the other will not, especially in a bright day and a clear water.

7. About the twentieth of this month comes in a fly called the horse-flesh fly, the dubbing of which is a blue mohair, with pink coloured and red tammy mixed, a light coloured wing, and a dark brown head. This fly is taken best in an evening, and kills from two hours before sunset till twilight, and is taken the month through.

MAY

... know therefore, that the first fly we take notice of this month, is called the turkey-fly;

1. The dubbing ravelled out of some blue stuff, and lapt about with yellow silk; the wings of a grey mallard's feather.

2. Next, a great hackle or palmer fly, with a yellow body ribbed with gold twist, and large wings, of a mallard's feather dyed yellow, with a red capon's hackle overall.

3. Then a black fly, the dubbing of a black spaniel's fur; and the wings of a grey mallard's feather.

4. After that, a light brown, with a slender body, the dubbing twirled upon small red silk and raised with the point of a needle, that the ribs or rows of silk may appear through; the wings, of the grey feather of the mallard.

5. Next, a little dun, the dubbing of a bear's dun whirled upon yellow silk; the wings, of the grey feather of a mallard.

6. Then a white gnat, with a pale wing, a black head.

7. There is also in this month, a fly called the peacock fly; the body made of a whirl of a peacock's feather, with a red head; and the wings of a mallard's feather.

8. We have then another very killing fly, known by the name of the dun-cut; the dubbing of which is a bear's dun, with a little blue and yellow mixed with it; a large dun wing, and two horns at the head, made of the hairs of a squirrel's tail.

9. The next is a cow-lady, a little fly; the body of a peacock's feather; the wing, of a red feather, or strips of the red hackle of a cock.

10. We have then, the cow-turd-fly; the dubbing, light brown and yellow mixed; the wing, the dark grey feather of a mallard. And note, that besides above-mentioned, all the same hackles and flies, the hackles only brighter, and the flies smaller, that are taken in April, will also be taken this month, as also all browns and duns; and now I come to my stone-fly and green-drake, which are the matadors for trout and grayling, and in their season kill more fish in our Derbyshire rivers than all the rest, ...

11. The artificial green-drake, then, is made upon a large hook, the dubbing, camel's hair, bright bear's hair, the soft down that is combed from a hog's bristles, and yellow camlet, well mixed together; the body long, and ribbed about with green silk, or rather yellow, waxed with green wax; the whisks of tail, of the long hairs of sables, or fitchet; and the wings, of a white-grey feather of a mallard, dyed yellow, ...

12. I should now come next to the stone-fly, but there is another gentleman in my way, that must of necessity come in between, and that is the gray-drake,... which fly is thus made, the dubbing of the down of a hog's bristles, and black spaniel's fur mixed, and ribbed down the body with black silk, the whisks of the hairs of the beard of a black cat, and the wings of the black-grey feather of a mallard.

13. This same stone-fly, _is to be made thus; the dubbing of bear's dun, with a little brown and yellow camlet very well mixed, but so placed that your fly may be more yellow on the belly and towards the tail, underneath, than in any other part; and you are to place two or three hairs of a black cat's beard on top of the hook, in your arming, so as to be turned up when you warp on your dubbing, and to stand almost upright, and staring one from another; and note that your fly is to be ribbed with yellow silk; and the wings long and very large, of the dark grey feather of a mallard.

14. The next May-fly is the black-fly; made with a black body of the whirl of an ostrich-feather, ribbed with silver-twist, and the black hackle of a cock all over; and is a killing fly, not to be named with either of the other.

15. The last May-fly is the little yellow May-fly; in shape exactly the same with the green-drake, but a very little one, and of as bright a yellow as can be seen; which is made of a bright yellow camlet, and the wings of a white-grey feather dyed yellow.

16. The last fly for this month (and which continues all June, though it comes in the middle of May) is the fly called the camlet-fly, in shape like a moth, with fine diapered or water wings, and with which I sometimes used to dibble; and grayling will rise mightily at it. But the artificial fly (which is only in use amongst our anglers) is made of a dark brown shining camlet, ribbed over with a very small light green silk, the wings of the double grey feather of a mallard; and it is a killing fly for small fish; and so much for May.

JUNE

From the first to the four-and-twentieth, the green-drake and stone-fly are taken.

1. From the twelfth to the four and twentieth, late at night, is taken a fly, called the owl-fly; the dubbing of a white weasel's tail, and a white grey wing.

2. We have then another dun, called the barm-fly, from its yeasty colour; the dubbing of the fur of a yellow-dun-cat and a grey wing of a mallard's feather.

3. We have also a hackle with a purple body, whipt about with a red capon's feather.

4. As also a gold-twist hackle with a purple body, whipt about with a red capon's feather.

5. To these we have this month a flesh-fly; the dubbing of a black spaniel's fur, and blue wool mixed and a grey wing.

6. Also another little flesh-fly; the body made of the whirl of a peacock's feather, and the wings of the grey feather of a drake.

7. We have then the peacock-fly; the body and wing both made of the feather of that bird.

8. There is also the flying-ant or ant-fly; the dubbing of brown and red camlet mixed, with a light grey wing.

9. We have likewise a brown-gnat, with a very slender body of brown and violet camlet well mixed, and a light grey wing.

10. And another little black-gnat; the dubbing of black mohair, and a white grey wing.

11. As also a green grasshopper; the dubbing of green and yellow wool mixed, ribbed over with green silk, and a red capon's feather over all.

12. And lastly, a little dun grasshopper; the body slender, made of a dun camlet, and a dun hackle at the top.

JULY

First, all the small flies that were taken in June are also taken in this month.

1. We have then the orange-fly; the dubbing of orange wool, and the wing of a black feather.

2. Also a little white-dun; the body made of white mohair, and the wings blue, of a heron's feather.

3. We have likewise this month a wasp-fly; made either of a dark brown dubbing, or else the fur of a black cat's tail, ribbed about with yellow silk; and the wing, of the grey feather of a mallard.

4. Another fly taken this month is a black hackle; the body made of the whirl of a peacock's feather, and a black hackle-feather on the top.

5. We have also another, made of a peacock's whirl without wings.

6. Another fly also taken this month, called the shell-fly; the dubbing of yellow-green Jersey wool, and a little white hog's-hair mixed, which I call the palm-fly, and do believe it is taken for a palm, that drops off the willows into the water; for this fly I have seen trouts take little pieces of moss, as they have swam down the river; by which I conclude that the best way to hit the right colour is to compare your dubbing with the moss and mix the colours as near as you can.

7. There is also taken this month, a black-blue dun; the dubbing of the fur of a black rabbit mixed with a little yellow; the wings, of the feather of a blue pigeon's wing.

AUGUST

The same flies with July.

1. Then another ant-fly; the dubbing of the black brown hair of a cow, some red wrapt in for the tug of his tail, and a dark wing; a killing fly.

2. Next a fly called the fern-fly; the dubbing of the fur of a hare's neck, that is of the colour of fern, or bracken, with a darkish grey wing of a mallard's feather; a killer too.

3. Besides these we have a white hackle; the body of white mohair and wrapped about with a white hackle-feather, and this is assuredly taken for thistle-down.

4. We have also this month a Harry-long-legs; the body made of bear's dun, and blue wool mixed, and a brown hackle-feather over all.

Lastly, in this month all the same browns and duns are taken that were taken in May.

SEPTEMBER

This month the same flies are taken that are taken in April.

1. To which I shall only add a camel-brown-fly; the dubbing pulled out of the lime of a wall, whipped about with red silk, and a darkish grey mallard's feather for the wing.

2. And one other for which we have no name; but it is made of the black hair of a badger's skin, mixed with the yellow softest down of a sanded hog.

OCTOBER

The same flies are taken this month as were taken in March.

NOVEMBER

The same flies that were taken in February are taken this month also.

DECEMBER

Few men angle with the fly this month, no more than they do in January; but yet, if the weather be warm (as I have known it sometimes in my life to be, even in this cold country, where it is least expected), then a brown, that looks red in the hand, and yellowish betwixt your eye and the sun, will both raise and kill in a clear water and free from snow-broth; but at the best, it is hardly worth a man's labour.

These flies would probably have been dressed on hooks equivalent to sizes 16-14. Both Cotton and Walton state the smaller sizes are best.

CHARLES COTTON'S WATERS AND FISHING TACKLE

The upper Dove is a narrow clear river with shallows, weed beds and low marginal vegetation. In places sheer limestone rock faces rear from the water but in the main the banks are low grassy flats and scree run ends. The lack of cover means that the angler can be easily seen by the fish.

The rods Charles Cotton used were between fifteen and eighteen feet long. Often there would be as many as six spliced joints, the rod being soft and whippy. Once assembled it would be stored set up unless the angler was travelling away from home. Hopefully the rod was light enough to use one handed but a day's fishing would be far more arduous than with today's equipment. The best of these rods were made by craftsmen in Yorkshire. The line was up to two yards longer than the rod and fixed to the tip. Often it would be tied with waxed silk to a point a little way down the rod in case the tip snapped. This was limited insurance against the loss of the line which was made of twisted horsehair, preferably from a white stallion's tail. Long glassy hair was eagerly sought by anglers. The line was built in a taper from the tip; first two hairs, then three, four and so on up to seven or eight hairs in thickness at the rod tip. Making such a line would be a complex and time consuming operation and its loss via a broken rod tip, very irritating.

One fly at a time was used, tied to a hair when it was dressed, sometimes at the waterside. Anglers usually took a dubbing bag with them on fishing expeditions. Often this would be carried, along with a creel and a net, by a boy or servant who accompanied them. This would be the case when Charles Cotton went fishing.

Anglers fished with the wind at their backs, allowing the fly to fall on the water as lightly as possible, whilst standing as far back from the water as the length of tackle would allow to cover fish. The fly was made to swim close to the surface with no drag or disturbance. This must have taken great concentration and skill. In effect the fly was dibbled or dapped. Wind direction largely determined where and how the angler fished. Upstream or downstream, across and down, across and up were the options. Casting was not easy and the management of the fly in the current crucial to success. If no fish were obvious, Cotton advised fishing the water with a small hackle. Once a catch had been made their gorge could be removed and examined for fly reference. Dapping was a popular method. A short line, probably with any excess wrapped round the rod top, was used for near bank fishing. Those fish moving further out were tempted by allowing the wind to blow the line and deliver the fly as loch fishers do today.

Striking the fish was not advised until it was seen to turn down and, having hooked the beast, he had to be landed. The long rod and line were a great disadvantage and this would be the point at which the assistant would be needed with the landing net to capture the fish. Some anglers, Izaak Walton and John Hawkins among them, stuck the rod in the ground. A spike on the rod butt facilitated this, the fish then being hand-lined to the bank. I imagine this would have been a very delicate operation. Gerald Heywood in *Charles Cotton and his River* (1928), reports Sir John's rod spike as being made from a piece of the greater end of a sword blade.

IDENTIFICATION OF CHARLES COTTON'S DRESSINGS

A Great Dun	*March Brown*
A Little Dun	*Red Spinner*
A Whitish Dun	*Pale Watery*
Thorn Tree Fly	*Hawthorn*
Blue Dun	*Olives*
A Little Black Gnat	*Black Gnat*
A Bright Brown	*Sedge. Cinnamon Fly*
Violet Fly	*Iron Blue*
The Whirling Dun	*Red Spinner*
A Yellow Dun	*Yellow Dun*
Horse Flesh Fly	*Blue Bottle*
A Peacock Fly	*Iron Blue*
Dun Cut	*Sedge*
A Cow Lady	*Marlow Buzz*
Cow Turd Fly	*Cow Dung*
The Green Drake	*Green Drake*
Camlet Fly	*Alder*
Owl Fly	*Moth*
Barm Fly	*Yellow Dun (Ronalds). Sedge*
Little Flesh Fly	*Housefly*
A Brown Gnat	*Needle Fly*
Orange Fly	*Soldier Fly*
A Blue Black Dun	*Iron Blue*

W H ALDAM

In 1876 a book was published unlike any previous angling work. Only one hundred, some say two hundred, copies were produced. From an old manuscript, W H Aldam reproduced the dressings of 26 flies recorded by *'an old man well known in the Derbyshire streams as a first class fly fisher a century ago.'* The manuscript, entitled *Flees, and the Art a Artyfichall Flee Making* was printed with its original spelling and language retained, along with Aldam's editorial notes and appendices. The book contains 26 dressings mentioned by the *'Old Man'*, and a further five of Aldam's own patterns. Sixteen flies described in the *'Old Man's'* manuscript are set up in sunken mounts, with the materials required to dress them alongside. A further five of W H Aldam's own patterns are also mounted with materials. Finally, two detached body mayflies, without a display of dressing materials, complete the illustrations.

Aldam had intended to tie the flies himself but failing eyesight resulted in his contracting the work out. The dressers he chose were Messrs Bowness and Bowness in The Strand, Mrs Mary-Ogden Smith of All Saints Terrace, Cheltenham and Mr David Foster of Ashbourne. Mary and David are referred to as 'perhaps two of the most accomplished provincial fly tyers in the Kingdom'.

The two mayfly dressings, mounted at the end of the book, are believed to be the work of James Ogden, the celebrated fly dresser who came from Matlock and moved to Cheltenham. He was the father of Mary Ogden-Smith and an acquaintance, if not friend, of David Foster. J W Hills in *A History of Fly Fishing for Trout* (1921) proposes that these dressings may be the earliest examples of floating flies in existence.

The original manuscript, which reappeared for sale at auction, was probably written between 1770 and 1800. The dressings described are in the Derbyshire style, which, by the time they were recorded, must have been established. The *'Old Man'* stresses the neat and delicate style of the dressings:

> *'When you have made a Artyfichall flee as nate as hand can make It is a thousand times behind a natural one when dresst with the natest meatearills – When we come to Examin those small beauty-full tender deliagate and nate water bred duns that ought to be the anglers coppiing – I can find no room for coace meatearills – the natest are very coace when compared.'*

He is equally clear about the colour of materials. His *'yellow carrited stuff,'* is used in four patterns, the recipe for the dubbing being very specific in its instructions:

> *'Take the white part of Hare of Rabbitts belley – then take one table spoonful of Aquafortis and tow of water mixt them togeather – then by the assistance of a ragg at the end of a short stick and a fark to keep your fingers from being bruned – lay the Hares belley upon a plate – and with acisstance of the fark hould it fast and wett it*

A QUAINT TREATISE

ON

"Flees, and the Art a Artyfichall Flee Making,"

BY AN OLD MAN

WELL KNOWN ON THE DERBYSHIRE STREAMS AS A FIRST-CLASS FLY-FISHER A CENTURY AGO.

PRINTED FROM AN OLD MS. NEVER BEFORE PUBLISHED, THE ORIGINAL
SPELLING AND LANGUAGE BEING RETAINED,

WITH

EDITORIAL NOTES AND PATTERNS OF FLIES,

AND SAMPLES OF THE MATERIALS FOR MAKING EACH FLY,

BY

W. H. ALDAM,

ARDINGLY, SUSSEX,

Founder, Honorary Member, and late Honorary Secretary of the Derwent Fly-fishing Club ; Promoter (with the late
Sir Joseph Paxton and William Condell, Esq.), and Honorary Member of the Chatsworth Fly Fishery ;
and Founder, Honorary Member, and late Honorary Secretary of the
Darleydale Fly-fishing Club.

WITH TWO CHROMO-LITHOGRAPHIC FAC-SIMILES

FROM WATER DRAWINGS BY JAMES POOLE, ESQ.

London :

LITHOGRAPHED, PRINTED, AND PUBLISHED BY

JOHN B. DAY, 3, SAVOY STREET, STRAND.

1876.

Title page (reduced) of W H. Aldam's Quaint Treatise, giving details of his membership
of several Derbyshire Fly Fishing clubs.

14

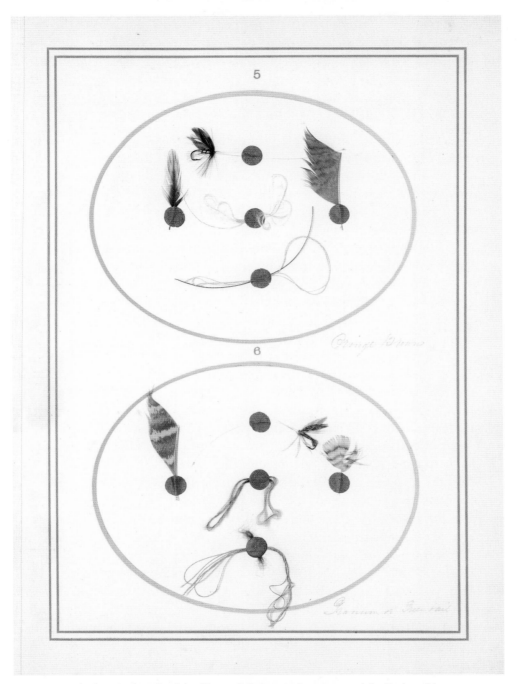

A plate (reduced) of the flies and their constituent materials displayed in
oval mounts in Aldam's *Quaint Treatise*.

well down to the roots with the mop – then hold it before the foir with the fark untill it is gone Yallow-when Yallow enough wash it well in Could water to kill the Aquafortis – and when droy it is fit for use-this and a little blue Rabbitt well mixt will be made to any shade suitable for all the Dun flees that is required in the Art a Artyfichall flee making – It makes your flee much nater and comes more to nature then than stiff brisley Dubbing – You find nothing coace in nature...'

These concise instructions not only give a detailed recipe, but also indicate the 'Old Man's' view of the natural world and his difficulties in imitating natural flies. His writings confirm him as a literate, observant angler and field naturalist. Further recipes are given for dyeing Green Drake feathers, making white wax for dressing silk and a moth killer. The latter contains two drams of '*White Hasnick*'. No doubt it was effective.

Of the 26 dressings given by the '*Old Man*', 23 are primarily presented as Derbyshire style hackles, 21 of these are also given with an alternative winged dressing. Ten of the flies in mounts are hackles and the rest winged. Much use is made of hen and gamebird hackles which give an attractive mobility in the water.

Observations of the life history and the natural appearance of each fly are given in a clear and interesting text. In the case of some flies, the Green Drake, Bank Flee and Ants for example, there are excellent descriptions of the habitats of the insects along with their behaviour. Advice regarding the time of year for their use and also the position they are placed on the cast is offered with the dressings. Two or three droppers were used, being recorded as 'Middle Anger' or 'Top Anger' in the manuscript. William Hurd Aldam set out to preserve, in a state as close to the original as possible, a record of Derbyshire flies and angling around a century before he set pen to paper. He did this in a way which indicates a man of considerable style and enthusiasm for his subject. He lived for some years at The Cottage in Matlock before moving to High Tor House, Matlock Dale, around 1864 and had considerable influence over the development of local angling. Founder and Honorary Secretary of the Derwent Flyfishing Club, he was also Promoter of Chatsworth Fly Fishery. In this enterprise he was partnered by Sir Joseph Paxton and William Condell, the Duke of Devonshire's doctor. Aldam also founded and was Honourable Secretary of the Darleydale Flyfishing Club.

The Derwent Club was founded in 1838 so Aldam's involvement with Derbyshire angling must have lasted much of his adult life. He was obviously a man of considerable means judging by the company he kept and his angling portfolio. In addition to Derbyshire and Staffordshire, he fished the Cumbrian Eden, Thames, Welsh Border rivers and the Wandle. His book has two illustrations presented by the artist James Poole. The dressing silks were presented by George Davenport of Leek and the mayfly hooks by Barleets of Redditch. One of Davenport's silk advertisements, Foster's *The Scientific Angler* (1882) records, '*Mr W. H. Aldam of Chilcomb Winchester, has a quantity of these silks...specially manufactured...by a personal friend at Leek...Mr. Geo. Davenport...*'.

Davenport specialised in tying silks to experts in fly dressing. The date of the item in the *Fishing Gazette* is October 1884. By this time Aldam had left Derbyshire and previous abode at Ardingley in Sussex where *A Quaint Treatise on Flies and Fly Making* was compiled.

Alfred Ronalds, David Foster and James Ogden were all known to W H Aldam. He corresponded with Ronalds over Ronalds's omission of the Blue Winged Olive in the early editions of the *The Fly-Fishers Entomology* (1836). The fly appeared as the dressing for the Red Spinner in the fifth edition. This irritated Aldam, blaming two 'friends' to whom he had divulged the pattern, for giving it to the unknown editor, 'Piscator'. There are those who think this was Ronalds himself, but it was almost certainly the Rev Barnard Smith. Could this have been a relative of the originator of the Indian Yellow, James Smith? David Foster and, very probably, James Ogden tied flies for Aldam's book. Another irritant to Aldam were Derbyshire Bumbles, which he claimed came from elsewhere.

Aldam took fly dressing very seriously. He and his wife bred poultry to provide plumage for fly dressing. He states that he only ever saw one hen, and that of his own breeding, which would be an acceptable substitute for dotterel hackles and plumage. Obviously by the late nineteenth century the dotterel was paying the price for Hofland's 'Dotteril Dun'. Aldam used Judson's dyes to produce substitutes for rare hackles such as Honey Dun and others. In his editorial comments he describes 'dibbling' live Oak and Wood flies. This was achieved by means of a fourteen foot spliced rod, five foot fixed line, a hook with a 'lead head' style shot attached, the fly impaled and lowered into likely spots. When a trout took the fly it was played with as much as three feet of the rod tip under water and hauled out! This same angler despised fishing at night; he was a grouse shooter who was content, after a day of action on the Glorious Twelfth, to go through the bag to select suitable under covert feathers from young grouse to wing the Indian Yellow fly. Dedication of a high order!

Aldam's Appendix to *The Quaint Treatise*, lists and illustrates in mounts, five patterns: the *Indian Yellow*, tied by James Smith of Sharrow near Sheffield, who Aldam assisted by providing silk for the body of the fly; the *Eden Fly*, similar to Ronalds' Little Sky Blue, which gave a good account of itself with Eden trout near Appleby. The fly was also rated highly by grayling anglers; Aldam's *Summer Dun* which he saw on Bakewell Meadows, dressed and on which he hooked a trout estimated at six pounds! Unfortunately, the dropper caught in the net as James Smith attempted to land the fish. The result was some strong language, the fish straightening the hook and '...gradually sinking out of sight...'; the *March Brown of Great Britain* to differentiate it from the 'Old Man's' March Brown dressing. In Derbyshire this fly was known as The Dun Drake; Aldam's *Jenny Spinner* with which in October 1852, he and William Condell caught a large bag of grayling from the Chatsworth water, along with a number of 'bright trout'.

W H ALDAM'S DRESSINGS

1   INDIAN YELLOW (Mid-May to September)

Hook: Kendal, 1 or 2.
Body: Silk (colour of new Russian Leather), slightly waxed with transparent wax, ribbed with bright yellow unwaxed silk.
Whisks: Two or three hairs from a 'rich buff Guinea Pig', or fibres from a bittern's feather, or from the hackle of a buff Cochin China fowl.
Wings: Under covert feather from the wing of a young Grouse.
Legs: Rich buff or ginger hackle from a Cochin China hen.
Head: Deep orange tying-silk slightly waxed, or very fine floss.

2   THE EDEN FLY (Mid-May to October)

Hook: No 0 or 1 Kendal Sneck bend.
Wings: Outside wing covert of the Sea Swallow, or lightest part of a Jay's wing quill feather.
Legs: Honey dun or light buff Cochin China hen's hackle.
Body: Pale buff or light straw-coloured tying-silk, slightly waxed with transparent wax.
Whisks: 2 or 3 fibres of buff Cochin China hen or cock, or a medium blue dun cock or hen hackle.

3   SUMMER DUN

Hook: 2 or 3 Kendal Sneck bend, long shank.
Wings: Lightest part of a young Starling's wing quill feather.
Body: Gold-coloured silk with buff Berlin wool dubbing, or fur from the buff part of a foreign Marten (Sable's gill).
Legs: Rich buff Cochin China hackle.
Whisks: From the Bittern or buff Cochin China cock or hen.

4   MARCH BROWN OF GREAT BRITAIN

Hook: 4, 5 or 6 of Kendal Sneck (No 3 long-shank for low water.)
Wings: The large under covert feather from a Woodcock's wing, or the secondary feather (quill) of the English Cock Pheasant.
Legs: Feather from the tail or one of the three secondary quill feathers nearest the body of a Jenny Wren; or a bright coloured feather from the back of a Partridge; or a rich, almost red, honey dun from the domestic cock or hen.

Body: Yellow silk and the red-brown fur at the back of a fox's ear, below the black tip; gold thread or gold coloured silk.

Tail: 3 fibres of the two centre brown mottled feathers of the tail or from the upper tail coverts of a Partridge.

5   JENNY SPINNER

Hook: No 1 or 0 Kendal Sneck.

Wings and Legs: A Bantam Hen's hackle, very slightly stained with Judson's slate colour; or a pale from the butt of the wing or back of a Sea Swallow or small Roseate Tern.

Silk: Mulberry.

Body: Middle part fine white floss silk, or horsehair of transparent watery whiteness.

Tag: Two or three turns of fine Mulberry floss.

Tails: 3 fibres white cockerel's hackle.

W H Aldam was probably the originator of The Eden Fly, Summer Dun and possibly the Jenny Spinner. A man of skill, imagination and of literary conservation, without his forethought a piece of Derbyshire's angling history would have been lost.

Here follows the legacy of W H Aldam, the dressings of the '*Old Man*' in his own words, put together under Aldam's title – '*A Quaint Treatise on Flees, and the Art a Artyfichall Flee Making*':

1   DERBYSHIRE MARCH BROWN

It is called many names – March Brown – Parteridge rump – Cuckoo Creel and Old Man.

I think this flee the best made if you hackle it from the Parteridge feather – one found upon the back betwixt the root of the wings the smallest you find – there are few birds that as a good one on them. If you wing it take the largest feathers from under the Woodcock wing the brownest and finest creeled – and a dark furness Cock hackle for Leggs Silk darke mayogany coulor – Hook No. 2 Dubbing the white part of a hare or rabbit belley part dyed The coulor of mayogany for want of furr gett a small patch of fine cloarth of the coulor and lint it Sometimes made with orange silk and the points of brown squirll furr – for the greetstone waters make it of the brown Moor game feathers – one from the bow of the wing or back If you wing it take from the quill parts of the woodcock for wings and a furness Cock hackle for legg – this flee is boath browner and larger on the greetstone waters than thoes on the limestone To be fished top or middle Anger.

(March onwards)

2   SPRING OR DOTTRILL DUN

I think this flee is best made from a brown dun hen or chicken feather if you can gett one to the coulor – they are much toffer and finer on the stem and make a nater flee One flee made from the Hen will fish longer than three from the dottrill Thoes you find on the ruff or back of Hen or chicken the coulor of dottrill – for want of Henfeathers make it of the dottrill – those you find on the bow of the wing or rump If you wing it take the Quill feather of the dottrill for wings Silke dark primrose - Hook No. 2 with a little yellow carrited Stuff and blue rabbit furr well mixt to the coulor for dubbing – and a small hackle from Hen or Cock of a dark straw coulor for leggs to be fished at the point.
(Late March to the end of May)

3   LITTLE CHAP

To be made from a Darke Dun Hen or Chicken feather from the Ruff Some angler think it Better made from the Longwing feather Silk Lead coulor - Hook No. 0 or 1 with a few laps of coppor Coulored paycock Harl for the Bodey If you wing it take the Quill feather from the Starling and small Hackle from the Ruff for leggs – to be fished at the point.

4   IRON BLUE OR WATCHETT

I think it is best made from a Jack Daw ruff or Tom Tit Tail Silk Lead or Darke purple coulor with a little Moules furr for bodey If you wing it take the Tom Tit tail and a small Cock or Hen Hackle the couler of straw for legs No. 0 or 1 for Hook The Wings are a verry Darke blue the coulor of New Garth Iorn – the Bodey of a Darke bluey Durty Drab with six leggs of a straw Coulor – the Head of a Darke reddy Coulor – to be fished one point and one Top Anger.
(Twentieth of April to end of June, cold stormy days)

5   ORINGE BROWN

To be made from the Woodcock feather – thoes found upon the bow of the wing Silk Oringe Coulor – Dubbing the brown parts of Squirl furr Hook No. 2 or 3 If you wing it take from the Quill feather of the Woodcock for Wings and a small darke furness Cock Hackle for leggs – to be fished Top Anger.
(Twentyfifth of May to the latter end of June)

6   GREEN TAIL OR GRANUM

To be made from a feather found under the Woodcock wing – silk lead coulor with a little furr from a Leveretts back well mixt Hook No. 2 If you wing it take from the same feather the wings and the point of the Parteridge rump feather for legg to be fished Top Anger and one point.
(Twentieth of April for fourteen days)

7   BLACK GNAT

To be made from a Hen Starling thoes feathers found upon the Brest or sides – with Lead couloured silk – with Tow laps of fine black ostridge nately twisted with the silk for Bodey If you wing it take the Quill feathers of the same Bird and a small hackle from the ruff for leggs To be fished at the point.
(Twentyfifth of May to the beginning of August)

8   TAILEY TAIL

To be made of a sootey Black Hen feather the coulor of the Long wing Hen feathers those from the Ruff make this Flee much sharper and nater and more Indewrable than the Long wing Silk darke fawne or flishey drab with a harl from a Brown Turkey Tail twisted with the silk for Bodey If you wing it take the Quill feather from the Long wing for wings and a small Hackle from the Starling neck for Leggs No. 0 or 1 Hook.
(From the twentyfifth of May to the beginning of August)

9   GREEN DRAKE

To be made from a fine creeled Drake feather dyed yallow the same feather will both hackle and wing this flee Silk – light primrose coulor – Dubbing yellow carried stuff and blue abbit furr well mixt to the coulor of Primrose Hook No. 6 long shanked with a Small Cock Hackle of a Blackish Brown for leggs – to be fished either Anger or Point.
(From fourth of June to the Twentyfourth of June in hot weather a short period or time)

10   DARK BLUE OR ORINGE HEADED DUN

To be made from a Darke blue Hen or Chicken feather from the Ruff or back – Silk lead Coulor with a little blue Rabbitt for dubbing Hook No. 2   If you wing it – take from the Blue or Merlin Hawk feather the wings and a small hackle of a darke straw Coulor for Leggs with or without Oringe head as you plase To be fished the middle Anger.
(Twentyfifth of April to the end of May)

11   ORINGE OR BUFF DUN

To be made from a middle dun Hen or Chicken feather – Silk feaded Oringe – Dubbing the fine parts of brown Squirll furr – Hook No. 1 If you wing it take from the Quill feather of the Starling for wings and a red Cock Hackle for Legg
To be fished Top Anger.
(June onwards. Good after Summer floods.)

12   LIGHT DUN

To be made from a Light Dun Hen of Chicken feather – or Sea Swallow or Gull   Silk Light Primrose Coulor – dubbing yellow carried Stuff and light blue Rabbitt furr well mixt to the Coulor of Primrose Hook No. 1 If you wing it take from the Sea Gull the

wings and the small hackle from Hen or Cock of a straw Coulor for Leggs   To be fished at the point.
(Beginning to end of July)

13   BIGG DUN

To be made from a Light Dun Hen or Chicken feather and ofen made from the Sea Swallow or Gull   Silk Light Primrose Coulor – Dubbing the same as the Green Drake   Hook No. 6 long shanked   If you wing it take from the Sea Gull feather for wings and a small hackle Coulor of darke straw for Leggs   This is the largest Dun that comes on the Darbyshire Waters   A Exilent flee for a rainey or Cloudy Day   To be fished Top Anger.
(Beginning of May to the end of June)

14   CROSSING BROWN

To be made from a Brown Hen feather of a darke sandey Coulor   Silk of a light Mayogany Coulor – Dubbing any fine furr of the Coulor of Mayogany – Hook No. 1   If you wing it take from the Quill feather of Corncrake the darkest parts and a small Cock Hackle of a darke furness for Leggs   To be fished Middle Anger.
(July but best in August)

15   SAND GNAT OR SPIDER FLEE

To be made from a Sandey dun Hen feather with black edges   If you wing it – take from the Quill feather of the Throssoll the wings and the large black Hen or Cock Hackle for leggs   Silk lead Coulor with a little blue Rabbit furr for Bodey   To be fished one at point and one Top Anger.
(End of April to the end of May)

16   BLACK ANT

To be made from a light Dun hen or Chicken feather – with black silk and black Ostridge Harl made thick at the Heel   If you wing it – take the Quill feather of a Fieldfare for wings and a Black Cock Hackle for Leggs – Hook No. 2 or 3   To be fished as a Anger.
(July, August and September)

17   LARGE RED ANT

To be made from a light Dun or Chicken feather – Silk feaded oringe or the Coulor of a Chusnut Horshare made thick at the Heel with the same silk   If you wing it – take the light part from the Quill feather of a Fieldfare wing and a small Ginger Cock Hackle for Legg to be fished as a Anger.
(July, August and September)

18   SMALL COMMON ANT

To be made from a Dun Hen or Chicken feather – Silk of a blood red with Copper Coulor paycock harl made thick at his Heel   If you wing it – take the wings from a Starling Quill feather and a small red Cock Hackle for Legg – Hook No. 1   to be fished at the point.
(July, August and September)

19   SMALL CATTERPILLER

To be made from a light Dun Hen or Chicken feather with a black Silk and fine black Ostridge made small and fine – If you wing it – take the light part of a Starling wing Quill feather and a small hackle from the ruff for Leggs – Hook No. 0 or 1   To be fished one at point and one Top Anger.
(Twentieth of May to the end of June)

20   LARGE BLACK CATTERPILLER

To be made from a light Dun or Chicken feather from the Back or Ruff – with black silk and black Ostridge for bodey – If you wing it – take the light part of a Starling wing Quil feather for wings and a Hackle from the Ruff for Legg – Hook No. 3   To be fished Top Anger.
(Twentieth of May to the middle of June)

21   BANK FLEE

To be made from a Landrail feather from the Bow of the wing – and feaded Orange Silk with a little reddy parts of the Squirll furr – Hook No. 3 – If you wing it – Take from the Quill feather of the Landrail and a long Ginger Cock Hackle for Leggs   To be fished as Anger.
(End of May to the end of August)

22   LITTLE SKY BLUE

To be made from a Hen starling feather from the brest or side – Silk sky blue – the Bodey to be made without dubbing with the same silk – Hook No. 0 – If you wing it – take from a Starling wing Quill feather the bluest part – and a fine Black Hen feather for Legge   To be fished as a Anger.
(May to August)

23   STREAM FLEE

To be made from a Jack Hawk or brown Cuckoo feather from the bow of the wing – and Lead Coulored Silk with a little Blue Rabbitts furr for Bodey – If you wing it – take the Quill feather from the Woodcock wing and a brown Hackle from Hen or Cock for Leggs   This is a killing flee when made and fished well   To be fished Top Anger – Hook No 2.
(Middle of June to the end of August in the evening after a hot day)

24   **WILLOW FLEE**

To be made from a white Hen feather from the Ruff and wing – dyed yallow with the same meateralls as the Green drake with yallow silk and Carritted Stuff for Bodey – Hook No. 2 To be fished as a Anger.
(End of May to the beginning of July)

25   **WHITE MOUT OR BUSTERD**

To be made from a White Barn Owl – if you hackle it – the Craim coulored feathers from the bowe of the wing – with buff silk and white Ostridge harl for Bodey – If you wing it take from the Quill feathers of the same Bird the wings and a small feather from the bowe of the wing for Leggs – Hook No. 6 To be fished at the point.
(Tenth of June to the middle of August late evening to early morning)

26   **BROWN MOUT**

To be made from a Wood Owl – If you wing it – take from the Quill feather the wings and the Leggs from the small feathers from the bowe of the wing – If you hackle it – take thoes feathers from the bowe of the wing that growe next to the Quill feather – and feaded Oringe silk with the harl from the Quill feathers for Bodey – Hook No. 6 To be fished as a Anger.
(June until mid August)

FLIES IMITATED BY THE 'OLD MAN'S' DRESSINGS

Local March Brown	February Red
Oringe Brown	Oak Fly; Downlooker; Ash Fly
Tailey Tail	Female Black Gnat
Oringe Dun	Blue Winged Olive
Crossing Brown	Bank or Sand Fly; Sedge
Sand Gnat	Long Legged Gnat
Small Caterpillar	Black Gnat
Large Black Caterpillar	Hawthorn Fly
Bank Flee	Cinnamon Fly; Sedge
Willow Flee	Yellow Sally
White Mout	Moth
Brown Mout	Moth

W H Aldam's editorial remarks are very useful, though in some cases he tends to alter the dressing somewhat. His was a lavish production which, in its way, was as innovative and revolutionary as that of the limited edition of Alfred Ronalds's *The Fly-Fisher's Entomology*, published in 1913. The flies are beautifully tied, perhaps with a little fly dresser's licence, but no matter.

In 1999 the original manuscript with William Aldam's editorial remarks appeared for sale. It gave the name of the *Old Man* as one Robert Whitehead. It seems odd that Aldam did not reveal the name of his source at the time of writing if the original manuscript was named. I have been unable to confirm details and Robert Whitehead has not been found in my research for the current work.

ALFRED RONALDS

For some of his life Alfred Ronalds lived in or near the town of Uttoxeter. His book *The Fly-Fisher's Entomology* (1836) reveals him as a man of considerable talent and possibly considerable means. When published in 1836 the book must have caused a sensation among both anglers and naturalists fortunate enough to gain access to a copy. For the first time anglers had a concise, illustrated handbook, which was well written and clear in every detail. A diagram of the Dove near Mappleton is accurate enough for a modern angler to fish the lies where Ronalds proposed fish to be found. He was evidently an excellent naturalist and observer, and a very able artist. It is likely that he etched the unsurpassed plates for his book prior to the printing process.

His enquiring mind led him to build an observatory of heather on the river Blythe close to Cresswell Station, near Uttoxeter. From this building, set low over the water, he conducted a series of experiments on the resident trout and their feeding activities. The observatory had three windows, each overlooking a different river feature – a scour, whirlpool and eddy. The river was fished as normal; otherwise the fish were left undisturbed. From his vantage point, unseen, Ronalds watched the fish and noted their behaviour. His experiments investigated hearing, sight, taste and smell. The former necessitated, in his view, the firing of a gun several times and also shouting in the vicinity of the fish. He controlled the former experiment, ensuring the river's inhabitants could not see the flash from the barrel when the gun was fired. He concluded that the fish could not hear the noise, commenting that sport would not be spoilt by friendly chat on the bank. The local population may well be less than enthusiastic about such 'experiments' in the area today.

Refraction diagrams, prepared by Ronalds, illustrate the probability of what fish can see above the surface, followed by brief remarks on keeping low and approaching fish from the rear when fishing. He presented flavoured baits to feeding fish, and whilst the results compared to unflavoured items were not decisive, all points to carefully planned and executed investigations. Autopsies are recommended as a definitive means of establishing the current diet of fish.

Having dealt with trout, Ronalds then discussed grayling. Their distribution, behaviour and sporting qualities are noted with care and enthusiasm.

Next Ronalds turns to rod, line and other tackle. The materials and action of rods was

The bridge over the river Blythe at Cresswell, where Alfred Ronalds
built his angling observatory.

obviously of importance to him and along with other tackle, clear instructions and advice are offered. He describes what may be the first 'automatic' reel – 'containing a spiral spring which acts in the manner of the spring in a window blind ...to wind up the line'. The temper and quality of hooks is stressed and the reader advised as to where to obtain suitable items.

Three types of fly are chosen to elaborate dressing techniques. The processes involved in the construction of Great Red Spinner, 'Buzz' fly and Palmer are described along with a plate of the processes and tools. In his instructions Ronalds stresses the importance of colour, shape and size regarding the flies tied. This section also gives eight recipes for dyeing the various feathers required to make up the patterns offered.

Angling instruction is given under 'Manner of Fishing for Trout and Grayling'. Casting, weather, choice of fly, short rises and landing are explained clearly and concisely. Indeed, much of the advice is similar to that given in a modern angling manual.

A month-by-month list of forty-seven artificial flies follows. Ronalds was the first angling author to use the Linnean system of classification for natural flies and whilst new science has now rendered his work somewhat inaccurate it was, when written and for decades afterwards, the foremost document of its time. His plates portray very accurate coloured drawings of the natural fly with its appropriate imitation alongside. This was a completely new departure in angling literature. It is often stated that the drawings have never been surpassed in quality; such was his skill in drawing and etching. Accompanying the plates are the actual dressings with further information. This includes details of emergence, weather conditions, angling methods and, where applicable, rivers on which the artificials are effective or popular.

The Fly-Fisher's Entomology, according to Donald Overfield, writing in *Famous Flies and their Originators* (1972), has run to twelve editions – one produced in 1913 in 250 copies, having a second volume containing actual flies in a similar manner to Aldam's *Treatise*.

Alfred Ronalds was a modest man, well read and educated. He was thorough but concise in every aspect of his publication and would, I think, have been a very pleasant angling companion. He obviously made some living from his writing and also sold his flies. Mr Eaton of 7, Crooked Lane, London, was commissioned to deal in his products of which anglers were advised to avail themselves.

Ronalds seems to have travelled the country in his angling expeditions, advising on patterns not only for the Staffordshire and Derbyshire streams but also those in the South, Yorkshire and Wales. In 1844 he moved to North Wales and four years later emigrated to Australia.

Between 1841, when David Foster came to Ashbourne and the year Ronalds moved to Wales, the two men lived close to one another and fished the same waters. The dicovery of the Red Caterpillar, and its subsequent publication, indicates a cooperation and consultation between the two anglers.

The preface to the fifth edition is written by an editor who signs himself 'Piscator' from

Thames Side, February 1856. At this date, Alfred Ronalds was still alive and Piscator wrote '*The present edition of The Fly-Fisher's Entomology has the full sanction of the Author, for whose approval the chief alterations were sent to him in Australia.*'

This was the last edition of the book produced in the author's lifetime. The identity of 'Piscator' excited some comment; it was thought it may have been Ronalds himself. H T Sheringham, the editor of the 1921 edition, reports R B Marston, editor of *Fishing Gazette*, as having researched the matter. Marston discovered that Rev Barnard Smith was paid ten pounds for the project. Sheringham researched further and believed him to be the author '*of the well known arithmetic*'. There was, apparently, no further contact with Alfred Ronalds, a talented man who gave an enduring contribution to angling literature.

Many of Alfred Ronalds's patterns are standards today. Of particular interest are some of the alternative hackled or 'buzz' dressings. In *The Fly-Fisher's Entomology* the remarks, advice and dressing are very detailed. Below is a transcription of the information.

FLIES FOR MARCH

NO. 1. THE RED FLY

Body. The dubbing is composed of the dark red part of squirrel's fur, mixed with an equal quantity of claret-coloured mohair, showing the most claret colour at the tail of the fly. This is spun on brown silk thread, to form the body.

Wings. From the softest quill feather of the pea-hen's wing which approaches thetint.

Legs. Of a claret-coloured stained hackle. No feather of its natural colour that I know of, is of the proper shade. Clip some of the upper fibres off, that the wings may lie flat.

Hook No. 2, short.

Remarks. This is the earliest fly in North Derbyshire. The tint of the wings is that of a cake of glue held between the eye and the sun. It is best made hackle-way, with the under covert feather of a woodcock's wing wound upon the above body. In Lancashire it is called 'Old Joan', and the body is made rough with claret-coloured German wool. Thus made it kills well in the Derwent.

NO. 2. THE BLUE DUN

Body. Fur of a hare's ear or face, spun very thinly on fine yellow silk, and wound on thickest at the shoulder. Some of the dubbing is then picked out to form legs.

Tail. Two fibres of a Dun Hackle.

Wings. From a quill feather of the starling's wing, which may be slightly stained in onion dye.

Legs. If a sufficient quantity of dubbing cannot be picked out for the legs, two or three turns of a Ginger Dun hackle can be added, and will help to keep the wings upright. Put these on last, whipping them on the bare hook, and finish at the head.

Hook No.2, Grayling.

Remarks.   This elegant fly kills well till June made as follows: Body of yellow silk waxed, with a very little Blue Dun fur from rat, mouse, mole, or rabbit, spun upon the silk so that the yellow shows through. Body tapering from shoulder to tail.

Legs.   A Honey Dun hackle; four or five turns.

Wings.   A starling's quill feather, put on last, on the bare hook, so as to stand up boldly.

Thus made, it is a good Fly for Parr. When you can put this fly together well you have reason to hope you are improving: for the Duns are delicate insects to imitate. Wax your silk lightly.

NO. 3. THE RED SPINNER

Body.   Thin, of bright brown silk, ribbed with fine gold twist.

Tail.   Two whisks of a red cock's hackle.

Wings.   Upright, from a mottled grey feather of the mallard, stained to match the colour of the natural wings.

Legs.   Plain red cock's hackle.

Hook, No. 2, Grayling.

Remarks.   Some of the best Derbyshire anglers make it thus:- Wing, upright from under covert wing feather of a young grouse. Body, silk, the colour of Russia leather, and ribbed with the finest yellow silk. Two dun fibres for tail. But after a frosty morning they make it as follows:-Wing, starling onion dyed; body, claret silk; legs, dead furniss hackle. Thus made it is called the 'Frost Fly'.

NO. 4. THE WATER CRICKET

Body.   Orange floss silk, tied on with black silk thread.

Legs.   Are made best of one of the two longest feathers of a peawit's topping. If this cannot be easily procured, a black cock's hackle will answer the body purpose and is easier to use. Either of these must be wound all down the body, and the fibres then snipped off up to the shoulder.

Hook, No. 0. or 1.

Remarks.   The rib may be formed with black silk, and the hackle fastened under the shoulder. This is an easier way.

NO. 5. GREAT DARK DRONE

Body.   Mole fur, ribbed over with black ostrich, when spun on black silk.

Wings and Legs.   Made buzz with a dun hackle, the tint a shade or two lighter than that of the natural wings.

Hook, No. 4, long.

When this fly is made with wings and legs not buzz, the dun feather of the wing of the mallard is used, and a grizzled hackle for legs, upon the same body.

Engraving from *The Fly Fisher's Entomology*
executed by Alfred Ronalds.

Remarks. The use of a smaller 'Spring Black' than the above is recommended in preference.

Body. Black ostrich herl.

Wings Purplish breast feather of a cock starling, wound on as a hackle.
and Legs. Hook, No. 1, long.

The larger black flies are seldom observed so early in the season.
But a black fly of one sort or another is seldom useless on your lash.

NO. 6. COW-DUNG FLY

Body. Yellow worsted, mohair, or camlet, mixed with a little dingy brown fur from the bear, and left rough, spun upon light brown silk.

Wings. From the landrail.

Legs. Of a ginger-coloured hackle.

The female is made buzz thus:

Body. Olive coloured mohair, or worsted, spun on silk of the same colour.

Wings Of a red cock's hackle, changed to a brown colour by putting it into a
and Legs. solution of copperas.

Hook, No. 3, short.

NO. 7. PEACOCK FLY

Body. Ruddy brown peacock's herl, dressed with mulberry-coloured silk.

Wings The darkest part of a wing feather of the starling.

Legs. A hackle stained dark purple; appearing black when looked down upon; but when held up to the light, having a most beautiful dark tortoiseshell hue.

Hook, no. 1 or 2, short.

Remarks. The Buzz form of this fly is a great Grayling killer, in spring and autumn, and is much prized on the Derwent, near Rowsley. It is made thus:

Body, the reddest strand of a peacock's feather.

Legs A lightish dun hackle; made with mulberry-coloured silk. It is called 'The
and Wings. Chap,' and is described with variations, by Arundo, in 'Practical Fly-fishing'.

NO. 8. MARCH BROWN

Body. Fur of the hare's face ribbed over with olive silk and tied with brown.

Tail. Two strands of a partridge feather.

Wings. Quill feather from the middle of the hen pheasant's wing, which may be found of the exact shade.

Legs. A brown mottled feather from the back of a partridge.

Hook, No. 2, 3, or 4, long.

Remarks. The female of this excellent fly must by no means be neglected; and observe that females are generally a few days later in their appearance on the water than the males.

Body.	Pale olive green wool, ribbed with fine gold twist.
Legs.	A honey dun hackle, that is less bright than a golden dun.
Wings.	Upright, the same as for the male; but the hackle will impart a lighter shade. This is a great killer on the Dove.

NO. 9. GREAT RED SPINNER

Body.	Hog's down dyed red-brown (or orange and brown floss silk mixed), spun on brown silk. It is ribbed with fine gold twist.
Tail.	Two long whisks of a bright amber red hackle.
Wings.	From an under covert feather of the starling's wing.
Legs.	A bright amber red hackle. Hook, No. 2, 3 or 4, long.

FLIES FOR APRIL

NO. 10. GOLDEN DUN MIDGE

Body.	Olive floss silk ribbed with gold twist, and tied with dun silk thread.
Wings.	From the palest feather of a young starling.
Legs.	A pure dun hackle, wound on in front of the wings. Hook, No. 1, Grayling.
Remarks.	No fly is more abundant, especially in showery weather, and just after rain. It is a prime favourite on the Dove. A delicate hand is required to make this fly handsomely, and the finest silk. Though shoemaker's soft wax is generally to be preferred, as most durable, colourless wax has an advantage for making delicate flies like this and the Jenny Spinner.

NO. 11. SAND FLY

Body.	Of the sandy coloured fur from the hare's neck, spun on silk of the same colour.
Wings.	From the landrail's wing made full.
Legs.	From a light ginger feather from the neck of a hen. Hook, No. 2, long.
Remarks.	A good variation of this fly is to use orange silk, and show it most at the tail; and instead of a light ginger hen's hackle, use one with a dark stripe down the middle. In any case cut off the upper fibres of the hackle that the wings may lie flat. The above is a good Grayling and Dace fly, in July and August.

NO. 12. THE STONE FLY

Body.	Fur of hare's ear mixed with yellow worsted or camlet, ribbed over with yellow silk, leaving most yellow at the tail.
Tail.	A strand or two of a brown mottled partridge feather.
Wings.	Quill feather from the hen pheasant's wing.

Legs.   A hackle stained greenish-brown: or a natural dark grizzle.

Hook, No. 4 or 5, long.

Remarks.   This fly kills best, when used in its natural state, either by dibbing with a short line in still deep water: or by wading up the streams, and throwing carefully with a few yards of line. Used thus, it kills the largest trout from early morning till late at night.

NO. 13. THE GRAVEL BED

Body.   Dark dun, or lead-coloured silk thread dressed very fine.

Wings.   From an under covert feather of the woodcock's wing.

Legs.   A black cock's hackle rather long, wound, twice only, round the body.

Hook, No. 0 or 1, long.

To make it buzz, a dark dun cock's hackle may be used, with a ginger tinge at the edges.

Remarks.   This fly kills well in May; weather bright, water clear, and when no other fly will raise fish. Some prefer the brightest outside (scapular) feather of woodcock's wing: and use the same feather, to make it buzz. The silk for the body should be of the most repulsive, ashy, livid hue that you can find.

NO. 14. THE GRANNOM

Body.   Fur of hare's face left rough, spun on brown silk. A little green floss silk may be worked in at the tail to represent the bunch of eggs there.

Wings.   Feather from the partridge's wing, and made very full.

Legs.   A pale ginger hen's hackle.

Hook, No. 2, long.

Made buzz with a feather from the back of the partridge's neck, wound upon the above body.

Remarks.   The Shell Fly, or Palmer, as this is sometimes called, kills well made buzz with a landrail's scapular feather. Body, pea-green German wool. Make with orange silk, shown only at the head. It is a good fly all the summer months, and into September.

NO. 15. THE YELLOW DUN

Body.   Yellow mohair, mixed with a little pale blue fur from a mouse. Or yellow silk thread waxed, and with the least blue rabbit fur spun upon it, and ribbed with yellow silk.

Wings.   Upright, from the lightest part of a young starling's quill feather.

Legs.   A light yellow dun hackle.

Hook, No. 2, Grayling.

To make it buzz, a lighter dun hackle is wound upon the same body. In either case make with primrose silk, and delicately.

Remarks. If made as a hackle, prefer a cock's hackle for Grayling, a hen's hackle for Trout; and rib with unwaxed yellow silk over the body, as above. When made with the feather of a dotterel as a hackle, it is called the 'Dotterel Dun,' a far-famed fly.

NO. 16. THE IRON BLUE DUN

Body. Blue fur from a mole. Reddish brown floss silk may be tied on for the head.

Tail. A whisk or two out of a yellow dun hackle.

Wings. From a feather of the under-side of the cormorant's wing; or, in default thereof, a feather from the breast of the water hen, the tip of which must be used. Or the upper end of the wing feather of a tomtit when in full plumage.

Legs. A very small yellow dun hackle.

Hook, No. 0, short.

It is difficult to find a hackle feather of the tint proper to make this fly buzz.

Remarks. A feather from the Merlin hawk's wing may be used, if procurable, to wing this fly (Arundo).

NO. 17. THE JENNY SPINNER

Body. White floss silk wound round the shank of the hook, &c. and tied on at the head and tail with brown silk, which must be shown.

Tail. A whisk or two of a light dun hackle.

Wings and Legs are best imitated by making them buzz, for which purpose the lightest dun hackle that can be procured should be used.

Hook, No. 0, short.

NO. 18. THE HAWTHORN FLY

Body. Black ostrich herl.

Wings. A feather of the starling's wing.

Legs. A black cock's hackle; or one of the two largest feathers from a peawit's top knot.

Hook, No. 2 or 3, long.

The fly cannot very easily be made buzz, unless the female is imitated, in which case a black hackle, wound over the above-mentioned black ostrich herl, will answer the purpose; and the fly so made is sometimes called the Black Palmer, or Black Caterpillar.

Hawthorn Fly

FLIES FOR MAY

NO. 19. THE LITTLE YELLOW MAY DUN

Body.	Pale ginger-coloured fur from behind the hare's ear, ribbed over with yellow silk thread.
Tail.	One or two whisks from a dun hackle.
Wings.	Mottled feather from the mallard, stained as for the Green Drake.
Legs.	A light dun hackle also very slightly stained yellowish in the same dye.
	Hook, No. 2, long.

The Light Amber Spinner, to which this fly changes, lives in its new state about four days. It is used successfully on the evenings of warm days.

NO. 20. THE BLACK GNAT

Body.	Black ostrich herl.
Wings.	The dark part of a feather from the starling.
Legs.	A black hackle.
	Hook, No. 0, or 1, short.
	To make it buzz, a light dun hen hackle may be wound upon the above body; and thus made, it kills decidedly best.
Remarks.	There is another imitation of the Black Gnat, of which Grayling are very fond.
Body.	Black ostrich herl.
Wings and Legs.	The purplish breast feather of a cock starling, wound on hackle-wise.

The Black Midge should be made like the winged imitation of the Black Gnat, but with the substitution of a thin black silk body. These black flies resemble many small beetles, and may be ranked among 'general flies'. In fine low water, after Midsummer, they are most useful, in the rapid parts of streams.

NO. 21. THE OAK FLY

Body.	Orange floss silk tied with ash-coloured silk thread, which may be shown at the tail and shoulders.
Wings.	From a scapular feather of the woodcock.
Legs.	A furnace hackle (i.e. a red cock's hackle, with a black list up the middle, and tinged with black also at the extremities of the fibres). This should be struck from tail to head, and the fibres snipped off nearly up to where the wings are set on, leaving a sufficient quantity for the legs.
	Hook, No. 2 or 3, long.
Remarks.	The small woodcock and grouse feathers (which can be used indifferently) make very neat hackle flies; and the beginner will find a pleasure in making the Oak Fly of various sizes in the following easy manner:-
	Body, orange floss silk, ribbed with fine black silk, which may be slightly waxed. Then form the head of your fly with your arming silk (brown), and

35

choosing a woodcock or grouse feather, whose fibres are the exact length of the hook, stroke it back, and tie it (upside down) by the tip to the arming of your hook, just clear of the head, and wind the feather round as a hackle, holding it by the quill, and fasten off under the shoulder.

NO. 22. THE TURKEY BROWN

Body.	Dark brown floss silk ribbed with purple silk thread.
Tail.	A whisk or two of a red cock's hackle, stained as for the legs.
Wings.	Tip of the brownest feather from a partridge's tail or, if well selected, a feather may be found on the back of the partridge.
Legs.	Red cock's hackle, stained a good brown with copperas.
	To make it buzz, a feather from the grouse may be tied on hackle-wise.

NO. 23. THE LITTLE DARK SPINNER

Body.	Mulberry-coloured floss silk ribbed over with purple silk thread.
Tail.	Three or four whisks out of the stained hackle feather which is used for the legs.
Wings.	From a feather of the starling's wing.
Legs.	From a purple stained hackle which appears black when looked down upon, but which shines with a dark tortoise-shell tint when held up between the eye and the light.
	Hook, No. 1, long.

NO. 24. THE YELLOW SALLY

Body.	Any yellowish buff fur ribbed with yellow or apple-green silk.
Wings.	From a wing feather of a white hen, or fieldfare, stained pale yellow.
Legs.	From an extremely pale ginger hackle, or a white feather dyed of a yellowish tint.
	Hook No. 2, short.

No. 25. SKY BLUE

Body.	Pale ginger mohair mixed with light blue fur.
Tail.	A whisk or two of the hackle used for the legs.
Wings.	From a feather of the sea swallow, or of a very light blue dun hen.
Legs.	Hackle stained a pale yellow.
	Hook No. 0, short.
	The body of the above-mentioned spinner is more brilliant than that of the Sky Blue; the wings perfectly transparent, and almost colourless; it is very little used.

NO. 26. THE FERN FLY

Body.	Orange floss silk.
Wings.	The darkest part of a feather from the starling's wing.
Legs.	A red cock's hackle.
	Hook No. 2, short.
	To make it buzz, a lightish furnace hackle is wound upon the above body. It kills very well thus made.

NO. 27. THE ALDER FLY

Body.	Dark mulberry floss silk, or peacock's herl, tied with black silk.
Wings.	From a feather of brown hen's or peahen's wing.
Legs.	Dark umber stained hackle, or, in case of need, a black cock's hackle will answer the purpose tolerably well.
	Hook No. 3 or 4, long.
	To make it buzz, a dark dun hackle tinged brown may be wound upon the above body.
Remarks.	Fine black German wool (a little) dubbed on dark reddish-brown silk makes the body of this fly very well.
	It is a good fly for dibbing in the natural state, when abundant.

FLIES FOR JUNE

NO. 28, A. THE GREEN DRAKE

Body.	The middle part is pale straw-coloured floss silk, ribbed with silver twist. The extremities are of a brown peacock's herl, tied with light brown silk thread.
Tail.	Three rabbit's whiskers.
Wings and Legs.	Made buzz from a mottled feather of the mallard, stained a pale greenish yellow.
	Hook No. 5, 6, or 7, long.
	To make it with wings in their state of rest, part of a feather similarly stained must be used, and a pale brown bittern's hackle, or in case of need, a partidge feather, must be wrapped round the same body under the wings.

NO. 28, B. THE GREY DRAKE

Body.	The middle part is of white floss silk, ribbed over neatly with silver twist. The extremities are of brown peacock's herl tied with brown silk thread.
Tail.	Three rabbit's whiskers.
Wings and Legs	Made buzz from a mottled feather of the mallard, stained a faint purple.

Hook No. 5 or 6, long.

To make it with wings at rest, the same pale purple stained feather may be used for them, and   a dark purple stained hackle for the legs, upon the above body.

THE BLACK DRAKE

Is the male green drake metamorphosed. Its term of existence is about the same as that of the male above mentioned. It is smaller than the female, and very much darker, and is erroneously supposed by some, who call him the Death Drake, to kill her. He is never in season without her, but is not here represented, because he is not so fat and tempting a bait.

NO. 29. THE ORANGE DUN

Body.	Dark orange silk, and the fly to be dressed with the same.
Tail.	Two fibres of a starling's feather.
Legs.	A dark dun hackle.
Wings.	The dark part of a starling's quill feather.

Hook No. 2, long or short.

This fly should be made small and fine. Its metamorphosis is believed to be of a pale lemon tint, which should be used in the evenings at the same season. Imitation similar to No. 32.

NO. 30. THE MARLOW BUZZ

Body.	Black ostrich herl twisted with peacock herl and made with red silk thread.
Wings	Are made buzz with a dark furnace cock's hackle.
and Legs.	There are other species, some much smaller, of Red Beetles, and Ladybirds which may be imitated in a similar manner, and used when numerous. This is one of the largest employed.
	To make it with wings at rest, the darkest part of the starling's wing and a red cock's hackle may be wound upon the above body in the same way as for the Fern Fly.
Remarks.	A famous fly for both Trout and Grayling, and may be used till the end of September.

NO. 31. THE DARK MACKEREL

Body.	Dark mulberry floss silk, ribbed with gold twist.
Tail.	Three rabbit's whiskers.
Wings.	From a brown mottled feather of the mallard, which hangs from the back over a part of the wing.
Legs.	A purple dyed hackle, appearing black when l ooked down upon, but of a dark tortoise-shell hue when held between the eye and the light.

38

FLIES FOR JULY

NO. 32. THE PALE EVENING DUN

Body.   Yellow martin's fur spun on pale fawn-coloured silk thread.

Wings.   From a very fine grained feather of the starling's wing, stained of rather a lighter yellow than that which is used for the Green Drake.

Legs.   Pale dun hackle.

Hook No. 1, short.

The brighter yellow-bodied spinner, to which this changes, lives four or five days, is fainter coloured, and more transparent in the wing. The change is not given, as the Dark Mackerel (No. 31) is very much preferable for the evening.

Remarks.   The hair of an abortive calf, which would have been red if born at the proper time, is of a resplendent gold colour, and forms a good material for the legs of Summer Duns. It is tied on in the manner of wings. Make the above. Small Red Spinner for June and July :- Body, clear yellow silk; Legs, a red cock's hackle; Wings, starling's quill feather, from the middle of the wing, and the bird a young one.

Hook No. 1, short.

NO. 33. THE JULY DUN

Body.   Mole's fur and pale yellow mohair, mixed and spun on yellow silk.

Tail.   Two or three whisks of a dark dun hackle.

Wings.   Dark part of a feather from the starling's wing, stained darker in strong onion dye.

Legs.   Dark dun hackle.

Hook No. 2, short.

To make it buzz, a lighter hackle may be wound upon the above body.

The tint of its metamorphosis is the same as that of the Dark Mackerel (No. 31). It will catch well late in the evening.

Remarks.   At this season several kinds of Dun will be found on the water together; and especially a lighter Blue Dun than No. 2, described above, and a Dark Orange Dun. The angler's own observation, or the experience of others who know the water, will be called into requisition here.

NO. 34. THE GOLD-EYED GUAZE-WING

Body.   Very pale yellowish green floss silk, tied on with silk thread of the same colour.

Legs.   The palest blue dun hackle which can be procured.

Wings.   Any transparent feather, stained slightly green.

Hook No. 2, long.

NO. 35. THE WREN TAIL

Body.	Ginger-coloured fur ribbed with gold twist.
Wings	Feather from a wren's tail, wound on hackle-wise.
and Legs.	Hook No. 1, short.

NO. 36. THE RED ANT

Body.	Peacock's herl tied with red brown silk.
Wings.	From a feather of the light part of a starling's wing.
Legs.	A red cock's hackle.
	Hook No. 00, 0, or 1, long or short.

The BLACK ANT is made of peacock's herl, and black ostrich mixed, for the body. Wings from the darkest part of the starling's wing, and legs a black cock's hackle.

NO. 37. THE SILVER HORNS

Body.	Black ostrich herl tied with black silk, and dressed off.
Wings.	Feather from the wing of the cock blackbird.
Legs.	Small black cock's hackle.
Horns.	Grey feather of the mallard.
	Hook No. 2, short.
	To make it buzz the body is ribbed with silver-twist upon the black ostrich herl and a nearly black hackle wrapped all down.

FLIES FOR AUGUST

NO. 38. THE AUGUST DUN

Body.	Brown floss silk ribbed with yellow silk thread.
Tail.	Two rabbit's whiskers.
Wings.	Feather of a brown hen's wing.
Legs.	Plain red hackle stained brown.
	Hook No. 2, short.
	It is made buzz with a grouse feather wound upon the above body.
	The Red Spinner, to which it changes, is very similar to that which the Blue (No. 2) turns to, and is a good fly on a mild evening.

NO. 39. THE ORANGE FLY

Body.	Orange floss silk tied on with black silk thread.
Wings.	Dark part of the starling's wing, or feather of a hen blackbird.
Legs.	A very dark furnace hackle.
	Hook No. 1, short.

NO. 40. THE CINNAMON FLY

Body.   Fawn-coloured floss silk, tied on with silk thread of the same colour.

Wings.   Feather of a yellow brown hen's wing, rather darker than the landrail's wing feather.

Legs.   A ginger hackle.

                It is made buzz with a red hackle from the grouse, or a red hackle stained brown with copperas, and tied on the same body.

                Hook No. 3, long.

Remarks.   So numerous are the species of Caddis Fly resembling the above, different on different waters, that the angler must use his own observation. A wren's tail feather, wound round a hare's ear body, will aid him in giving the rich brown tint common to many of the genus, and the landrail's quill feather will be sufficiently dark with this hackle.

                The Sheffield anglers use a fly they call Partridge Rump, which may be noticed here as proper for this part of the season.

                Hook No. 4, long; body, yellow silk (not floss); feather, partridge rump. The head is formed with copper-coloured peacock's herl. A good killer in Derbyshire waters. It is the yellow-bodied Harry-long-legs.

FLIES FOR SEPTEMBER

NO. 41. THE BLUE BOTTLE

Body.   Bright blue floss silk tied with light brown silk thread, showing the brown at the head.

Wings.   Feather of the starling's wing.

Legs.   Black hackle from a cock wrapped down the principal part of the body.

                Hook No. 3, short.

                To make it buzz, a dark dun hackle may be wound upon the above body.

Remarks.   The House or Shade Fly may be noticed here. A first-rate angler used to make it thus, for July:-

Wings.   From under covert feather of waterhen's wing.

Legs.   Blue starling feather.

Body.   Light brown and pea-green wool mixed.

Head.   Green peacock's herl, and three laps under the wings.

                Hook No. 2, short.

                A first-rate killer.

Mayfly

NO. 42. THE WHIRLING BLUE DUN

Body. Squirrel's red brown fur mixed with yellow mohair, tied with yellow silk thread well waxed.

Tail. One or two whisks of a pale ginger hackle.

Wings. Feather from a starling's wing not very light.

Legs. Pale ginger hackle.

Hook No. 2, Grayling.

NO. 43. THE LITTLE PALE BLUE DUN

Body. Very pale blue fur mixed with a very little yellow mohair.

Wings. Feather from the sea swallow.

Legs. The palest blue hackle to be had.

Hook No. 1, Grayling.

To make it buzz, a sea swallow's feather only may be wound upon the same body.

The metamorphosis of this fly has very transparent wings. It is too delicate to be imitated.

Remarks. This is called by some anglers the 'Willow Fly.'

NO. 44. THE WILLOW (OR WITHY) FLY

Body. Mole's fur (a very little) spun upon yellow silk.

Wings and Legs. A dark dun hen's hackle with the edges strongly tinged a copper colour; sometimes called a golden dun feather, or a yellow dun.

Hook No. 1, Grayling.

Remarks. As the fishing at this season, and in October is, or should be, for Grayling exclusively, the hackle form of No. 7 may be recalled to the angler's notice, as now coming again into season, and killing the largest fish.

This and the Willow Fly, made as above, or with the addition of wings from the dark part of a starling's quill feather, are good killers in the Derwent till November.

PALMERS FOR THE FISHING SEASON

NO. 45. THE RED PALMER

Peacock herl with a red cock's hackle wrapped over it, and tied with light brown or red silk thread. This corresponds also with the larvae of the Drinker Moth.

It may be varied by a ruby stained hackle; which answers well on the Dove.

Hook No. 6, Palmers.

NO. 46. THE BROWN PALMER

Mulberry-coloured worsted spun on brown silk, and a brown stained cock's hackle wrapped over the whole.
It may be varied by making the body of ostrich herl, of a drab colour, and winding a grizzled hackle over.
Hook No. 6, Palmers.

NO. 47. THE BLACK AND RED PALMER

Black ostrich herl ribbed with gold twist, and a red cock's hackle wrapped over it. This Fly may be made large.... The feather at the shoulder should be a large furnace hackle from the rump of a game cock, and the ostrich herl should be wound thickest there. The gold twist should be shown clearly at the tail, and the tailhook should be large and strong.
Hook No. 7, Palmers.
Show plenty of gold at the tail; and let your feather be a good black near the head, and shade off to a rich game red. A fly of this kind falls more lightly, and shows more life in the water, than other large flies. The elastic fibres of the hackle open and close as it is drawn across the stream, and it displays its colours to the best advantage. A hackle fly is never on its back. The Black and Red, or Large Red, Palmer will ever be a standard Trout fly. For a Dropper, a smaller fly of similar materials, on a single hook (No. 7), will be found a good accompaniment. That this is taken for a beetle of some kind by the Trout is highly probable.

PATTERNS MENTIONED BY ALFRED RONALDS SPECIFICALLY FOR DERBYSHIRE WATERS

Red Fly	Partridge Rump
Frost Fly	July Dun
March Brown	Cinnamon fly variant
Red Spinner variant	Little Pale Blue Dun
Little Chap	Caterpillar
Orange Dun	

There are twenty 'Buzz' dressings and a further ten Hackles in Ronalds's list. For the rivers he fished these were evidently a successful and popular style of fly. On a number of dressings an upright wing is made, all these being in the Derbyshire style of fly dressing.

The influence of Ronalds was enormous. His work has been used as a benchmark for the presentation of angling literature up to the present day, his patterns are commonly used by anglers worldwide and he established the need for a system of scientific classification of flies imitated by anglers.

JOHN TURTON

John Turton was a Sheffield angler and tackle maker who, in 1836, wrote *The Angler's Manual or Fly-Fisher's Oracle*. He had thirty years angling experience throughout England and Wales, but particularly on the streams of Southern Yorkshire and Derbyshire. His preferred style of angling was by artificial fly. However, he by no means eschewed other methods. In his work he writes with authority on Bottom Fishing, also on the use of worm, minnow, natural fly and pike fishing. Dibbling was a very popular method and Turton recommended dun drake, grasshopper, stonefly, mayfly, bluebottle downlooker and daddy long legs as live bait, often with a pellet attached to the cast to sink the fly in what is now termed 'pocket water'. He mentions 'Ant Egg Fishing' as being much used by the 'natives of Derbyshire' when the rivers ran 'high and black'. By this method large numbers of trout and grayling were caught from turnholes – eddies and deep still water. The eggs were obtained from the large nests of wood ants; several were used to bait the hook and they were then fished under a float, usually in the form of a dyed cork. After rain, riverbanks were often lined with anglers using ant eggs, who took hampers – creels – full of fish on this bait.

The Angler's Manual details many species of fish along with suitable baits and tackle to deceive and overcome them. There is clear instruction on fly dressing, suitable and unsuitable weather for angling, weather forecasting, cooking the catch and angling style. Turton insisted on subdued clothing, cautious approach and fishing 'fine and far off' – inevitably. In respect of fly dressing he considered size, shape and colour relative to natural flies as being of importance and recommends wetting a sample of material prior to use to ensure an accurate colour match. Body colour, he thought, is of primary import.

John Turton was a skilled rod maker, fly dresser and manufacturer of lines spun from silkworm, gut and horsehair mixtures. These were tapered, ending in single hair 'lashes' tied with water knots. Rods were often constructed of lancewood with up to five joints to allow transport in pocket or carriage box! They would be between ten and twelve feet long, though for smaller streams Turton favoured a rod of nine feet. When practical, rods of two sections were preferred with a spliced whalebone tip of several inches 'to improve the strike'. Such models were often used by Lancashire anglers fishing Derbyshire waters, with a deep narrow reel used to store the tapered line.

Turton's description of a landing net points to a sophisticated model. The rim folded and was detachable to facilitate storage in the pocket; its handle two-piece, terminating in a spear and hook to rescue tackle from trees and herbage; the whole also acting as a wading staff. He carried a tackle case with silks, tinsels, hooks, scissors, wax and file contained in pockets. Parchment books, also stored in pockets contained feathers from, in Turton's case, thirty four bird species and one with dubbing fur from some fifteen mammals in different colours, including everyone's favourite – hair from abortive calves.

John's angling began as a child on local dams which were used to supply the water-

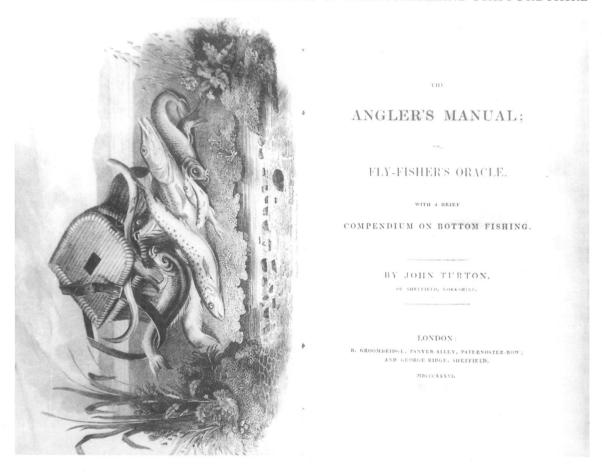

Frontispiece and title page of John Turton's book
The Angler's Manual or Fly-Fisher's Oracle

power to drive the grinding wheels and drop hammers of the 'Little Mesters' workshops in the steep valleys around Sheffield. The waters were stocked with fish and he reports there were plenty of trout in them. From here he graduated to the upper river Don in the company of his grandfather – a man of independent means – and an expert fly-fisher of some fifty years experience.

This allows the possibility of the older man beginning his angling career as early as 1760, giving insight, via John Turton, to dressings used in a largely unrecorded period of Derbyshire and Staffordshire fly fishing. Turton was supplied with flies by his grandfather and, no doubt, also acquired their dressings. Access to materials was fairly easy – his grandfather was a shooter. Aged fourteen, John was considered by his tutor to

45

be a good fly fisher eventually inheriting the old man's fishing tackle and, perhaps more importantly, his fly book. From the latter he was able to tie flies to patterns very probably used in the distant past.

Coarse fishing experience came initially from visits to the river Rother and local canals. Here, Turton fished for 'scale fish', pike, chub and the few trout which inhabited the waters. He was also able to indulge his fondness for the fly on the river's chub population – an activity he much enjoyed. A large lake near Chapel-en-le-Frith attracted notice too. This contained '...*an immense quantity of perch and very large trout...*'. One visit there with a companion yielded sixteen trout together weighing thirty three pounds, taken on Brown Watchet, Upwinged Dun, Small Black and Dun Drake. John's companion, a bottom fisher, used worm to catch sixty perch, which totalled sixteen pounds.

The river Derwent at Darley Dale was popular water with 'Sheffielders'. Turton regularly fished the river, staying at the Grouse Inn, which provided both accommodation and access to the water.

One of his clients - a middle aged, independent, single gentleman – was so pleased with flies dressed by Turton that he invited John to share a three week excursion in April and May on the rivers of Derbyshire and Staffordshire! The pair began on three preserved dams in Darley Dale, one of which had been stocked with grayling. Turton comments that this is the only lake in his experience with the species present, (today the only similar water I am aware of is Gouthwaite in Nidderdale).

From here they fished up the Derwent from Matlock to Rowsley where they spent time at the Peacock Inn. They next fished through Chatsworth to Baslow, catching trout, grayling, chub and dace. Turton records the presence of very large barbel 'all up the river'. Next through Grindleford and Padley to Hasleford Bridge where they lodged at 'Widow Eyre's'. Evenings were spent yarning with her son, a good angler, about fish, fishing and the Duke of Rutland's waterkeeper, Jonathon Bamford. He in the past, prior to then problems with poachers, had caught large numbers of fish. Side streams and the river were then fished to Mytham Bridge and on up to the Ashopton Inn, the next hostelry.

They then returned to Rowsley, to begin their expedition up the river Wye to Bakewell. Good numbers of excellent trout and grayling were caught from well-kept and highly stocked water. Lathkill was crossed and described as '...the clearest stream, and which breeds the finest and reddest coloured trout in the country'. Gentlemen anglers haunted the Rutland Arms in Bakewell, particularly in the 'drake season', and the two anglers made the inn their base. Ashford and Monsal Dale both afforded good sport, Monsal after rain, 'being so full of trout that a person may tire himself with sport'. After fishing the small streams up to and near Buxton the next destination was Ashbourne and then Dovedale, where they spent two days in wonderful scenery with no shortage of fish.

It was a visit which Turton and his host greatly enjoyed. He describes with pleasure the discussion among anglers of the day's sport, sharing both knowledge and anecdote. The flies used on the visit are listed as:- March Brown, Dark Dun, Cockup Dun, Dun Drake,

Snipe Dun, Cow Dung Dun, Brown Watchet and Small Black; coupled with his further advice of flies made with a martin feather hackle and sparse silk bodies of black, sky blue purple and flesh colours, this is a formidable Derbyshire/Staffordshire flybox!

The fly list is organised in three sections. The first consists of twenty four standard patterns and these, he states, should be available in various sizes to suit the state of the water. If no fish show, he proffers the advice to use dark duns on bright days and light duns on gloomy days. These are the 'certain killers in any trout river' of John Turton:

1. WINGED – March Brown.
Used all March and April: made with orange silk; the wing of partridge, red mottled, top of tail or rump feather; legs of wren's tail feather; body brown down, from fox's ear, twisted on the orange silk. It comes into use several times after rains in summer, but changing its colour; it must then be made with a hackle from the feather outside of a woodcock's wing, which is grey mottled, and grey at the end, with Devonshire brown silk and dark brown tammy dubbing: an excellent fly in dark waters.

2. HACKLE – Barm Dun.
For March and April: approaching to a furness; made with red silk; wing a cock's hackle, tinged a bann colour; dark-red brown dubbing, from fox's ear, close to the black part; it gets darker towards the end of April, and is called Black Red or Furness Fly, and kills all the season: made with red silk; body, black silk at tail, and a lap or two of green peacock feather close under the wing; a black-red cocked hackle feather, red at the edges, and a black list up the middle; sometimes in black waters the body is quite black, and a dark furness feather, reddish at the underside only, and made with black silk and black dubbing.

3. HACKLE – Brown Watchet.
By some anglers called the Orange Brown. It kills all the year, and is made with light orange silk; wing, a wren's tail feather; body, bright light orange silk; head, green peacock's feather. In dark water, with a little green peacock's feather under wing. This is so noted a fly to kill with, that anglers, when asked what the fish are taking, frequently say – "Wren's tail and orange for ever!" A little brown bear's down is used at the spring of the year, twisted round the silk.

4. HACKLE – Hawthorn Fly.
For March and April: made with black silk; body, black ostrich's herl; legs, black hen, from neck; wing, lightest or bottom part of a starling's quill feather; sometimes in summer, red legs. In May use the jay's wing quill feather for wing: this will be the Black Caterpillar Fly. In June, the sea swallow's feather, for wing, makes it the Black Ant Fly.

5. HACKLE – Whirling Dun.
Comes on early in April: it is made with yellow silk; wing, the middle dun of cock's hackle feather, tinged at the edges with the down of a fox's cub; ash-colour at the roots; twisted thinly round the yellow silk, so as that the ribs may be seen. Some use a pale dun mallard feather; it comes on toward the end of June, after rains.

6. WINGED – Dun Drake.

For March and April: is made with yellow silk; body, brown down from fox's ear, ribbed with yellow silk; legs, a dark grizzled dun cock hackle feather; wing, the dark shaded feather under woodcock's wing. It frequently comes on after rains, and is called by some anglers the Old Man: it must then be made with a bright ash-coloured body; the legs of light ginger-coloured cock hackle; and wings, dark grey mottled mallard feather. It is a large fly, and kills the largest fish.

7. WINGED – Cock-up or Upwinged Dun.

Kills all the season: it is made with ash-coloured silk; wing, of starling's wing quill feather; legs, the lightest ginger cock hackle feather that can be got; body, bright ash-coloured silk, having a shade of green in it; ribbed with a black horse-hair, and two black horns. It changes colour as the weather alters, sometimes having red and at other times yellow legs: which anglers must notice, as the flies are younger or older. This fly is the surest killer that is thrown on the water: too much cannot be said in its praise, for either trout or greyling [*sic*], particularly on cool gloomy days.

8. HACKLE – Red Spider Fly.

For March and April: is made with yellow silk; wing, a red mottled partridge rump feather; body, hare's ear, dark coloured at bottom, and grey at top, twisted round the yellow silk. In summer, for dark waters, yellow dubbing is used. A very good fly and often wanted.

9. WINGED – Brown Spider Fly.

Comes into season about the 20th of April, and lasts all May: wing, the large brown feather outside woodcock's wing; legs, black hen's feather from neck; body, bright lead-coloured silk. A good fly, and found on sand-beds by the river side; by some called the Sand Fly.

10. WINGED – Stone Fly.

Comes on toward the latter end of April, and lasts three or four weeks; it comes on a second time in July. It is found under flat stones by the river side, and is as large as a house cricket, and not unlike one. It is artificially made with yellow silk; wing, a very dark grey mallard's or pheasant's wing quill feather; legs, brown moor game, out of neck; body, bear's dun, with brown and yellow mohair mixed; most yellow underneath, and toward tail; ribbed with yellow silk. Kills large fish late at night; also in strong streams, and on rough windy days.

11. HACKLE – Orl Fly.

For May and June: is made with red silk; wing, a dark grizzled cock hackle feather; body, copper-coloured peacock's herl. A good fly.

12. HACKLE – Down Looker.

Used in May, and lasts till the end of August: it is made with orange silk; wing, the brown feather outside woodcock's wing; body, light bright orange silk, ribbed with a thick black horse-hair; made small at tail; dark brown down, from fox's ear, under wing. In discoloured water, this is as good a killer as can be used, and takes the largest fish.

PLATE I
JOHN TURTON FLY DRESSINGS

ORL FLY

Wings
& Legs: Dark grizzled cock hackle
Body: Copper coloured peacock herl
Silk: Red

BROWN SPIDER FLY

Wings: Large brown feather from
    outside of a woodcock's wing
Body: Bright lead coloured silk
Legs: Black hen's feather from neck

ORANGE BLACK

Wings
& Legs: Black hen hackle
Body: Bright orange silk
Silk: Orange

RED SPIDER FLY

Wings
& Legs: Red mottled partridge
    rump feather
Body: Hare's ear fur
Legs: Yellow

49

13. WINGED – Primrose Dun.
For May and June: is made with primrose silk; wing, light starling's quill feather; body, bright primrose silk; legs, brimstone-coloured mohair. A good fly in clear water.

14. HACKLE – Black Gnat.
In June: made with black silk; wing, a small light starling's under wing feather; body, black ostrich and pewit's cap feather. This fly does not touch the water, and the fish is said to look above the water; the artificial fly falls into the water, and this is supposed to be the reason they so often refuse to take the made fly.

15. HACKLE – Yellow Spider Fly.
In June: it is made with yellow silk: wing, light brown mottled moor-game's feather; body, light yellow silk and yellow marten's fur from the throat. Good in clear low water.

16. WINGED – Green Drake.
Comes on about the 20th of June, and lasts all July; it is a large fly, made with pea-green silk; wing, a mottled mallard's feather from the top side of the thigh, dyed a yellow green; body, pea-green dubbing, ribbed with yellow silk; yellow-green mohair legs, and three black horns. This fly takes the best of fish: it is very often used in its natural state and thrown on the water. In their season, these flies come from the rivers in such quantities, that a stranger would be astonished: boys can gather small drake baskets full of these baits in a very short time: these they sell to gentlemen to fish with.

17. WINGED – Red Ant Fly.
In June and July: Made with light orange silk; wing, the light or bottom part of a starling's quill feather; legs, ginger-coloured cock hackle; head and body, peacock's feather, made thick at tail and thin in the middle of the body. An excellent fly, and used in September, on bright sunny days.

18. HACKLE – Orange Dun.
In July: made with light orange silk; wing, the light dun feather under young moor-game's wing; body, light bright orange silk, and orange mohair dubbing under wing. Good in black or disturbed waters.

19. HACKLE – Tail to Tail, or Knotted Midge.
In July and August: is made with purple silk: wing, pewet's topping or cap feather, headed with magpie's green feather from tail; body, hare's scut, a mazarine blue. These flies come down the streams two together, tail to tail, and the fish rise very fast at them, refusing all other kinds when they are in season; the largest trout take them.

20. WINGED – Bank Fly.
From July to September: made with orange silk: wing, a corncreak's quill feather; legs, wren's tail; body, bright light orange silk. Seldom takes before three or four o'clock in the afternoon; a good killer late at night, and in dark waters.

21. HACKLE – Brown Shiner.
In August: made with light orange silk: wing, light brown mottled moor-game's feather from bottom of neck; body, light orange silk at tail, and green peacock's feather close under the wing, headed with green peacock. At particular times, especially after rains, it is made with mulberry-coloured silk, and dark brown tammy twisted upon the silk for body; wing, a grouse's feather, nearly black. This is a great killer after rains and in black waters; by some anglers called Old Joan.

22. WINGED – Proud Tailor Fly.
In August: made with orange silk: wing, the darkest brown feather of a landrail, or corncreak; legs, brown cock hackle feather; body, bright pale orange silk untwisted. A large fly, and kills in low clear waters.

23. HACKLE – Purple Midge.
For September and October: it is made with purple silk: wing, the blue feather, shaded with green at edge, out of an old cock pheasant's neck; body, black down, twisted on the purple silk.

24. WINGED – Little Pale Blue Dun.
For September and October: made with ash-coloured silk: wing, sea-swallow's outside wing feather; legs, a pale blue hen hackle; body, light blue rabbit, and a little yellow fur mixed. Good for grayling.

After the 'drake season' when fish have become glutted the following patterns are offered: '...a very light dun, made with a bright yellow silk body; a middle dun, with light ash-coloured body; a blue dun, with a bright orange silk body; and a very dark dun with bright purple body, must then be used; and a small black dun at night'.

It is perhaps no accident that these are the body colours of several North Country spider patterns. The next group of flies, John Turton thought requisite for anglers who have practised well with the previous twenty-four. These, too, apparently rarely fail to catch fish! Many of them are imitations of specific insects.

25. HACKLE – Red Palmer.
Used all the season in strong waters: made with red silk: wing, a red cock hackle feather; body thick, of black ostrich's feather.

26. HACKLE – Great Red Palmer.
Used all the season in strong waters: made with red silk: wing, red cock hackle feather; body, black ostrich's feather, ribbed with gold twist.

27. HACKLE – Whirling Blue.
For March and April: wing, feather from under water-hen's wing: made with yellow silk and mole's fur, twisted thinly on the silk.

28. HACKLE – Black with Red.
All the season: made with red silk: wing, black hen's feather from neck; body, black silk at tail, and black down close under wing.

29. HACKLE – Green Tail.
For April: made with orange silk: wing, light-brown mottled woodcock's feather from bottom of neck; body, hare's ear, the brown part ribbed with brimstone-coloured silk; head, green peacock's herl; and tip of tail, dark-green silk. A very good fly, but lasts only about a week.

30. HACKLE – Snipe Dun.
For April and May: made with yellow silk: wing, a full snipe's underside wing feather; body blue, rabbit's down, twisted on the silk. An excellent greyling fly.

31. HACKLE – Red Shiner Fly.
For April: made with orange silk: wing, red woodcock's feather from butt end of wing; body, light bright orange silk, ribbed with green peacock's feather, and peacock's head. A good killer after rains. It changes these colours; - if there be bright days, the red owl's feather, from butt end of wing, is used for wings; if a dark day, the brown owl's feather must be used from side of wing; if clear low water, the partridge's rump feather is best.

32. HACKLE – Cow-dung Fly.
In May: made with pea-green silk: wing, feather from underside of a jay's wing, and pea-green mohair twisted on the silk.

33. HACKLE – Black May Fly, or Silver Palmer.
Made with black silk: wing, a black hen's hackle feather; body, black ostrich's feather, ribbed with silver twist.

34. HACKLE – Oak Fly.
In May: made with yellow silk: wing, partridge's rump feather, without moon; body, yellow silk, ribbed with a strong black horse-hair, light brown under wing.

35. HACKLE – Iron Blue Fly.
In May: made with yellow silk: wing, outside or butt end of merlin hawk's wing; body, dark water-rat dubbing ribbed with yellow silk. An excellent fly, and frequently comes on after showers of rain.

36. WINGED – Small Black Midge.
In May: made with black silk; wing, fieldfare's quill feather; body, black ostrich's feather; legs, blue starling.

37. WINGED – May Imp.
Made with yellow silk; wing, the yellow feather out of a green linnet's tail; legs, yellow plover's feather; body, waxed yellow silk. A good fly in brooks after rains; seldom taken in clear water. The Little Yellow Drake is made the same way, only with a bright yellow body.

38. WINGED – Yellow Legs.

In May and June: made with yellow silk: wing, a jay's wing quill feather; legs, yellow plover's feather; body, bright brimstone silk. Both trout and greyling take this fly well in discoloured waters.

39. WINGED – Grey Drake.

In June: made with yellow silk: wing, a blue shaded green feather from a white grouse; legs, a middle dun grizzled cock's hackle feather; body, blue and yellow dubbing mixed, ribbed with black, and three black horns.

40. HACKLE – Purple Gold Palmer.

In June: made with purple silk: wing, a red cock's hackle feather; body, purple mohair, ribbed with gold twist. Takes large fish in rough streams and dark waters.

41. WINGED – Red Spinner.

In June: made with yellow silk: wing, starling's quill feather; legs, red cock's hackle feather; body, red-brown squirrel's down, ribbed with gold twist.

42. WINGED – Small Red Spinner.

In June: made with yellow silk: wing, starling's wing quill feather; legs, a red feather from a cock's neck; body, yellow marten's fur from the throat, twisted on the silk. A capital killer; takes large greyling.

43. HACKLE – Netted Fly.

In June: made with yellow silk: wing, light mottled partridge's feather out of the horse-shoe mark on the breast; body, yellow silk, and yellow marten's fur close under wing.

44. HACKLE – Gold-coloured Dun.

In June: made with gold-coloured silk: wing, yellow or golden plover, from outside of wing; body, gold-coloured mohair, twisted on the silk, close under wing. Best early in a morning and late at night.

45. HACKLE – Brown Gnat.

In June: made with very light brown silk: wing, feather under starling's wing; body, lightest brown and violet down mixed, twisted on the silk. A good fly in clear water; made long, and very thin. By some anglers it is called the Fern Fly.

46. WINGED – Small Ant Fly.

In June: made with orange silk: wing, martin's quill feather; legs, wren's tail feather; body, bright reddish orange silk, headed with green peacock's feather. Best on bright days, and in low clear water.

47. HACKLE – Grasshopper.

In June: made with pea-green silk: wing, a red cock's hackle feather; body, green and yellow dubbing mixed, ribbed with green silk. A very good chub fly.

48. WINGED – Sky-coloured Blue.
In June and July: made with sky-blue silk: wing, starling's quill feather; legs, yellow mohair; body, blue and yellow dubbing mixed. Most taken in clear water.

49. HACKLE – Buff-coloured Dun, or Stream Fly.
In June and July: made with buff-coloured silk; wing, a buff-coloured dun hen's feather; body, buff-coloured mohair, and yellow dubbing mixed close under wing.

50. HACKLE – Blue Gnat.
In June and July: made with yellow silk: wing, a pale blue cock's hackle feather, tinged at edge: body blue, fox's cub and yellow down mixed, twisted on the silk. A very good trout fly.

51. WINGED – Small White Moth.
In June, and, at evenings, to the end of the season: made with yellow silk: wing, a white duck's feather; legs, white hen's hackle feather; body, white part of hare's scut, ribbed with yellow silk.

52. WINGED – Shade Fly.
In July, and on bright days, to the end of the season: made with orange silk: wing, water-hen's underwing feather; legs, blue starling's feather; body, light brown and pea-green dubbing mixed, with about three laps of green peacock's feather close under wing; head, green peacock. An excellent fly, and kills either in clear or discoloured waters; good for all sorts of fish that take flies.

53. HACKLE – July Blue Dun.
Made with ash-coloured silk: wing, bluecap's tail, or a dark blue pigeon's feather; body, mole's and marten's fur mixed, twisted on the silk.

54. HACKLE- Violet Midge.
In July: made with violet silk: wing, jackdaw's neck; body, pale pink silk, and water-rat's down close under the wing.

55. HACKLE – Stone Midge.
In July: made with sky-blue silk: wing, pewet's topping feather; body, fibres of blue heron's feather; a silver colour, headed with green peacock's feather.

56. HACKLE – Orange Black.
In July: made with orange silk: wing, black hen's hackle feather; body, bright orange silk.

57. HACKLE – Wasp Fly.
In July: made with light brown silk: wing, starling's underwing feather; body, brown bear's hair, ribbed with yellow silk.

58. HACKLE – Black Palmer Fly.
July to September: made with dark orange silk; wing, black hen's hackle feather; body, copper-coloured peacock's feather; after rains, ribbed with silver twist.

59. HACKLE – White Dun Midge.

In July: made with white silk: wing, blue dun heron's feather; body, white mohair, very small. Taken early in a morning, and in the evening.

60. WINGED – Red Clock Fly.

In July and August: made with dark orange silk: wing, red partridge's tail feather; legs, blue starling; body, large peacock's and black ostrich's feathers mixed. On some days, a red freckled partridge's tail feather must be used for wings.

61. WINGED – Black Wood Fly.

In August and September: made with red silk: wing, blackbird's wing quill feather; legs, black hen's hackle feather; body, purple mohair, ribbed with black ostrich's feather; head, green peacock.

62. HACKLE – Yellow Spider Fly.

In August: made with yellow silk: wing, the large mottled feather of a sandpiper, or snipe; body, yellow marten's fur, twisted on the silk.

63. WINGED – Mill Dun.

In August: made with light orange silk: wing, lightest starling, bottom of quill feather; legs, light ginger cock's hackle feather; body, one rib pink and one purple silk; a little light brown down close under legging.

64. WINGED – Small Black-clock Fly.

In August: made with black silk: wing, a yellow throstle's wing quill feather; legs, blue starling's feather; body, peacock's and ostrich's feathers mixed.

65. WINGED – Stone Gnat, or Dark Watchet.

In August and September: made with plum-coloured silk; very small: wing, martin's wing quill feather; legs dark, tinged at edge, dun hen's feather from top of neck; body, dark water-rat's down. This is a fly most anglers are at a loss about: it comes on after rains, and is taken in the turn-holes and still, deep places; it looks very dark coloured, and may be seen carried down the rivers by the current; it is the best fly that can be used for trout and greyling in dark waters.

66. WINGED – Little Whirling Blue.

In August and September: made with yellow silk: wing, starling's quill feather; legs, red feather from a cock's hackle; body, blue and yellow dubbing mixed, twisted on the silk.

67. HACKLE – Grey Dun Midge.

In September: made with yellow silk: wing, light woodcock's feather under wing; body, yellow silk; head, green peacock. On some days, the outside wing feather of the dotterill is used for wing.

68. HACKLE – Willow Fly.

In September and October: made with yellow silk: wing, a blue grizzled cock's hackle feather; body, blue squirrel's fur and yellow down mixed, twisted on the silk. Best on cold stormy days.

69. HACKLE – Winter Brown.
In October and November: made with orange silk; wing, woodcock's underwing feather; body, bright orange silk, headed with magpie's green tail feather.

The final eight patterns are those which Turton used for coarse fish, especially chub. He recommended that the flies be tied large for large fish! Along with these, Drakes, Downlooker, Brown Shiner, Purple Midge and Ant Flies will be found successful. In use the fly was often tipped with a caddis or maggot.

70. HACKLE – Moor-Game Brown.
Made with red silk: wing, a large dark-brown mottled moor-game feather, from top of thigh; body, black down, ribbed with gold twist. Some anglers use a brown mottled hen's feather for wings; and for body, brown part of fox's ear, with orange silk.

71. HACKLE – Brown Moth Fly.
Made with orange silk: wing, mottled cock pheasant's breast feather, red edged; body, green peacock's herl, ribbed with gold twist.

72. WINGED – Great Moth Fly.
Made with orange silk: wing, hen pheasant's mottled tail feather; legs, a red cock's hackle feather; body, green peacock's herl, ribbed with gold twist.

73. WINGED – White Moth Fly.
Made with white silk: wing, a white mottled barn-owl's feather; legs, white hen's hackle feather; body, white part of a hare's scut, ribbed with yellow silk or gold twist. This is an excellent fly, and is frequently taken by the largest trout after hay-harvest and during the night.

74. WINGED – Black Fly.
As No. 61, for trout, but very large in August; it must be ribbed with silver twist.

75. HACKLE – Harry Longlegs, or Large Spider Fly.
Made with yellow silk: wing, partridge's long top tail or rump feather; body, pale buff or nankeen-coloured silk, with red down from squirrel's thigh close under wing.

76. HACKLE – Large Bank Fly.
Made with orange silk: wing, the largest feather from under corncreak's wing; body, light orange silk, with blue and brown down mixed from fox's ear.

77. HACKLE- Purple Palmer.
Made with purple silk: wing, corncreak's feather from top or outside of wing; body, bright purple silk, and purple mohair dubbing close under wing. This is an excellent fly for the latter end of the season.

56

Of all these patterns forty-seven are hackles, six of these being Palmers, the remainder are winged. Many are very close to the dressings of Charles Cotton, Aldam's Old Man (Robert Whitehead) and Alfred Ronalds. It is probable that many of these patterns were handed on from angler to angler or in handwritten documents. The flies have a North Country bias and a Sheffield fly dresser would be in an admirable position to take his business from the rivers of Derbyshire along with the Dales of Yorkshire.

The Angler's Manual is a fount of advice and humour. Under *Signs of Rain, or Prognostics of the Weather* are to be found :-

> *If two rainbows appear together*
> *If corns pain your feet more than usual*
> *If Mam Tor keeps its nightcap on in the morning*
> *If very large black thick clouds appear in the West*

And *Amusement for Leisure Time*

Anglers when they have leisure may be recommended:-
> *To look over their rods...*
> *To spin and repair their reel lines...*
> *To examine lashes of gut...*
> *To cut up old flies... and make new ones...*
> *To look over and dress any feathers...*
> *To wash bait bags and fish hampers quite clean...*

FLIES REPRESENTED BY JOHN TURTON'S DRESSINGS

Barm Fly	Yellow Dun
Brown Gnat	Soldier Fly; Igneumon Fly
Brown Spider Fly	Gravel Bed; Sand Fly
Cock-Up	Cock Winged Dun
Downlooker	Oak Fly; Ash Fly
Dun Drake	March Brown
Green Tail	Grannom
March Brown (local)	Possibly February Red as Aldam
Orange Dun	Blue Winged Olive
Orl Fly	Alder Fly
Red Clock Fly	Terrestrial Beetle; Heather Fly
Small Black Clock	Beetle
Snipe Dun	Olive
Stone Gnat	Iron Blue
Whirling Blue	August Dun
White Dun Midge	Caenis; Angler's Curse

In John Turton's own words:

'What can be more delightful to an angler than to look from the hills into the beautiful valleys where three of the principal Derbyshire rivers – the Dove, the Wye and the Derwent – take their course! – to see rocks, woods, pleasant groves, and in some places the fine streams in which he is going to fish, abounding as they do with trout and greyling. Surrounded by such scenery, while angling for these fish with the fly in the charming Month of May is indeed enjoying one of the sweetest pleasures of outdoor life...'

WILLIAM SHIPLEY

There were two men, father and son, by the name of William Shipley, who were tackle makers and professional anglers in Ashbourne. William senior was born around 1760 and fished the Dove all his life. He died in or near 1830. His son, William, was probably born in the late 1790s. The elder man was well known, and rated by locals and clients as '...the best fly fisher that appeared on the banks of the Dove during the last fifty years...'. For much of his life he kept both notes and a diary of his angling activities, this eventually forming the basis of his son's publication. Both Shipleys acted as guides on local rivers to clients. Sir Humphrey Davy, a friend of David Watts-Russell of Ilam Hall, frequently fished the Dove and Manifold. When staying at Ilam, Davy was guided on his expeditions by William Shipley senior, and he offered assistance in writing up the sum of his guide's knowledge. This was never done but left to William Shipley junior and Edward Fitzgibbon years later.

The younger William Shipley was a tackle maker and fly dresser. Although he had served a thirty year 'apprenticeship' on the Derbyshire and Staffordshire rivers, he considered help was required in detailing his own experience and the recorded wisdom of his father. Whilst visiting relatives in Nottingham he met Edward Fitzgibbon who wrote under the pen name of 'Ephemera'.

'At a single interview, at the hospitable board of a relative, ...and reading shortly after certain sketches of fly-fishing in Derbyshire, which appeared in a celebrated sporting London journal, and from certain allusions in them knowing them to be his, I resolved (forgive the vulgar flippancy of the expression) to hook him. The world shall never know the bait I used, but he took it freely; and I had the pleasure, towards the end of last January, of landing him safely under my humble roof...'.

The partnership of author and editor was thus sealed and work began on their important and influential work, *A True Treatise on the Art of Fly-Fishing* (1838). The enthusiasm of the two men is amply demonstrated in their preface remarks. Fitzgibbon told Shipley that without Shipley's knowledge and his father's notes, he alone could not

A

TRUE TREATISE

ON THE ART OF

FLY-FISHING,

TROLLING,

ETC.,

AS PRACTISED ON THE DOVE, AND ON THE PRINCIPAL
STREAMS OF THE MIDLAND COUNTIES;

APPLICABLE TO EVERY TROUT AND GRAYLING
RIVER IN THE EMPIRE.

BY WILLIAM SHIPLEY.

EDITED
BY EDWARD FITZGIBBON, ESQ.

LONDON:
SIMPKIN, MARSHALL, AND CO.;
SOLD ALSO BY THE AUTHOR AT ASHBORNE,
AND BY ALL BOOKSELLERS.
1838.

Title page and frontispiece of William Shipley's *A True Treatise on the Art of Fly-Fishing*.
For the purposes of art the river flow has been reversed!

have produced the work. After discussing the project, reading the elder Shipley's work and subjecting Shipley himself to a rigorous interview he announced '...with the blessing of God, we should manage a good and useful book on fly-fishing betwixt us'. The book includes opinions and contributions from others. Particular references to Alfred Ronalds, Professor Rennie, G C Bainbridge and Sir Humphrey Davy are made, along with suitable acknowledgement – the latter being a courtesy in which William Shipley was most particular. He published the work by subscription and a list of the two hundred and thirty four subscribers who took two or more copies is included.

Shipley's writings deal principally with angling on the 'Dove, and on the Principal Streams of the Midland Counties', though 'applicable to every trout and grayling river in the Empire'. In the last chapter he gives name to these principal streams, along with brief descriptions of their qualities and suitable angling methods. Included are the rivers Derwent, Wye, Lathkill, Churnet, Blythe and Manifold. Brooks listed include Bradbourne, Cubley, Boylestone, Foston, Brailsford, Longford and Barton. In Shipley's time all these waters held a head of trout.

A quote from Byron's Don Juan is used by William Shipley to highlight the anti-angling lobby of the 1830's:

> 'And angling, too, that solitary vice,
> Whatever Izaak Walton sings or says:
> The quaint old cruel coxcomb in his gullet
> Should have a hook and a small trout to pull it.'

Shipley points out that fly fishing is a difficult art but one which takes the participant to the best of countryside and torments no living thing. The fish are included as, according to the opinion of Sir Humphrey Davy, they feel no pain in their cartilaginous mouths. He recommends angling as a benefit to both healthy mind and body, pointing out that no anglers feature on the Newgate list. His delight in the use of delicate and light tackle is very obvious. At that time fly fishing was, according to Shipley, a peculiarly British sport.

As a tackle maker William Shipley was interested in modern developments of his age, and his accounts of tackle used are detailed and accompanied by critical appraisal. Once more the adjectives 'light' and 'delicate' are applied; this time the subjects of description are rods, reels, lines and flies. Rods used by Shipley's father would probably have been up to eighteen feet long, with fixed lines. The younger man may well have served his time with such tackle.

By 1838 Shipley advised a much shorter rod. He considered twelve feet very adequate, but certainly no longer than thirteen and a half feet. Such a rod could be used to throw a fly in a delicate manner. Equally important was the construction. The butt was made of well-seasoned ash, cut before the winter solstice, bored out to house a spare tip to the rod. For less muscular anglers and beginners, willow also made a good first joint, being lighter and almost as pliable, hickory being used for the next two joints rather than lancewood. The best tip joints were formed of bamboo cane with the option of a six inch length of whalebone at the tip. The latter Shipley did not deem necessary, as the cane could be tapered sufficiently. The joints were fixed together by means of brass ferrules. Loops were bound on in line next to the ferrules to enable the joints to be tied in place by silk thread.

The rods were furnished with rings to carry the line. Shipley gives a formula for the size of these rings, advising that they should diminish in size toward the rod tip. The taper of the rod is accorded great importance to enable it to do its best work. It was completed by the addition of a removable butt spike, to enable the rod to be fastened in the ground whilst dealing with fish, tangles or fly changes.

Reels, when used, had been held on the rod by being screwed on or by a plate. Shipley notes that the modern rods had brass hoops to receive the reel, and were, perhaps, preferable. He used a multiplying style of reel with a four to one retrieve and stresses that the gears should be of iron or steel. Some anglers fished with the reel on top of the rod but the preferred method was to have it underneath the butt and close to the end. He advocated four inches.

Lines, as always, attract much discussion. For the Dove Shipley thought a twenty yard line suitable; on smaller streams fifteen yards was plenty long enough. He did not like lines made of pure silk as they became waterlogged and difficult to cast. Hair lines were difficult to twist and became kinked. The best lines, he considered, were a mix of both materials. These were constructed to a formula based on one silk thread and four strands of different coloured horsehair which tapered from butt to tip. There were different formulae for lighter or heavier lines. Each line was speckled by the mixed threads and '...suitable for the generality of waters'. Of the hundreds of different lines made, Shipley used his own specified formula and no other. A seven and a half foot casting line or leader was made, by knotting sections of silkworm gut. This was carefully selected to be round and fine. Knots were formed by the 'old angler's knot', peculiar to Derbyshire and Staffordshire. I think this is the fisherman's knot, perhaps derived from the Staffordshire knot? Droppers, if used, were placed about twenty inches apart and were two inches long. A link of four twisted stallion tail hairs was used to join the reel line to the gut casting line. This resulted in much improved casting. Shipley used Kendal hooks in sizes which now seem very large. For the Dove in warm weather, his advice was a Kendal No 1 – equivalent to a Redditch size 10. Much is made of hook styles and making.

The angler's tackle was completed by a creel of suitable dimensions made of osier, a 14" diameter landing net with five and a half foot handle and a clearing ring for retrieving snagged tackle. The latter was a spring-loaded ring of 2½ diameter, which was attached to, and slid down the line to the snag. By pulling on a cord attached to the ring the tackle was freed or the snag pulled to shore. Every angler should carry one!

Later William Shipley advised shorter rods of eleven feet with stiffer tips to facilitate casting and to allow a fly to drop naturally to the water surface.

It is in his style of fishing that William Shipley is at his most innovative. After an exhaustive explanation of casting a fly and facilitating its arrival on the water in a delicate manner, the beginner is advised not to try casting into the wind. This can only be done by an old practitioner with a stiff rod and hair line, and even then not always satisfactorily. The use of the wind either from behind or the side is advocated. He then goes on to describe a process, which can only be upstream dry fly fishing, but this in 1838, some years before even James Ogden described the technique.

Fly dressing was an important part of the business of William Shipley senior and his son, berating the plagiarists who claim the dressings of others as their own. He assures the reader only dressings 'known to ourselves and which have killed fish by dozens' will be offered. Comprehensive lists of materials, wings, hackles, herls, ribbing and feathers are given. Along with these is advice on selection of hackles and suitable furs. All fly dressers have their own special materials. Shipley adopted Cotton's greyhound dubbing and visited the skinners' yards but what is special about the fur on a hedgehog's belly?

His fly making instructions are given under what are described as 'eight rules'. These 'rules' take the form of various fly dressings. They are: plain hackle, palmer fly, ribbed palmer, winged fly with dubbed body, grouse or wren's hackle, winged fly with hackle legs, winged, dubbed and hackled fly, and finally a winged, dubbed, hackled and ribbed fly. A vice was not used by Shipley and he, like Ronalds and Foster, was fastidious in attempting to copy form and colour from nature. Interestingly, he states that Derbyshire anglers considered the addition of tinsel 'useless'.

Professor Rennie, says Shipley, did not consider the imitation of natural flies as essential. He thought a more general form, coupled with movement, sufficient attraction. Shipley disagreed with this thesis, preferring to copy nature as closely as possible but with sparse delicate dressings. Whisks were not used as they were considered to interfere with the hooking abilities of the fly. The following flies are the patterns used by William Shipley's father. The advised hook sizes are Kendal No 2 for the Dove, and for smaller warmer streams a Kendal No 3. They come with impeccable references; Sir Humphrey Davy invariably used Shipley flies in preference to all others. There are seven hackles, three palmers and just two sedges from the total of fifty seven patterns. Shipley explains that the list begins in January to allow those anglers who enjoy early spring fishing sufficient information on flies.

THE FLIES OF WILLIAM SHIPLEY

JANUARY

RED-BROWN FLY
The body of this fly is to be dubbed with dark-brown mohair. The wings are to be made of the feather from a starling or dotterel's wing. It is to be tied on or dressed with red silk. Will kill from eleven to three o'clock.

BLUE DUN
The body of this fly is to be formed of the straw-coloured silk, with which it is dressed. A blue-dun cock's hackle for legs, to be wound round the hook under the wings three times.

The wings from the feather of an old starling's wing.

This fly must be made rather full in the body, and in the winter months, and when the water is high, it must be dressed on a No. 3 Kendal hook. It may with safety be accounted a standard fly.

LIGHT-BLUE DUN

The body to be of greenish-yellow silk; legs, a soft hackle-feather of a light-blue-dun colour, to be wound round the hook close to the wings four times, and in a way that the silk may be clearly discerned. Wings, the feather of an old starling.

GOLDEN OSTRICH, OR GOLDEN PALMER-FLY

The body, a black-ostrich herl ribbed with gold-twist; a dark-red cock's hackle for legs. To be dressed sometimes with orange, sometimes with puce-coloured silk. A famous fly for grayling. Hook, Kendal No 3. Will kill all day long.

ESTERHAZY DUN

Bright Esterhazy-coloured silk for body; blue-dun hackle for legs; wings, from the feather of the fieldfare's wing. An extremely killing fly on a cold windy day, from half-past ten to three o'clock.

PEACOCK FLY

Peacock herl for body; a bluish-dun hackle for legs. To be dressed with greenish Pomona silk.

Let us here remind the reader, that the flies that will kill in the beginning of the year, will also kill at the latter end. Thus, then, the flies that are taken in January, February, and March, will also be taken in November, October, and September; making the months correspond in the way we have written them down.

FEBRUARY

The flies that we recommended for last month will be found serviceable in the begin ning, and frequently throughout the whole of this month.

DARK DUN

Body of dark-plum-coloured silk; legs, a blue-dun hackle-feather; wings, of the feather of a fieldfare. This fly kills well in all the cold months.

PLAIN PALMER

Black-ostrich herl for body; over that a red cock's hackle for legs. To be dressed with red silk. Hook, Kendal No. 3.

RED FLY

Body, dark-red dubbing, to be chosen from the hair found in tan-yards; cock's hackle of the same colour for legs. To be dressed with orange-coloured silk. Wings, a starling's feather, or if you wish to be still more exact, the dun covert feather of a mallard's wing. A good grayling fly, and it will kill both in March and April.

ANOTHER BLUE DUN
A very small portion of the water-rat's fur, spun round yellow silk for body. A blue-dun hackle for legs. Wings, from the feather of a starling. There cannot possibly be a more killing fly than this during all the cold months.

RED DUN
Esterhazy-coloured silk for body; reddish-dun hackle for legs. Wings, from the feather of the fieldfare.

FURNACE FLY
Body, orange-coloured silk; legs, cock's furnace hackle. Wings, a fieldfare's feather. A standard fly, killing well all the year through.

MARCH

The same description of flies, but dressed of a smaller size, that were recommended for last month, will be taken in this.

ANOTHER BLUE DUN
A small quantity of water-rat's fur, twisted round straw-coloured silk for body; a blue-dun cock's hackle for legs. Wings, of the light fibres from the feather of a fieldfare's wing. This fly kills well on cold windy mornings.

DARK-CLARET FLY
Body, deep-claret-coloured silk; legs, a cock's dark-red hackle; wings, from the feather out of the wing of the land-rail.

ANOTHER DARK DUN
Esterhazy silk for body; blue-dun hackle for legs; wings, of the feather of a starling.

WINTER BROWN
Body, puce-coloured silk; legs, a dark furnace hackle; wings, from the feather of a fieldfare.

THE MARCH BROWN, OR DUN-DRAKE
We dress this fly as follows: Body, orange-coloured silk, or deep-straw-colour, on which wind for dubbing the fox-coloured fur taken from a hare's poll; legs, a honey-dun hackle; wings, the top of the light or inner fibres stripped from the feather of the hen pheasant's wing. Rib with gold-twist for your tail-fly; let your dropper, when you use one, be without any twist.

'Ephemera,' Shipley's editor, writing in *A Handbook of Angling,* in 1848 records this pattern as '...perhaps the best fly that can be used from the middle of March to the middle of April, and sometimes up to May.' He recommends a tail fly and dropper, only the former being ribbed with gold twist. In addition he stresses the wing to be tied standing erect. When the fish are particularly interested, the use of a further dropper is advised, each being different in size and colour. Suggested hook sizes are eight to ten, old numbers. Whilst fishing the river Dove on the twenty third of March 1836 with William Shipley, they caught sixteen trout and one grayling. Sometimes two fish were hooked at once to tail fly and dropper. The slaughter ceased when, '... an accident occurred to our tackle.'

MARCH-BROWN DUN-FLY
Body, hare's fur from the back of the neck, twisted round primrose-coloured silk; legs, a brownish-dun hackle; and wings from a hen pheasant's wing-feather.

APRIL

ORANGE DUN
Body, orange-coloured silk; legs, a blue-dun hackle; wings, a fieldfare's wing feather.

COW-DUNG FLY
Body, yellow lamb's-wool, mixed with a little brown mohair; legs, ginger-coloured hackle; wings, from the wing-feather of a land-rail. To be dressed with orange-coloured silk. This is a killing fly on windy days, and on them only.
The Golden and Plain Palmer flies are to be used this month, tied on a No. 2 Kendal hook.

THE GRANNOM, OR GREENTAIL
The body is made of the dark fur from a hare's ear, mixed with a small portion of blue fur; the tail is made of the green herl taken from the eye of a peacock's feather; the legs, a pale-ginger hackle; and the wings, of a hen pheasant's feather.

LIGHT-BLUE DUN
This fly is to be dressed exactly like that of the same colour recommended for January, except that the hook must be a No.2 Kendal.

YELLOW DUN
Body, yellow silk; legs, a yellow-dun hackle; and wings from a feather of the red-wing.

STONE FLY
Body of the fur from the dark part of a hare's ear mixed with a little brown and yellow mohair, and ribbed over with yellow silk rather closely towards the tail; legs, a dark-grizzled cock's hackle of great length; wings, which must lie flat upon the body and not be longer, or at least very little longer, than the body, to be made of the dark-mottled feather of a hen

pheasant or pea-hen; tail, two rabbit's whiskers. This fly is in season from the beginning of April until the middle of June, and is a killing fly early and late in rough streams, and in pools during a strong wind. Hook, No. 4 Kendal.

SAND FLY
Body, from the fur off the hare's poll; legs, a ginger or light-red hackle; wings, from the feather of the land-rail's wing. To be dressed with bright-orange-coloured silk on a No.3 Kendal hook.

This is a first-rate fly, and is justly a great favourite with anglers, since it will kill well for at least three successive months, namely April, May, and June.

MAY

SPIDER FLY
Lead coloured silk for body; for legs, a wood-cock's hackle, wrapped three or four times round the hook.

IRON BLUE
Body of the blue fur of the water-rat or monkey, warped on with purple silk, and afterwards neatly picked out. Wings, from a tom-tit's tail. An excellent fly.

ANOTHER DARK DUN
Body, a small quantity of the blue fur of a water-rat warped on with yellow silk; legs, a blue-dun hackle; wings, of the feather from under the water-hen's wing. If delicately dressed, a very killing fly.

ANOTHER SORT OF PALMER
Body, brown peacock's herl; legs, a dark-red hackle. To be dressed with red silk.

LITTLE YELLOW MAY-FLY
Body of yellow silk; legs, a light-ginger hackle; wings, a fieldfare's feather stained yellow.
Another way:
Body, yellow monkey's fur; wings, from the feather of a dotterel's wing. To be dressed with lemon-coloured silk. Both these little flies are capital killers.

SILVER-TWIST HACKLE
Body, of a black-ostrich herl, ribbed with silver-twist; legs, a black cock's hackle. To be dressed with puce-coloured silk.

FERN FLY
Body, the brown fur from a fox's breast; legs, a pale-dun hackle; wings, of the palest fibres from the feather of a thrush's wing. To be dressed with orange-coloured silk. A killing fly for grayling.

JUNE

THE GREEN-DRAKE, OR MAY-FLY
Body of an ostrich herl died a straw colour, and ribbed with gold-twist; legs, a ginger hackle; wings, a mallard's feather from the side under the wing, died a dingy yellow colour; two whips of a brown peacock's herl between the wings and the shank of the hook, to form the head of the fly.

GREY DRAKE
Body, puce-coloured silk ribbed with silver-twist; legs, a dark-blue-dun hackle; wings, a sooty-grey mallard or widgeon's feather. Hook, No.9 Redditch.

BLACK GNAT
Body, the feather from the green-plover's crest; wings, a fieldfare's feather. To be dressed on a No.1 Kendal hook, with dark-purple-coloured silk.

PEACOCK FLY
Body, a peacock's herl; legs, a bluish-dun hackle. To be dressed with Pomona green silk.

LIGHT MACKEREL FLY
Body light-orange silk, ribbed with gold-twist; legs, light-red hackle; wings, light-grey feather of a mallard.

JULY

DARK MACKEREL FLY
Body, purple silk ribbed with gold-twist; legs, a dark furnace hackle; wings, a darkish grey mallard's feather.

ASH FLY
Body, orange-coloured silk; legs, a furnace hackle; wings, from a woodcock's wing-feather.

ORANGE DUN
Body, bright orange-coloured silk; legs, a light-blue-dun hackle; wings, from a fieldfare's feather.

RED ANT FLY
Body, bright-brown peacock's herl; legs, bright-red cock's hackle; wings, starling's feather. To be dressed with bright-red coloured silk.

BLACK ANT FLY
Body, black ostrich herl; legs, a dark hackle; wings, of a fieldfare's feather. To be dressed with silk of a dark-puce colour.

WREN'S HACKLE

Body, light-brown silk; legs, the feather of a wren's tail. This little fly will kill at all times – especially during the summer months when the water is low and clear.

GROUSE HACKLE

Body, deep-orange coloured silk; legs, the reddish-brown mottled feather of the male red grouse. Will kill in July, August and September.

AUGUST

OAK FLY

Body, a black-ostrich herl, wound thinly round the hook; legs, a dark-red hackle, stained deeper than the natural colour; wings, from the feather of a woodcock's wing. To be dressed with orange-coloured silk. This fly will kill from the latter end of April to the beginning of September.

LITTLE WHIRLING-BLUE

Body dubbed with hare's fur from the back of the neck, mixed with a little yellow mohair; legs, a blue-dun hackle; wings, a starling's wing-feather. To be dressed with primrose-coloured silk.

SUMMER DUN

Body, of greenish-yellow silk; legs, a soft light-blue-dun hackle, to be wrapped three times quite close under the wings, so as to show the silk body well; wings, from the wing-feather of a starling just fledged. Let this fly be dressed as delicately as possible, and it will be found a very killing one.

PEACOCK FLY

This fly should be repeated, but it should be dressed on a No. 1 Kendal hook.

BROWN FLY

Body of yellow silk, of the finest twist possible; legs, a red cock's hackle, whipped twice round the body under the wings, which are to be from the feather of a land-rail's wing.
All the flies for July will kill more or less in this month.

SEPTEMBER

LITTLE PALE BLUE

Body of a minute portion of pale-blue fur from the water-rat, mixed with a little fine fur of any sort, died yellow; legs, a very pale-blue hackle; wings, a young starling's feather. To be dressed very delicately, with fine pale-yellow silk. A good killer.

WILLOW FLY

Body, a small portion of monkey or water-rat's fur spun sparingly on yellow silk; legs, a dark-blue-dun hackle; wings, a fieldfare's feather. This fly will also kill on fine days in February.

GOLDEN DUN

Body, deep-straw-coloured silk, ribbed with gold-twist; legs, a honey-dun hackle; wings, the palest feather of a young starling. This little fly will also kill well on warm days towards the end of May.

CINNAMON FLY

Body, any sort of dark-brown fur; a pale-ginger hackle for legs; wings, the pale-reddish-brown feather of a hen. A good fly both during this month and the last, on a windy day, or in a smart shower.

NB The same sort of flies that killed in April will be found equally serviceable during this month. For October, use the same flies you fished with in March; for November, the same sort of flies that were recommended for February; for December – do not fly-fish at all.

NIGHT FLIES

The flies used for night-fishing are generally imitations of moths. We can recommend no more than three of them.

THE WHITE MOTH

Body, a white ostrich-herl; legs, a white cock's hackle. Wings, from the feather of the white owl. To be tied with white silk on a No. 4 Kendal hook. When you fish with this fly put a gentle on the hook.

BROWN MOTH

Body, dark-brown bear's fur; legs, a brown hackle; wings, the brown owl's feather, to be dressed with dark-brown silk, on the same sized hook as that for the last fly. A cad-bait on the point of the hook will render the lure more enticing.

CREAM-COLOURED MOTH

Body of any fine cream-coloured fur; legs, a pale-yellow hackle; wings, the feathers of the yellow owl of the deepest cream-colour.

BLACK CLOCKER

Body, black-ostrich herl, thickly warped round the hook; legs, a large black hackle; wings, the darkest fibres of a wild-goose's wing-feather.

Further chapters detail the physiology, distribution and habits of both trout and grayling. Shipley spends more time on the grayling despite '...*he is not so general a fish as the trout nor to me so good to eat or angle for...'*. Much of the information in these sections is accorded to Sir Humphrey Davy writing in *Salmonia* (1828).

Several of Shipley's observations are of interest. He remarks on grayling being undisturbed by bankside activity but easily put down by unsuitable tackle. He also records his father catching four two pound grayling on a Red-Brown Fly between Norbury Weir and Dove Leys in January. A Mr Powell regularly minnow fished for large grayling and was, by Shipley's reckoning, successful in his endeavours.

WILLIAM SHIPLEY'S RECOMMENDED GRAYLING PATTERNS

Black Gnat	Yellow Dun
Willow Fly	Ants
Grannom	Alder Fly (Orl Fly)
Red Palmer	Black Palmer
Red Fly	Light Blue Dun
Blue Dun	Bluebottle
Spider Fly (Gravel Bed)	Golden Ostrich

Shipley's Golden Ostrich may well be the origin of John Fosbrooke's Golden Earwig. The dressings are very close in material and form.

As do other earlier writers, Shipley gives advice on minnow fishing for trout, trolling for pike, dibbling and dapping. He fished for grayling using a leaded hook with a grasshopper attached. This was lowered into deep pools and was a good fish catcher. He also describes fishing live fly. Mayflies, stoneflies, bluebottles, housefly, oak flies and March Browns were all used later in the season after the Drake hatch. Rods of up to sixteen feet were used to dibble. Even longer rods, up to twenty feet, in conjunction with blow lines were used to dap flies on big pools. Dibbing was considered an easy way of fishing, often being used by children. The live flies were stored in osier baskets, with twigs inside left uncut. This allowed the insects to perch and be easily picked off with dry fingers to ensure flotation. Such fly baskets were made in Ashbourne.

This work by William Shipley and Edward Fitzgibbon has a wealth of advice, information and anecdote. It is difficult to believe it was penned nearly two centuries ago, such is its practicality of application. William Shipley and Edward Fitzgibbon produced a clear detailed record of Derbyshire and Staffordshire angling in the late eighteenth and early nineteenth centuries. Remarkably, such was their perception and innovation, most of it is applicable to fishing the Dove and Manifold today.

DAVID FOSTER

David Foster as portrayed
in *The Scientific Angler*.

David Foster was born in Burton on Trent in 1815. He began his working life in the angling trade as a part-time hook maker and brazier with Samuel Allcock of Redditch, the town then being an important centre for tackle manufacture. An article in *'Classic Angling'* in September 2002 by John Knott says Foster was first apprenticed to a jeweller and certainly the skills extant in both occupations are similar and transferable. As a young man he was evidently an avid angler and no doubt the waters of the lower Dove and mid-Trent provided plenty of scope for his piscatorial activities in the immediate environs of his home town. Further, his work with Allcocks would have provided contact with new developments in angling, skilled tackle makers and fly dressers. He was to go on to become a noted fly dresser and angler of his generation.

In the early 1830's Foster moved to Ashbourne, then an important centre for those who fished the rivers Dove, Manifold and their associated tributaries. Here he began work as a tackle maker though it is unclear exactly when he set up his business. Foster Bros. bi-centenary publication issued in 1963, states that the business, then run by Fosters, was established in 1763 –

'–*When George III was King the firm of Foster Bros. was founded, 1763. The manufacture of fishing tackle has been carried out through the reign of nine sovereigns. It is recorded that in 1763 J Barton had a business in Ashborn for the sale of fishing tackle.'*

J Barton has proved rather elusive, but there is the possibility David Foster may have acquired Barton's business at some stage thereby giving credence to the 1763 foundation date in the 1963 publication.

At the time Foster came to Ashbourne William Shipley was established in the town, having taken over from his father as a barber, tackle maker and angling guide. There is no mention of William Shipley in the Foster bi-centenary booklet, but there was probably considerable business and personal rivalry between them. David Foster was an ambitious and innovative businessman along with his considerable skills as both angler and fly dresser; not the man to suffer competition readily. As with Barton's business, there is no available record of the demise of William Shipley. John Knott's proposal that Foster acquired one or both businesses seems a real possibility.

By the early 1840's Foster's activities were in full flow. A number of inventions and innovations appeared under his name or auspices. Lines, drawn gut, the dry fly, rods, nets and lures were all subject to his attentions over the years. Some of these were remarkably similar to products described by other companies, but then the Victorians were well used to elaborate and excessive claims by advertisers. The similarities between folding nets and 'Kill Devil Minnows' manufactured by David Foster and James Ogden of Cheltenham are remarkable!

A further example of David Foster's ambition was reported in *The Derby Mercury* of August 22nd, 1849 and remarked upon by John Knott in '*Shedding a Little Light on Foster*'. David Foster issued a challenge to take on anyone in a fishing match on a specific length of the River Dove for a ten pound purse. It was probably a direct challenge to William Shipley but was not taken up despite the wager being increased to a hundred pounds, underwritten by an associate of Foster, Mr. Pike Watts-Russell of Ilam.

David Foster's premises were first in the Market Square and later at 27 Church Street in Georgian buildings some way down from the Old Grammar School. Ashbourne's reputation as the angling centre for the upper and middle reaches of the Dove was reinforced by excellent waters, available tackle, guides and flies, coupled with hotels and good, modern, public transport access for its time. All this contributed to the success of Foster and the further development of angling in the locality. Foster not only retailed tackle but also continued to develop and manufacture products, supplying rods, reels, lines, lures and flies of its own brand; eventually after David's death in 1881, winning medals in the 1880s and 1890s in international exhibitions. Foster rods were advertised as being supplied to well known anglers including T E Pritt and Dr Brunton, the inventor of 'Brunton's Fancy'.

David Foster had contact, if not friendship, with many of the well-known anglers of his time: Alfred Ronalds, James Ogden, T E Pritt and C W Gedney are all mentioned in familiar terms in his work, *The Scientific Angler*. This book was published posthumously in 1882 by his sons, William and David, from manuscripts he prepared before his death. These were referred to in his obituary in the Ashbourne Parish Magazine. The book was widely acclaimed and in its time became the only angling work, other than *The Compleat Angler*, to be published in America.

Despite David Foster's contribution to fishing 'The Dry Fly' the book was perhaps somewhat eclipsed by the new creed of F M Halford on Southern waters.

Foster's angling experience was extensive considering the constraints of running a business and travel conditions. He knew the waters of Derbyshire and Staffordshire well, but also fished southern streams such as the Kennet and Test. He caught grayling in Yorkshire waters, also visiting Scottish lochs and rivers, and even the Hebrides in search of his sport.

He was one of the earliest to use and supply dry fly patterns to the angling public, but it is as a grayling angler that most applaud his skill. T E Pritt's *Book of the Grayling* (1888) provides an illustration of David Foster's favourite grayling cast, 'Silver or Winter Dun, Steel Blue Bumble and Cock Winged Dun', along with those of Bradshaw, Walbran, Pritt and Lupton.

The Scientific Angler is, in its later editions, a book of twenty chapters. It is supplemented with work from William Foster, C W Gedney, B W Murdock and James Taylor, but is largely the work of David Foster. The work covers the field of freshwater angling, with seven chapters relating to fly fishing. There are coloured plates of natural flies along with their relevant artificial imitations after the style of Ronalds, though not so accurate. The book also has black and white plates, diagrams of tackle, flies and equipment.

The chapter on Piscatorial Entomology describes flies to be found on the water. Foster's personal observations, made over fifty years of angling, led him to an oversimplified opinion of the classification of insects taken by trout as food. He acknowledges only four species of upwinged insects – Ordinary Olives, Iron Blue Duns, Large Browns and Mayfly or Green Drake. He accords the differences in the number of apparent species as being related to '... *the prevailing temperature of the atmosphere and water at the time of the larva and pupa arriving at the stage of maturity...*'. Foster thought that the body colour was governed by these different conditions. This view was also shared by others. Sir John Hawkins, who produced the fifth edition of *The Compleat Angler*, and Sir Humphrey Davy in *Salmonia* had similar views. Interestingly, according to Tony Hayter in *F M Halford and the Dry Fly Revolution* (2002), Halford, too, was of a similar opinion for some time. Perhaps all saw the natural history of aquatic flies from the perspective of an angler, rather that that of a critical scientist? Nevertheless, from these flawed ideas, David Foster developed his classification of natural flies and his range of artificial patterns – which of course caught trout and grayling.

Herewith, an extract from the Ordinary Olive as an example.

MONTH	FLY STYLE	BODY COLOUR
*February	Blue Dun	Dead lead
+Few weeks!	Cock Winged Dun	A shade lighter!
*April		Olive Colour: Yellow rib.
		Muscat grape bloom
-Dull days	Yellow Dun of April	Rust like fungus–ruddy

-Cold Water esp on limestone	Pale Blue Dun	Light blue tint
+few weeks	Yellow Dun of May	Light delicate olive
-In poor weather	Hare's Ear Dun	Several shades darker
*June – hot weather	Yellow Dun of May	Several shades lighter
and so on to November and February		Dull blue

Entomological reality is possibly simpler to understand than the variables extant in this system; but, even today, comparatively few anglers grasp the nettle of studying insect life thoroughly. One thing is certain; Foster was a good observer of both insect life and weather conditions. Otherwise, the formulation of his classification would not have been possible.

There are some sixty fly patterns recorded in *The Scientific Angler*. Included are representations of upwinged, flatwinged and terrestrial insects. When fly making, writes Foster, 'a natural specimen of the fly' should be available. Viewing the fly, both in the hand and against light is vital to accurately assess the relevant colour. The wing should be dressed erect and the fly be sparse in structure – advice which forms a common theme with several other Derbyshire/Staffordshire authors. Several (15) of Foster's patterns are very close in structure to those of Alfred Ronalds. The two men knew one another and there would almost certainly have been contact or even co-operation over methods of angling and fly dressing. Certainly, over one pattern - the Red Caterpillar – the two men had contact.

Foster was an advocate of fishing the 'Bumble' and his references and patterns are the first records I have found of the flies named as such. R B Marston writes in the *Fishing Gazette* of July 1915,

> '*The Derbyshire Bumbles have long been favourites of mine ever since I first bought some from Mr David Foster in his shop at Ashbourne over 30 years ago.... I think Old David Foster was the first to publish the dressings of the famous Derbyshire Bumbles and to christen the Honey Bumble.*'

David Foster died in April 1881. The company was continued after his death by his sons, and became D & W H Foster. Many writers have praised his angling skill. Writings and the obituaries in *The Field*, *Fishing Gazette* and *Sportsman* are generous in their assessment of a notable angler.

PATTERNS FROM THE SCIENTIFIC ANGLER – *DAVID FOSTER*

THE FEBRUARY AND NOVEMBER SHADE (commonly known as the Blue Dun)

Body, a small portion of blue fur spun sparingly on yellow silk; wings, from the field-fare's wing feather; legs, a light dun hackle.

Fly plate from *The Scientific Angler* showing
David Foster's shades of natural and artificial flies.

MARCH AND OCTOBER SHADE (Cock-winged Dun)

Body, a small portion of water-rat's fur, spun sparingly on full yellow silk; wings, from an old starling's quill feather; legs, a bluish dun hackle, freckled with yellow, or a blue dun hackle, slightly stained yellow.

THOSE OF APRIL AND SEPTEMBER (Olive or April Dun)

Body, small portion of pale blue fur, spun on yellow silk; wings, palest part of a young starling's wing feather; legs, a light dun hackle, freckled with or stained yellow.

(Dark April Dun) Rust-coloured fur to be used in lieu of the pale blue for body. In September the rust-like shade of body here alluded to is yet more conspicuous. It is then termed in some localities the

(Whirling Blue Dun), the body being formed by still more pronounced ruddy fur; legs, a dull ginger hackle. This latter is very difficult to procure. An ordinary ginger Cochin hen's preserved neck, steeped in copperas water, will be found to answer admirably.

(Pale Blue Dun)

Body to be dressed or formed with pale blue silk; legs, a pale dun hackle; wings, from a starling's short quill feather.

MAY AND AUGUST SHADES (Yellow Dun of May)

Body, palish yellow mohair mixed with a little pale blue fur, spun upon palish yellow silk; wings, young starling's or fieldfare's quill; legs, a light dun hackle, freckled with yellow.

(Hare's Ear Dun)

Body, blue mole's fur, dressed with silk of a pronounced yellow; wings, from the redwing's quill; legs, hare's fur from behind the ear.

IN JUNE SHADE (Golden Dun)

To be tied or dressed with deep yellow silk, neatly ribbed with fine gold wire; wings from a young starling's longer fiberia quill; legs, a palish dun hackle, freckled with yellow.

The common Yellow Dun is the same dressing, minus the gold tassel, the waxed tying silk being used for the formation of the body.

THOSE OF JULY (Pale Evening White)

Body, a little white fur spun on pale buff-coloured silk. Wings, the palest part of a young starling's wing feather; legs, a pale dun hackle.

(Pale Evening Dun)

Body, yellow marten's fur, spun sparingly on yellow silk; wings, starling, slightly stained yellow; legs, a brassy dun hackle. A pale blue hackle, stained in weak yellow dye, forms an excellent substitute.

(July Dun)

Body, blue rabbit's fur, mixed with yellow mohair; wings, the bluest part of a fieldfare's wing, stained slightly yellow; legs, a darkish dun hackle. Tying silk, yellow.

The Iron-Blue Dun Family of Order may be dressed as under:—

FOR APRIL AND MAY, also SEPTEMBER AND OCTOBER (Iron-Blue Dun)

Body, blue fur from the owl, spun around mulberry-coloured silk; wings, from the male merlin hawk's wing; legs, a freckled blue dun hackle, stained slightly by brown dye. Tying silk, mauve. For the light shade, the body should be dressed with a strip of a quill feather, stained the desired hue, or the tying silk only may serve for the purpose.

AUGUST AND SEPTEMBER (Little Pale Blue)

Body, a small portion of pale blue fur, mixed with a little yellow mohair, spun upon pale yellow or primrose-coloured silk; wings, from the quill feather, or from the small feathers upon the knob of the wing of the sea-swallow—a pair of the latter to be used back-to-back; legs, a pale dun hackle.

OCTOBER AND NOVEMBER (October Dun)

To be dressed from same material as the shades of the Olive Duns for April. The size the same as the Iron Blue, and therefore one-half that of the olive order.

GENERAL FLIES

Red Spinner

Body, copper-coloured silk, ribbed with round gold thread; whisks, three strands from a red feather from the back saddle of a game cock; legs, fiery brown hackle, from the neck of the same bird; wings, from an old starling's end quill.

Dark Spinner

Same as the Red, but the floss silk for body, and the hackle for legs, should be a shade or two darker, the latter approaching a claret.

Golden ditto

Body, gold-coloured silk, to be ribbed the same as the red spinner; legs, sandy hen's hackle; wings, fieldfare quill.

Jenny Spinner

This is, perhaps, the most delicate fly to copy correctly of the whole species of aerial and aquatic insects that become food for fish. We find it kills best when dressed buzz or hackle-wise. The body should be formed with floss silk of two shades, the ground-work being white, with a bright crimson band near the head and tail. It may also be tied with crimson silk, so as to form a head of that colour. The hackle may be a white hen's, or a small white feather from the knob of a pigeon's wing.

The first three shades of spinners are the transformation of the Olive Dun Order. The last given is the metamorphosis of the iron blue.

For the large browns (ephemeral) the following are given:

FOR MARCH AND APRIL (March Brown)
Body, fur from the back of a hare's neck, spun on reddish buff-coloured silk, ribbed with fine gold twist; tails, two strands of a feather from the back of a partridge; legs, a partridge's neck feather.

FOR MAY AND JUNE (Light shade, commonly known as the Turkey brown)
Body, light drab fur, ribbed with gold twist; wings, light partridge quill; legs, grisly dun.

FOR AUGUST (Commonly termed August Dun)
Body, to be tied on, or dressed with pale brown silk, ribbed with yellow silk; wings, from a cock pheasant's wing feather; legs, a pale dull brown cock's hackle.

Green Drake
Body, straw-coloured mohair, ribbed with gold twist; wings, from a mallard's mottled feather, slightly dyed yellow; legs, honey-dun cock's hackle; the head of the fly to be formed with a peacock head or copper-coloured silk. To make this fly buzz, a mottled feather from a mallard, stained as above.

For the grey copy, we give the following:

Grey Drake
Body, white floss silk, ribbed with silver twist, tied on with brown silk; tails may be made from hair from under the jaws of a brown horse; wings, mottled feather from the mallard; legs, a dark dun or black cock's hackle. To make this fly buzz, a dark mottled feather from the mallard. This fly may be used with success from six o'clock until twilight.

For the Dark Mackerel
Body, copper-coloured mohair, ribbed with gold twist; wings, from the brown mottled feather of a mallard; tails may be got from under the jaws of a brown horse; legs, a dark mulberry-coloured stained cock's hackle.

To take the various species of flies in their proper order, we come next to the Phryganidae order, which ranges as follows:—

February Red, or Red fly
The body of this fly is dubbed with dark-brown mohair, mixed with claret-coloured mohair; wings, from the hen pheasant, or dotterel wing feather; legs, dark-brown feather from a pale partridge's neck, or a cock's hackle of the same colour.

Sand fly
Body, fur from the back of a hare's neck spun sparingly on pale orange silk; legs, a pale dull-coloured ginger hackle; wing, from a landrail's wing feather.

Cinnamon fly

Body, fur from a hare's neck, mixed with a small portion of sable fur, spun on pale dull orange-coloured silk; wings, from a brown hen's wing feather; legs, a pale dull ginger-coloured cock's hackle.

Grannum, or Greentail

Body, fur from the hare's neck, spun on fawn-coloured silk, with two laps of green floss-silk on the tail; legs, a pale ginger hackle; wings, the palest part of a hen pheasant's wing feather.

The above being what are usually termed flat-wings, should be dressed as in the old method, i.e.,wings last, so as to resemble the naturals.

The Perlidae order ranks next. Some of these it is best not to wing at all; the dun hackle from the knobs of wings of various birds forming an excellent substitute for legs and wings when carefully wound on like an ordinary hackle.

Stone fly

Body, dark-coloured fur, spun with full yellow silk, to be ribbed with some silk of same colour, unwaxed; wings, from the quill-wing feather of a cock pheasant, or may be cut from a sheet of gutta-percha (pure), dyed in cold blue dye; legs, a black cock's hackle stained yellow; this, if rightly made will form an excellent artificial fly, not to be excelled by any combination of feathers and fur alone.

Willow fly

Body, water rat's fur spun sparingly on yellow silk; legs and wings made buzz, from a dark dun hackle, with a brownish tint in it, or a small dark feather from the merlin hawk's wing.

Needle fly

Body, sable fur spun upon yellow silk, dressed hackle with small brown feather from the knob of a fieldfare's wing. This fly may be formed by a strip of the enamelled quill of a peacock's feather, which forms the alternate shades of ribs beautifully. This has been introduced by a clever southern angler.

Yellow Sally

This should never be dressed winged; it falls upon the water like a heavy beetle would be supposed to do, therefore the wings not being extended are not seen by the fish. The most killing way is to hackle it palmerwise, with a white hen's hackle dyed light yellow, or by the small feather round a white pigeon's wing, stained as above; the body to be yellow mohair.

The casual killers amongst the land flies may be dressed as follows:—

The Cowdung fly

To be dressed or tied on with pale dun orange-coloured silk; body, yellow lamb's wool, mixed with a little green mohair; wings, from a landrail's wing feather; legs, pale dull ginger-coloured hackle.

Oak fly, or Down-looker
Body, pale orange floss silk, tied on with pale lead-coloured silk; wings from the wood-lark's wing feather; legs, a furnace hackle.

Marlow Buzz, Coch-y-bondu, of Wales
Body, peacock herl, hackle with bright furnace feather. The red tag (fancy fly) is formed by the simple addition of a red tag, or tuft of wool or feather at the tail.

Brown Palmer, Bracken's Clock
Body, black ostrich herl, ribbed with round gold twist, hackled with red cock's hackle stained.

Blue Bottle, or Beef Eater
Body, light blue floss silk, ribbed over with black ostrich herl and silver twist, tied on with brown silk; wings, from an old starling's wing feather; legs, a black hackle.

Wrentail
Body, amber-coloured floss silk, or ginger-coloured fur from a hare's neck, ribbed with gold twist; legs and wings made buzz from a wren's tail feather.

Red Ant
To be tied or dressed with orange-coloured silk, which may be shown at the tail; body, copper-coloured peacock's herl; legs, a red cock's hackle; wings, from a redwing's feather.

Black Ant
To be tied on or dressed with pale dull fawn-coloured silk, which may be shown at the tail; body, black rabbit's fur, well mixed with copper-coloured mohair; legs, a dark furnace hackle.

Black Gnat
Body, ostrich herl; wings, from a starling's wing feather; legs, a dark blue dun, or black hackle.

Grey Gnat
Body, grey mohair, or wool hackle, with sea-swallow feather.

Red Palmer, or Caterpillar
Body, copper-coloured peacock's herl, tied with brown silk, ribbed with gold twist, a bright brown red-stained cock's hackle, having a gold-colour when held between the eye and the light.

The Alexandra fly
Body, flat silver twist, hackled with bright feather of green or blue hue, from the neck of a peacock; wings (if any) from the turkey's wing.

Black Palmer
Hackle, black cock's, ribbed with fine silver twist; tying silk, black.

Golden Palmer
Hackle, bright furnace; body, peacock herl, ribbed with gold twist.

Grey Palmer
Hackle, cock's with black centre and whitish grey edge, ribbed with fine round silver tinsel; tying silk, black.

A variety of palmers may be made by intermixing the materials here given for the different shades.

Dun Cut
A fly for evening to imitate moths. Body, drab fur, ribbed with silver twist; hackle, double, dun and brown hen's breast feathers, the outer being the dun.

There are a number of recommendations in *The Scientific Angler* made by David Foster for casts and seasonal fly patterns, including those for dry fly fishing and grayling. It is very possible that some of these may be the opinions of his sons, who compiled the book from David's notes after his death.

An early spring cast: Red Fly, Blue Dun and Rough Bumble.

David Foster's grayling cast: Winter Dun, Steel Blue Bumble and Cock Winged Dun. Both these casts contain Bumbles which do not feature in the original fly lists. The dressing for the Steel Blue Bumble is given by T E Pritt as:

Hook: 1 or 2 (15 or 14)
Body: Formed by twisting light and dark orange, and cerise, or rose coloured silks and laying them on as alternate ribs, with peacock herl as intermediate or alternate ribs. Over this a pale, or steel blue hackle is palmereddown from the head to the bend end of the body.

The Rough Bumble tie is not to be found in Foster's book, but Roger Woolley, who must have known Foster's sons, gives this tie:-

Hook: 0 – 2 (16 –14)
Body: Yellow floss, ribbed peacock herl and red silk.
Hackle: Medium blue dun hen from shoulder to tail.

Grayling flies, which Foster found successful, included Bumbles, Winter Dun, Grasshopper, Iron Blue, Grey Palmer, Little Chap, Black Gnat and Willow Fly. He specified that small grayling patterns should be tied.

Undoubtedly, the list of patterns contains many not invented by Foster. The reference to 'a southern angler' in the pattern lists amply demonstrates this fact. The discovery of the Red Caterpillar here, and its subsequent development, is also testimony to dressings being acquired rather than created.

The patterns for the shades of Olive and Iron Blue, together with the Bumbles, are very probably original to David Foster and, as such, could well be considered 'local' patterns of Derbyshire, if not specific to the Dove.

A brief summary of tackle David Foster used may be of interest. He fished from the 1830s until the 1870s. The rods he advised were three piece, each joint of three feet six inches, making ten and a half feet. The butt was hickory or washaba, the middle joint washaba, greenheart or blue mahoo, the top of snakewood or best jungle cane; similarities here too with the recommendations of James Ogden.

Foster designed a reel built into the rod butt, to avoid the problem of line wrapping round the reel. The illustration of this also shows the rod butt as having a bank spike on the end. The reels were made of bronze or brass with the handle attached to a revolving plate. Lines were of waterproofed plaited silk, Foster's 'Acme' line incorporating a fine strand of copper wire. Casts were of gut, 'two Staffordshire knots' being the recommended means of joining the pieces together.

Olive Dun

82

CHAPTER TWO

FLY DRESSING IN THE DERBYSHIRE STYLE

Next, pouch must not fail,
Stuff'd as full as a mail,
With wax, cruels, silks, hair, furs and feathers,
To make several flies
For the several skies
That shall kill in spite of all weathers.

The Angler's Ballad *Charles Cotton*

Charles Cotton, Aldam's '*Old Man*,' Alfred Ronalds, John Turton, William Shipley and David Foster dressed flies in times when most anglers fished only on their local streams and rivers. The fly patterns of these writers will have been those found by them and their contemporaries to be successful. The flies were certainly important enough to have been preserved in the lists. No doubt some of these dressings will be from other anglers and authors as all these men, despite the difficulties of travel, fished widely. Anglers, then as now, would be anxious for success and as a consequence gave much thought and trial to their dressings.

Without exception, their source of inspiration was the natural fly life they observed on the rivers. All recommended copying from life as far as possible when tying flies. At times patterns were often dressed at the waterside as insects appeared. Variations in dressings point to experiment and modification, the successful flies becoming standard patterns, the unsuccessful disappearing in the evolutionary process. Several writers give patterns with alternative dressings, usually winged or hackled.

In the process of copying natural flies on similar, if not the same, rivers it is not unexpected for many patterns to be similar and often with the same name. There are differences in materials used but all dressers realised the importance of presentation, colour and size in deceiving their discerning quarry.

Charles Cotton's dressings are generally considered to be a collection of his own developments along with a number of much older patterns probably handed on verbally. For around a hundred and forty years after Cotton, no definitive work on Derbyshire angling was published. It is thought that over this period various manuscripts, such as

83

that of Aldam's '*Old Man*', circulated among local anglers. Patterns would also be passed from parent to child by word of mouth. As anglers often killed their catch to become part of their day to day diet, those flies which caught fish would earn a great reputation. As now, the more often a fly is fished the more fish it tends to catch, and gradually a tradition of dressing emerged. The anglers of the past probably lived much closer to the natural world than we do today, and whilst they may not have been aware of scientific classification, their knowledge and observation of local insects would have been both acute and accurate. In addition there would have been far more awareness of weather, season and moon phases; all factors which affect feeding cycles of living things.

The rivers of Derbyshire and Staffordshire tend, in the main, to be rough water shallow streams with pools and runs. Some are limestone rivers such as the Dove, Wye and Lathkill. These have been modified, in places, for angling. Others, the Derwent and Manifold, are of a different nature, rising on the shales or acid grits. All before the mid-nineteenth century were fished in much the same manner by use of a subsurface hackle or wet fly. To enable the flies to reach the fish rapidly they needed certain qualities in common with the North Country patterns of Yorkshire, Lancashire and the Clyde.

Tradition has it, over centuries of trial and error, for a slender body, often tied short of the hook bend but not beyond the point where the bend begins. Soft hackles from hen poultry or game birds are used, these dressed with few turns and being long in the fibre. The hackles on flies are often Palmered or tied 'Buzz;' those on Palmer flies often being cock hackles, those on Bumbles and wet flies taken from hen capes. When a wing is used on a dressing it is set upright and kept slim. Some authors separate the wing into two; others do not. A completed fly should be slim, neat and delicate. These are the words used by all the writers when describing patterns.

Body materials are selected and blended carefully to achieve translucency when viewed against the light. Charles Cotton was most particular about this process. Colour, too, is accorded great importance, and very detailed recipes for dyeing feathers are given in the texts. The sources of some materials in respect of colour are astonishing; a good example being the visits of Alfred Ronalds to the skinners' pits for the hair of abortive calves!

Not all the traditional features are present in every pattern. They are simply the basic principles of dressing flies in their local Derbyshire and Staffordshire form. Many dressings of Alfred Ronalds have wings which slope backward somewhat, but he also often offers a 'Buzz' alternative, this being very much a feature of Derbyshire style. Charles Cotton chose to make fun of heavily dressed Southern or 'London' flies, setting one up as an object of ridicule. All the old Derbyshire and Staffordshire writers stress spare dressing of patterns. Occasionally they defy their own advice but not often. This same advice has been brought through into comparatively modern times in the dressings of a far-famed Derbyshire fly dresser, Roger Woolley.

In the turbulent waters of the Peak District rivers, sparse soft hackles move in an attractive manner, particularly so when fished upstream and allowed to drift and tumble in the current. Such patterns suggest dead and injured flies, along with those which have failed to emerge correctly. The Derbyshire style of dressing is very similar to the North Country patterns of Yorkshire and Lancashire. The 'Yorkshire School of Flydressing' was consolidated in the early nineteenth century. This is admirably recorded in Leslie Magee's *Fly Fishing The North Country Tradition* (1994). In fact, John Turton, one of the writers already discussed and chosen for his 'Derbyshire' patterns, lived in Sheffield. It is perhaps only a matter of one's perception of county boundaries as to where a pattern originates.

The means of fishing a fly relates directly to the way it is dressed. Those to be fished across and down may well need wings and hackles to be tied flatter as the fly will then tend to sink faster and be combed by the current. This will create a nymph-like profile and give less movement to various appendages. When fished upstream, as already described, the hackles are tied upright, as if the wing is present. These flies remain high in the water with appendages working in the flow. Patterns tied 'Buzz' without wings create surface attraction as would a hatching nymph or emergent insect.

The Derbyshire style of winging creates a rather unusual looking pattern. It consists of a pair of feather slips tied closely together in an erect, or slightly forward posture. This device enables the fly to remain just subsurface for a longer period, 'hanging' in the current creating the impression of an emerger.

W H Lawrie in *English and Welsh Trout Flies* (1967) summarises four important lessons of the past when tying successful fly patterns. The use of best quality feathers and fur is to be strongly recommended. Little is gained from economy as the fly is the essential link with the fish. All the great fly dressers give considerable importance to colour, shape and size of flies and only good materials complement these features. The way a fly behaves in the river, or even in its presentation on being cast, can be spoiled by poor hackles or dressing. Already the sparse tying of tradition has been laboured. If the creatures to be imitated are small, neat and delicate then their representations should mirror this structure.

Locally created fly dressings have survived because they work on local waters, fished in a specified manner. Trout followed by anglers are quick to reject unsuccessful dressings and it has long been that way. Patterns used for centuries will work when fished appropriately. Charles Cotton's 'Black Flie' still catches its share of fish from both Dove and Derwent. Should new patterns be thought necessary then the inclusion of the main principles of their forerunners is a sound basis on which to begin.

When dressing the bodies of flies, fur, hair or feather dubbed onto a silk thread gives sparkle, translucency and colour variation which is difficult to improve. Dubbing needs to be sparsely and evenly applied to enable the silk colour to 'grin' through. The shape of the body, and thorax if required, is built up by winding even turns.

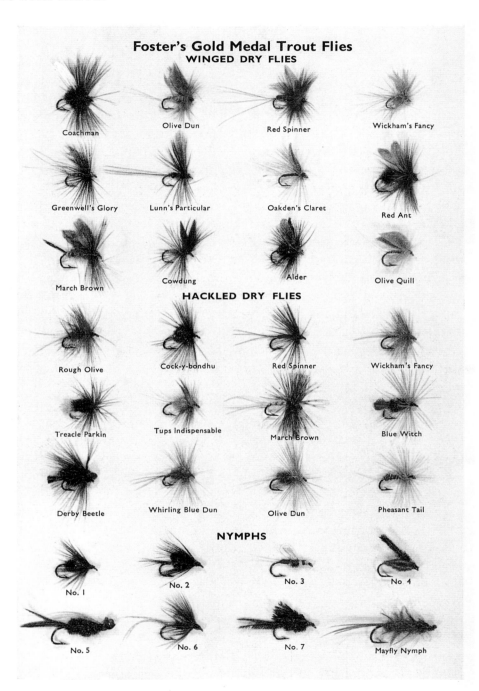

A selection of flies offered in Foster Bros 1964 catalogue

Foster's Trout Flies

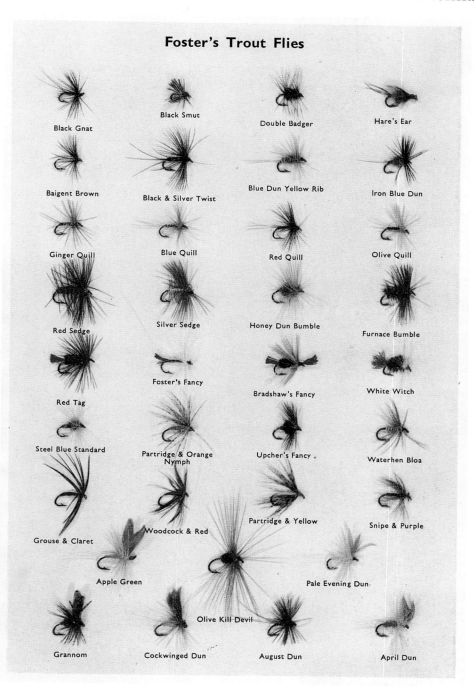

Black Gnat

Black Smut

Double Badger

Hare's Ear

Baigent Brown

Black & Silver Twist

Blue Dun Yellow Rib

Iron Blue Dun

Ginger Quill

Blue Quill

Red Quill

Olive Quill

Red Sedge

Silver Sedge

Honey Dun Bumble

Furnace Bumble

Red Tag

Foster's Fancy

Bradshaw's Fancy

White Witch

Steel Blue Standard

Partridge & Orange Nymph

Upcher's Fancy

Waterhen Bloa

Grouse & Claret

Woodcock & Red

Partridge & Yellow

Snipe & Purple

Apple Green

Pale Evening Dun

Grannom

Cockwinged Dun

Olive Kill Devil

August Dun

April Dun

FLY DRESSING MATERIALS

Current wildlife legislation has been updated in recent years. Fly dressers and anglers should be aware of these changes. The possession of certain feathers, furs and body parts is illegal, as is the acquisition of birds and animals found dead. Organisations such as the Royal Society for the Protection of Birds will give advice and information. Aside from the law, there is a duty of care to both the environment and wildlife by anglers. Correct disposal of waste line and retrieval of lost tackle are essential responsibilities for the protection of birds, animals and our sport.

Materials anglers and fly dressers used in the past would, in the main, be supplied by their immediate environment. Feathers from domestic poultry and local game, perhaps supplemented by surreptitious pilfering from the hats of their respective ladies, no doubt added to their store. Fur and dubbings could be obtained from domestic stock, wild fauna and, in the cases of Cotton, Ronalds and Shipley, a visit to the Shambles.

The number of bird species used by Charles Cotton is relatively few when compared to the other five authors considered. This may be to do with the inaccuracy of his firearm or perhaps simply that he had a sufficient variety of feathers for his needs.

I do think that the advent of reliable shotguns in later times is related to the range of fur and feather available. Until the twentieth century there was no protection for wild species except that of the close seasons and conscience. Leslie Magee proposes that T C Hofland's publicity of the dotterel as a source of feathers for the fly dresser resulted in the bird deserting Yorkshire as a breeding species. The corncrake is often considered to have been eradicated on the mainland of Great Britain by modern agriculture, but I wonder if the influence of fly dressers speeded it on its way.

Thread, silks, tinsels and twists for embroidery and dressmaking would have been available in most homes. Many people made, or at least repaired, their clothing until comparatively recent times. Complex embroidery was commonly practised as a leisure activity, even by children, who made samplers. Beeswax was used to waterproof thread and to polish furniture or boots, thus many essentials were to hand.

Tools used by anglers to make flies are not well documented. Many tied without the aid of a vice. As late as the twentieth century, Roger Woolley of Hatton considered that holding the fly by hand gave a better feel to the dressing process. When tools are mentioned, small pliers, needles and fine scissors are the most common. Hofland lists 'a small hand slide vice' but David Foster tied by holding the fly in his fingers.

The following lists give an indication of the materials used by anglers from Cotton to Foster.

	1676 Cotton	1836 Ronalds	1836 Turton	1838 Shipley	c1800 Aldam	1882 Foster
BIRD PLUMAGE						
Barn Owl				X	X	
Blackbird			X	X		
Bittern		X			X	
Bluetit		X	X	X		
Cock	X	X	X	X	X	X
Coot	X					
Cormorant		X				
Dotterel		X	X	X	X	X
Fieldfare		X	X	X	X	X
Golden Plover			X	X		
Goose				X		
Green Woodpecker						X
Grouse		X	X		X	
Hen	X	X	X	X	X	X
Heron	X		X	X		
House Martin			X			
Jackdaw					X	
Jay			X		X	
Landrail		X	X	X		X
Lapwing		X	X	X		
Mallard		X	X		X	X
Magpie			X			
Merlin		X	X		X	X
Moorhen		X	X			

	1676 Cotton	1836 Ronalds	1836 Turton	1838 Shipley	c1800 Aldam	1882 Foster
Ostrich	x	x		x	x	x
Partridge		x	x		x	x
Peacock	x	x	x	x	x	
Peahen		x				
Pheasant cock			x		x	x
Pheasant hen		x	x	x		x
Pigeon	x					x
Ptarmigan			x			
Redwing			x			x
Sea Swallow (Tern)		x	x		x	x
Snipe			x	x		
Song Thrush			x		x	
Starling		x	x	x	x	x
Tawny Owl			x		x	x
Turkey					x	x
Widgeon				x		
Woodcock		x	x	x	x	
Wood duck						x
Woodlark						x
Wren		x	x	x	x	x

ANIMAL HAIR

Badger	x					
Bear	x	x	x	x		
Calf - Abortive	x	x	x			

	1676 Cotton	1836 Ronalds	1836 Turton	1838 Shipley	c1800 Aldam	1882 Foster
Camel	x					
Cat	x					
Cow	x					
Dog	x			x		
Fox	x		x	x	x	
Guinea Pig					x	
Hare	x	x	x	x	x	x
Horse			x			x
Lambswool				x		x
Marten (Pine)		x	x	x	x	x
Mohair	x	x	x	x		x
Mole		x	x	x	x	x
Monkey				x		
Mouse		x				
Pig	x	x		x		
Rat		x		x		
Rabbit	x	x			x	x
Sable					x	x
Squirrel (Red)	x	x	x		x	
Water Vole			x	x		x
Weasel	x					
Wool (any)	x				x	

COLOURS AND DYEING

Anglers are particular about the colours of the materials used to dress their flies. This has long been the case, and for some the search for materials never ceases. In the old books there are often recipes which are used to produce colours or effects on feathers and hair.

Mixtures to produce various dyes are given by Ronalds, Aldam's '*Old Man*' and Foster. Those colours of most interest to fly dressers tend to be shades of yellow, olive, green, brown and black. Often the required shade needs to be muted or even 'dirty.' As a consequence, natural dyes were used even after the introduction of aniline chemical products, as the latter tended to give sharp colours. It is also important that the by-products of the dye industry were some of the principal pollutants of rivers, something the river Churnet in particular suffered.

Natural dyes were largely based on various types of hardwoods having their origins in South America, the West Indies or Africa. Infusions were made of one or more woods, often mixed with metallic sulphates which, according to the volume added, muted or darkened the shade of the dye. The materials to be coloured were added to the dye, having been degreased first. They were then removed and placed in a chemical mordant to fix the colour. Some of the mordants were mineral acids or other unpleasant chemicals.

The woods used by most anglers to produce their chosen colours were:-

Black: Infusion of logwood chips and ferrous sulphate.

Brown: Fustic wood and logwood chips infusion. Soaking in a solution of ferrous sulphate.

Dark yellow: An infusion of walnut chips.

Fiery brown: Camwood and logwood infusion.

Green: Infusion of fustic of wood and sulphuric acid.

Olive: Camwood and fustic wood infused with the addition of ferrous sulphate. Boiled onion skins.

Purple and red: An infusion of brazil wood and logwood. The material boiled with camwood chips gives a similar result.

Yellow: Boiled onion skins. Turmeric solution. A barberry bark infusion.

It needs to be stressed that the chemicals used in these processes, while not readily available, are both corrosive and poisonous. In addition, the infusions are also dangerous if imbibed.

Yet more radical colouring involved the use of sulphuric and picric acids; the former as a mordant, the latter, which has explosive qualities, to create an olive shade on heron or goose quills. The recipe for 'yellow carried stuff' used by Aldam's '*Old Man*' required the use of nitric acid and he felt it necessary to warn the user to protect his fingers by using a 'fark' to handle the material on a mop. Perhaps it was Charles Cotton who began the pilgrimage to the skinners' pits and shambles in the search for materials. Ronalds, Turton and Shipley also list materials which they obtained there, along with less macabre products. The abortive red calf hair used by three of these anglers, when tanned gave a 'resplendent gold colour', according to Alfred Ronalds. The hair of tanned skins often produced interesting shades; the process also tended to waterproof the materials. Hair pulled from the fabric of lime plaster walls had similar colours and water resistant properties.

Fashion played its part in the acquisition of exotic materials. Victorian ladies enjoyed hats dressed with feathers and garments made from, or trimmed with fur. It would be a fly dresser of high moral fibre who could resist such temptations whilst his wife was looking the other way. The import of such materials along with the passion for taxonomic collections of skins and taxidermy gave enormous choice to those able to afford such exotics. Supply of feathers and furs was the sideline of at least one taxidermist. Samuel Rodgers of Alfreton, my great grandfather, certainly sold materials to anglers for fly dressing.

Poultry, until comparatively recently, were farmyard or back garden birds. 'Feeding the fowls' was the job of many a child in the morning before school, within living memory. Some of these birds would be specific breeds, but others were thoroughly mongrelised. This, as a consequence, gave rise to capes and plumage of interest to those who sought coloured feathers. Some anglers, W H Aldam and Roger Woolley among them, bred birds of specific colours to provide material for flies. To obtain these colours and styles today we have resorted to genetics or import capes from India and China where poultry are often still kept in a traditional manner.

Included with the recipes for colourings are usually those for fly tying waxes and moth killers. The wax recipes are often quite involved, the moth killers very poisonous, white arsenic being a common ingredient.

WINGING TECHNIQUES

A feature of Derbyshire fly dressing is an upright slender wing or wings. This appears to have been developed after Charles Cotton's time. There is a gap in the literature between the late 1600s to the early 1800s when no real record exists of Derbyshire angling. It was during this period when the upright style of wing dressing emerged.

Cotton's dressings are in two styles. Winged flies with dubbed bodies and no hackle; the legs on these flies being picked out of the dubbing with a needle. Secondly, hackled flies with a herl or dubbed body. These are sometimes palmered and ribbed.

CHARLES COTTON'S WINGING

The link of two or three hairs is first whipped to the hook. Next, a strip of feather sufficient to form both wings tied in with its upper surface facing downwards to the hookshank. Enough fibre is left over the end of the hookshank for the length of wing required. Two or three turns of silk are taken around the root end of the feather fibres and hook. The waste is cut away and the silk lapped to the beginning of the hook bend. A half hitch is made and the silk dubbed with the body material and taken back up the hook to where the wings are set. The wing feather is divided in two with a dubbing needle ensuring each half of the wings is turned outwards and backwards toward the bend. Two or three more turns of dubbed silk in front of the wings will make them stand and slope towards the bend of the hook. This also forms the shoulder and legs of the fly. The dubbing is now raised with a needle to finish off.

ALFRED RONALDS'S WINGING

Ronalds's wing dressing is illustrated with an elaborate plate and instructions. Once more, the gut is tied to the hook, first of all singeing it to prevent slipping. The silk is then wrapped down the body to tie in the tail whisks. The rib, if used, is added next. Dubbing is applied to the silk and the body formed up to the shoulder and ribbed. A hackle is tied in, the waste trimmed and two or three turns wound, pulled into a beard and tied down. Finally two wing slips are tied in 'firmly and neatly' at the point where the hackle was tied off. If required, they are parted, the butts bound down and trimmed. The fly is finished off at the head end. When dressing a fly with wings at rest the hackle was dispensed with and the legs represented by teasing out the dubbing with a needle. Ronalds tied palmers by dressing the hackle from the tail of the fly having tied it in by the point.

WILLIAM SHIPLEY'S WINGING

Shipley's technique begins the fly by tying in the gut and next the wings. Strip a sufficient quantity of feather fibres, place it on the back of the hookshank with the roots pointing towards the bend and the points of the feather towards the right hand. The silk is next bound twice around the feathers and hook a short distance from the end of the shank. Using the right thumb nail, force up all the wing which lies to the right of the silk binding. The fibres are next divided 'equally and exactly' into two on each side of the shank. This makes two wings of 'exact proportion the one with the other'. The silk is then brought under the nearer wing and back through the wings. Next it is brought round the wing on the right hand side of the shank in the direction of your left hand fingers. In effect a figure of eight lashing. The wing roots are now cut away. Bend the points of the wings between thumb and forefinger down toward the bend of the hook. Holding them firmly there, wrap two or three turns of silk between the bent-down wings and the point of the shank. This forms the head of the fly and prevents the wings from falling back, retaining them in an upright position. The hackle is added, if required, the body formed and the fly finished off at the tail.

This, as are the dressings of Cotton and Ronalds, is tied on a sneck hook tied direct to gut.

DAVID FOSTER'S WINGING

Construct the body and rib of the fly leaving one fifth of the hookshank bare at the head end. This is to accommodate the hackle and wing. David Foster rarely put tails on flies as he believed they interfered with hooking.

A suitable amount of quill feather fibre is prepared. Half an inch breadth for a March Brown, two thirds this amount for an Olive Dun and half this quantity for Iron Blue Duns. The fibre is doubled to form separate wings when it is tied in, the length being similar to that of the hook and a little longer than the body. The means of separating the wings is not detailed in *The Scientific Angler*, but it is assumed by some authorities that figure of eight turns are used. The hackle is next wound underneath the wings in such a manner as to make them stand 'nearly upright'. This is supported by a few turns of well planted tying silk. Excess dubbing is nipped off between finger and thumb and the fly tied off.

ROGER WOOLLEY'S WINGING

Roger Woolley lists ten different ways of winging flies in *Modern Trout Fly Dressing* (1932). He normally used two of these to produce a very durable wing and a light, sparse dressing. The first of these is the 'Glanrhos' wet fly wing made known by Mr Graham Clarke.

The wing and legs of the fly are made from the same hackle. A single upright wing is made from the hackle tip, the remainder being wound to create the legs of the fly.

A further method, credited to Mr John Henderson and used by Woolley, will make either split or spent wings. Stripped hackle fibres are tied in as for a wet fly. By the careful use of figure of eight lashing either split upright wings or flat spent wings can be formed.

These five anglers, spanning almost three centuries, all tied their flies without the use of a vice. Roger Woolley considered, even though he was tying on a commercial scale, a better feel and balance was achieved by holding the fly in the fingers. The final remark of this section is his: '*To be able to wing correctly a small dry fly is the height of attainment in trout fly dressing and is the most difficult part of the art...*'

CHAPTER THREE

DERBYSHIRE AND STAFFORDSHIRE
FLY PATTERNS

The flies in this chapter are presented in four groups. Those originally peculiar to Derbyshire and Staffordshire which were developed from palmered patterns, the quaintly named 'Derbyshire Bumbles'. Next come the 'Traditional' patterns. Many of these are ancient dressings. All those selected appear a number of times in the lists of Charles Cotton, W H Aldam, Alfred Ronalds, John Turton, William Shipley and David Foster.

The fly dressings invented or adapted by local anglers to fish local waters are listed under 'Speciality' patterns. This is an expression used by W M Gallichan in *Fishing in Derbyshire and Around*. He refers to the 'Specialities' of John Fosbrooke and I have adopted the term. Here it encompasses dressings both old and new. From such flies as these traditional patterns and dressing styles eventually evolved. Many of the more recent 'Specialities' invented by local Derbyshire and Staffordshire anglers are dry or emergent patterns.

The standard and modern patterns are included for reasons of comparison and completion. An 'Adams' or a 'Grey Wulff' cannot be considered local or even British patterns but are much used by anglers on the Dove and Derwent watersheds.

DERBYSHIRE BUMBLES

The anglers and rivers of Derbyshire have given rise, since the times of Charles Cotton, to a style of fly dressing peculiar to the county. The Bumble, in its various forms, is well known and documented but generally little used. A number of famed anglers in the past have rated the series highly so this appears rather curious.

Bumbles can be fished wet or dry, but their origins lie as wet flies. They probably developed from the Palmers of Cotton or even earlier anglers. Referring to Cotton's Green Grasshopper and Peacock fly dressings Gerald Heywood in *Charles Cotton and his River* (1928) says, 'From these latter may, one fancies, have descended the Derbyshire Bumbles...'.

The style of the Bumble is of a herl, silk or wool body ribbed with either herl or silk, and overall a palmered hen or cock hackle. This gives a range of alternatives but two distinct types have emerged, those with peacock herl bodies ribbed with coloured silk and those with a silk body ribbed with herl. Later developments give more variation with the use of two differently coloured hackles carefully intertwined to add translucency and brightness.

96

When fished either as a point fly or dropper, the Bumble drifts in the current allowing the hackle fibres to work. In calm water a draw does tend to induce takes. The flies are generally considered to be grayling patterns but have been well used as trout flies in hot weather. Some Bumbles were tied as dry flies and were much used on southern waters.

In his contribution to *The Compleat Angler* Charles Cotton gives nine patterns with palmered hackles. He evidently found this style of dressing useful. One, the 'Peacock-flie', has a peacock herl body, a feature of Bumbles, in its dressing. Others have bodies of spaniel fur, ostrich herl or wool. They are ribbed with gold or silver twist and have a shoulder to tail body hackle. The dressings are so similar in style to the Bumbles that it seems logical to assume the latter developed from the former.

Alfred Ronalds, a Staffordshire man, published his *Fly-Fisher's Entomology* in 1836. In this remarkable book he lists three Palmers as imitations of various caterpillars. One of these has a peacock herl body, the others, dubbed worsted and ostrich herl respectively. One of these – the Red Palmer – he recommends for fishing the Dove. Ronalds's dressing for the Grannom, which he calls the Shell Fly, is palmered. The Shell Fly is one of the dressings listed in a much older publication, *A Treatise of Fishing with an Angle*, attributed to Dame Juliana Berners and written in 1496. Ronalds says this fly is good in the summer months and September, though this is long after the main hatching of the Grannom (Leslie Magee). Ronalds's other patterns are, in the main, winged though nineteen of them have an alternative tie to make them 'buzz'. This involves either partially or completely palmering the hackle of the fly – in effect making it 'Bumble like'. Perhaps it is from such dressings that the rather drab Palmers of Cotton acquired their brighter liveries of coloured silks and lighter hackles.

William Shipley and Edward Fitzgibbon's Golden Ostrich or Golden Palmer Fly is of interest. It has a black ostrich herl body, ribbed with gold twist. The fly is dressed with orange or puce coloured silk. Flies dressed in this way allow the silk colour to 'grin' through the herl as in Bumble patterns. There are similarities in this dressing to David Foster's Ordinary Bumble. William Shipley was a tackle maker in Ashbourne.

The second edition, 1848, of Edward Fitzgibbon's book, *A Handbook of Angling* lists dressings for eight Palmers. He considered they '... kill better in England than in any other part of the Empire'. He fished them in smooth rivers flowing through flat districts rather than in mountain waters. Whilst the title 'Bumble' is not appended to any of them several are similar in pattern, if not size, to those of David Foster, George Eaton and Roger Woolley. All are dressed on hook sizes between four and nine, though for low water they should be, '...small and sober...'. Dark days and coloured water warrant their being, '...larger and more conspicuously coloured...'.

Fitzgibbon says most writers limit the number and size of Palmers unnecessarily. He evidently used them as larval imitations and considered anglers should vary the dressings in any way they please to effect the catching of fish.

THE PALMERS OF EDWARD FITZGIBBON

No. 28. BLACK PALMER-HACKLE
Body, black ostrich harl, ribbed with gold twist. Black cock's hackle wound over the whole.
Hook, No. 4,5,6 or 7.
When palmers are dressed large they may be tied on two hooks, whipped lengthways, bend to shank, on the gut.

No. 29. BROWN PALMER-HACKLE
Body, brown floss silk, or brown fur, or mohair of a deep amber, or a rich brown ostrich harl, ribbed alternately with gold and silver twist; legs, a red cock's hackle.
Hook, No. 4,5,6 or 7.

No. 30. A PLAINER BROWN PALMER
Body, mulberry-coloured worsted, spun on brown silk thread; legs, a fiery brown cock's hackle wound over the whole of the body. These last two palmers kill well when the water is clearing after a flood.

No. 31. RED PALMER-HACKLE
Body, dark red coloured mohair, with a little richly-tinted red fur intermixed, to be ribbed with gold or silver twist; legs, a blood red cock's hackle.
Hook, No. 4,5,6 or 7.

No. 32. A PLAINER RED HACKLE
Body, a peacock harl with a red cock's hackle wrapped over it, and tied with dark brown thread.

No. 33. GOLDEN PALMER-HACKLE
Body, green and gold peacock harl, ribbed with gold twist; legs, a bright red cock's hackle, worked with a green silk.
Hook, No. 5,6,7 or 9.

No. 34. PEACOCK PALMER-HACKLE
Body, a rich full fibre of peacock harl, ribbed with wide silver platting. Make a head to this palmer with a bit of scarlet mohair. Legs, a dark grizzled hackle, dressed with red silk.
Hook, No. 5 or 6.
This hackle, dressed very large, will kill Thames trout and chub of the largest size.

No. 35. A GOOD GENERAL PALMER
Body, long and tapering, of yellow mohair; legs, a good furnace hackle wound on from tail to shoulder; head, black ostrich harl.
Hook, 4,5,6 or 7.

James Ogden, describing a day's fishing at Rowsley around 1864, mentions patterns in his fly book dressed for Derbyshire waters. They comprised several shades of duns, red palmers, small orange and clarets. He explains the locals renamed the Palmers, Bumbles. These were fished downstream, drifting and working in the current, '...edging the side well and carefully...', before recasting. This method had been used by Ogden's father Frank many years before. Hackles used to dress the patterns were yellow dun, honey dun, dark brassy dun and furnace. Ogden lists his favourite Palmers for a three fly cast. Whilst rather large they are dressed in the Bumble style.

POINT FLY
Hook: No. 6
Body: Sparse bronze peacock herl ribbed with gold thread.
Hackle: Bright red cock or furnace, palmered alongside the thread showing the herl between the hackle.

MIDDLE HOPPER.
Hook: No. 4.
Body: Bright orange floss silk with a strand of magenta peacock herl wrapped down the body at intervals.
Hackle: Honey dun, brassy dun or grizzle dun with or without gold.

THIRD FLY.
Hook: No. 4. Black Palmer.
Body: Black ostrich herl ribbed with narrow silver tinsel
Hackle: Black cock wrapped by the tinsel.

David Foster was an all round angler of great experience. For most of his adult life he too was a tackle manufacturer in Ashbourne, fishing the rivers of Derbyshire regularly. He recommends three palmers and five bumbles. One palmer is similar to Cotton's Black Fly, the other two much the same as Ronalds's palmers. This is probably the first time Bumble dressings had been described as such, despite it being very likely that Foster sold the patterns for years to clients. He evidently thought very well of the series. His flies have peacock herl bodies, palmered hackles and are ribbed with coloured silk. They were intended to be fished as wet flies and tied with soft hackles. They were dressed on smaller hooks than palmers and were used principally as grayling flies though Foster regularly used a Honey Dun Bumble as a summer trout fly. He also mentions success with the patterns when dace fishing. Whatever the quarry or time of year it seems Bumbles featured on his casts.

The Marquis of Granby, who fished and owned much Derbyshire water, commends the Bumble as a grayling fly for his home rivers. His Bumbles are of a different style to those of David Foster. The bodies were of orange or crimson silk, ribbed with herl and dressed with cock hackles. They may have been provided by Foster's firm as the two men were acquainted, Granby praising the skill of Foster as an angler.

In 1886 F M Halford published *Floating Flies and How to Dress Them*. He lists four Bumble patterns but tied as dry flies to, no doubt, accommodate his principle of imitative dry fly angling. Halford's Bumbles have silk bodies and are ribbed with peacock herl – the reverse of Foster's, but similar to those used by Granby. Two of them have the further addition of a flat gold rib and cock hackles. All are promoted by Halford as invaluable hot weather flies for trout and three of the four as good grayling flies. Such was the success of one on the Test, the Orange Bumble, that it became known as the 'Priceless Bumble'. Foster and Halford had some contact – not always cordial. Tony Hayter in *F M Halford and the Dry Fly Revolution*, records comments in Halford's own copy of *The Scientific Angler* as being 'trenchant and peppery'; in addition is a marginal comment 'Bosh!'. As far as I can ascertain F M Halford does not specify which exact flies the Bumbles he included in his lists imitate.

By this point the Bumbles had proven to be good rough stream patterns and successful chalk stream dries. They had become smaller than their probable ancestors, the Palmers, acquiring more colour and brightness but retaining the 'buzz'.

Walter Gallichan, another angler of wide experience, recommends the use of the various Bumbles on the Dove, Manifold, Wye and Derwent. He in the main considered them as grayling patterns. Those he found successful include Claret, Furnace and Fiery Bumbles but he does not specify the dressings. Perhaps the style of the fly is more important than its colour. One fly which is mentioned a number of times by Gallichan is the Golden Earwig tied by John Fosbrooke of Hartington. This is not designated a 'Bumble' but is in fact in exactly the same style. A feature shared by Roger Woolley's dressing of 'Steel Blue'. Fosbrooke was a grocer in Hartington, a waterkeeper and fly dresser of 'Specialities'.

In Matlock three generations of 'Professional fishermen' and tackle makers had been in business over a considerable period of time. All were named George James Eaton, and were excellent fly dressers and anglers. The two elder men promoted Bumbles to their clients and also fished the patterns themselves. The frontispiece of Eric Taverner's *Fly Tying for Trout* (1939) portrays a Bumble illustration tied '...after the prescription of Old Eaton'. The fly appears to have a peacock herl body. A. Nelson Bromley used 'Eaton's Honey Bumble and 'Eaton's Orange Bumble' when fishing the Dove at Ashbourne in his youth. He includes the Orange Bumble in his list of favourite flies.

Roger Woolley, the well known fly dresser from Hatton, lists six Bumble dressings in *Modern Trout Fly Dressings* under 'Grayling Flies' and the Golden Earwig as a 'General Fly'. He considered the flies of sufficient merit to include instructions as to how they should be dressed. Mulberry, Honey Dun, Light, Rough, Ruby and Yellow Bumbles are listed. Woolley's own favourite is often quoted to be the 'Steel Blue' or 'Grayling Steel Blue'. This is given under 'Fancy Wet Flies' in his book.

The series was offered for sale by many different companies during the early to mid twentieth century. Hardys, Allcocks, Cummins and Fosters all had their selections of the patterns.

An Irish form of Bumble was developed by T C Kingsmill-Moore for sea trout angling. He spent a good deal of time and experiment on his patterns in the search for translucency and brightness in the fly. He had observed both characteristics not only in the in the Traditional Irish Patterns but also in Derbyshire Bumbles. His work eventually led to the use of two carefully matched hackles of different colours entwined and wound to create a 'halo of light' around the fly. To increase and aid this the body materials include tinsel and seal fur rather than peacock herl. A similar effect has been created in the nymphs of Conrad Voss Bark by the use of coloured hackles.

Opinions differ widely as to what the Derbyshire Bumbles represent. Foster claimed Caterpillars, Eric Taverner favours a hatching larva, some think beetles, others nymphs in eclosion. In some ways a Bumble is not unlike a freshwater shrimp – the speculation can go on and on. Certainly, the word 'buzz' is a very adequate description of these patterns. It gives the feeling of disturbance in, or beneath, the surface of the water. It is perhaps also of note that a very buzzy bee has acquired the name of Bumble! The dressing enables the fly to hang in the water, the current agitating the fibres and displaying colours for a longer period than faster sinking patterns.

Writing in *Fly Fishing The North Country Tradition*, Leslie Magee proposes that palmers were followed by 'half-palmered' hackle flies. In these patterns the hackle is wound partly down the body in the manner of Stewart Spiders. These flies '...were used in Devon and Derbyshire and became known as Bumbles or dressed Buzz'. From these patterns the 'Modern North Country' fly developed by the 'substitution of hen, game or soft hackle bird feathers for cock hackle'. Magee also provides a quote from T E Pritt's notes:-

'August 30th 1884 The Famous Derbyshire Bumble is not much used on Yorkshire rivers.'

Used or not, a pair of dressings follow –

'Tying Orange floss ribbed with peacock harl and a light blue hackle over and a similar fly with a ruby body with a dark blue hackle'.

T E Pritt fished the Derwent at Chatsworth in 1884 and was a client of Fosters. His name is used in a rod advertisement in *The Scientific Angler*, and it is very likely he obtained Bumbles from them on his Derbyshire visits.

In Pritt's *Book of the Grayling* (1888) is a plate with five grayling casts illustrated in colour. Among the exalted grayling anglers of the day – Walbran, Bradshaw, Lupton and Pritt - is that of 'The Late David Foster'. Named as his favourite cast, it consists of Silver or Winter Dun, Steel Blue Bumble and Cock Winged Dun. Interestingly, there is no tie for the Steel Blue Bumble in *The Scientific Angler*.

Writing in 1939 W Carter Platts comments on the changing fashions in the section of flies. He observes '...a noticeable change...on the Derbyshire streams where, in the latter part of the last century, the various Bumbles had great vogue. Since then they have distinctly waned in general repute'.

There follows a considerable number of Bumble patterns. Many are similar but there are differences of stress which may be of interest, or even significance, to anglers if not to grayling and trout.

DAVID FOSTER'S PATTERNS

These may well be the first Bumble patterns formalised and written down as such. The dressings are taken from *The Scientific Angler*, seventh edition.

BUMBLE, ORDINARY
Hackle, white hen's slightly stained blue; body, peacock herl, ribbed with orange and puce-coloured silk (floss); tying silk, brown.

MULBERRY BUMBLE
Hackle, dun hen's; body, peacock's herl, ribbed with mulberry-coloured floss silk; tying silk, claret.

RED BUMBLE OR EARWIG
Hackle, red cock's, stained; body, peacock herl, ribbed with gold silk; tying silk, dark brown.

HONEY DUN BUMBLE
Hackle, honey dun hen's; body, peacock herl, ribbed with orange floss silk; tying silk, yellow.

FURNACE BUMBLE
Hackle, furnace cock's; body, peacock, or black herl, ribbed with dark orange silk; tying silk, red brown.

These flies were probably dressed on size twelve or fourteen hooks.
Fosters, as a family company, obviously continued development of the Bumble series. W L Foster, David's grandson, writing in his book *Fishing Tackle*, published in 1929, mentions Steel Blue, Light and Orange Bumbles. Honey Dun, Furnace and Derbyshire Bumbles are listed in Foster Bros. catalogues up to, and probably beyond, 1964.

DAVID FOSTER'S BUMBLE DRESSING
The body is begun by winding a base of tying silk from the shoulder to the hook bend. One strand of peacock herl is tied in at the tail, along with either tinsel or silk for the rib. The tying silk is now returned to the shoulder of the fly and the peacock herl wound over the silk base and secured at the shoulder. An appropriate hackle, prepared by removing the soft flue, is tied in at the shoulder by its butt and wound in open turns to the end of the body. The hackle is then secured by ribbing over it with the tinsel or coloured silk and secured.
An option is to have close winding at the shoulder or even to use a collar hackle in addition to the body hackle. A variety of patterns can be made by intermixing different materials.

F M HALFORD'S PATTERNS (Taken from *Dry Fly Entomology* 1897)

YELLOW BUMBLE
Hook: o or oo long (16 or 17 LS)
Hackle: Pale Blue Dun Cock
Body: Primrose floss silk, ribbed with strand of peacock sword feather

CLARET BUMBLE
Hook: o or oo long (16 or 17 LS)
Hackle: Medium Blue Dun Cock
Body: Claret Silk, ribbed with a strand of peacock sword feather

ORANGE BUMBLE
Hook: oo to 1 (17 – 15)
Head Hackle: Honey Dun Hen Hackle
Shoulder Hackle: Honey Dun Cock Hackle
Ribbing Hackle: Honey Dun Cock Hackle
Body: Condor or peacock dyed orange and ribbed flat gold.

This fly, the one known as the 'Priceless Bumble', was very successful on the Test, hence its 'nom de plume'.

FURNACE BUMBLE   Substitute Furnace Hackles for the Honey Dun, otherwise tie exactly as the Orange Bumble.

F M Halford was very specific about the dressings for his flies. The green peacock sword feather used would probably make these patterns effective as grayling flies given the fish's alleged favour of green. Halford's Orange Bumble, whilst different in structure, is very similar in materials to David Foster's Honey Dun Bumble, nor are the two furnace patterns dissimilar.

Francis Walbran, the celebrated Yorkshire angler, fished Bumbles for grayling. His chosen patterns were Halford's Orange Bumble, Honey Dun Bumble and Claret Bumble. Sylvester Nemes in *Two Centuries of Soft hackled Flies* (2004), reports Walbran mentioning the Honey Dun Bumble, Mulberry Bumble and Grey Palmer in his *'Fishing Gazette'* article of September 12th 1855. All the patterns are tied in the style of David Foster.

ROGER WOOLLEY'S PATTERNS (Taken from *Modern Trout Fly Dressing* 3rd Edition)

Roger Woolley's notes on Bumbles begin, 'A Bumble is a palmered fly that is chiefly used for grayling. The body is plump made of one or two colours of floss silk...'. An exception then to the normal advice for Derbyshire flies, of a slim body.

As a grayling angler of repute, Roger Woolley was an advocate of the Bumbles. Below are his six ties:-

MULBERRY BUMBLE
Hook: sizes 0-2. (16 – 14)
Body: Mulberry-coloured floss, ribbed peacock herl.
Hackle: Medium dun hen from shoulder to tail.

HONEY DUN BUMBLE
Hook: sizes 0-2. (16 - 14)
Body: Orange floss, ribbed green peacock herl.
Hackle: Honey dun hen from shoulder to tail.

ROUGH BUMBLE
Hook: sizes 0-2. (16 – 14)
Body: Yellow floss, ribbed peacock herl and red silk.
Hackle: Medium blue dun hen from shoulder to tail.

LIGHT BUMBLE
Hook: sizes 0-2. (16 – 14)
Body: Pale yellow floss, ribbed peacock herl and red silk.
Hackle: Pale dun hen from shoulder to tail.

RUBY BUMBLE
Hook: sizes 0-2. (16 – 14)
Body: Ruby floss, ribbed peacock herl from eye of feather.
Hackle: Pale blue dun hen from shoulder to tail.

YELLOW BUMBLE
Hook: sizes 0-2. (16 – 14)
Body: Yellow floss, ribbed green peacock herl.
Hackle: Pale blue dun hen from shoulder to tail.

A favourite of Roger Woolley was the Steel Blue – sometimes called Grayling Steel Blue. He often used this fly on his cast when beginning to fish in the absence of any feeding activity.

STEEL BLUE
Hook: sizes 1-2. (15 – 14)
Body: Thin peacock herl, ribbed gold wire, with three turns of orange silk at tail end.
Hackle: Well grizzled bright blue cock, from shoulder to tail.

I include one more pattern from Roger Woolley. Listed under Sea Trout Flies, it could possibly be a pattern he brought home from his days as a coachman in Ireland. From this origin it may form a link with Derbyshire Bumbles and those developed by T C Kingsmill-Moore. The possibility is extremely tenuous – Woolley lists the fly as 'An Irish Pattern'.

AN IRISH PATTERN
Tail: Tippet fibres.
Body: One-third at tail orange floss, remainder green floss, ribbed gold oval.
Hackle: Yellow and Orange intermingled.
Wings: Tippet fibres and brown mallard over.

Very likely, the whole thing is a figment of the writer's imagination! It does have intermingled hackles similar to T C Kingsmill-Moore's flies.

ROGER WOOLLEY'S BUMBLE DRESSING

The body is plump made from one or more colours of floss silk with ribbing of peacock herl, wire or tinsel. Prepare a hackle by removing the flue and stroking the remaining fibres downward from the tip. The hackle is then tied in by its tip at the tail of the fly. Stress is laid on tying in the materials so that the one tied in first is used last as this will ensure a neat body and fly.

Tie in the hackle, rib, peacock herl and body silk in order. Wrap the silk and rib it with the peacock herl, wire or tinsel. Now follow alongside the peacock herl with turns of hackle giving two or three close turns at the shoulder, tie off the stem, trim and finish the head.

Woolley says this is different from the 'old way' of tying the Bumble. It is odd that the hackle in his tie is not protected by a rib.

In *A Dictionary of Trout Flies* (1973), A C Williams quotes, 'The Bumbles are famous Derbyshire patterns of the wet palmer type which are deadly for grayling... As trout flies they often kill well in hot weather whilst in Ireland they are favoured for sea trout fishing'. Listed are Claret (or Mulberry), Orange, Honey Dun, Steel Blue and Yellow Bumbles.

One of David Foster's favourite grayling patterns for the Derbyshire rivers is given as the Honey Dun Bumble.

THE HONEY DUN BUMBLE

Body: Salmon coloured floss silk ribbed with a strand of peacock sword feather.
Hackle: Honey Dun hen's from tail to shoulder. Hook 12-14.
Hook: 12-14.

The dressing is at variance with Foster's tie in *The Scientific Angler*. The dressing given for the Steel Blue Bumble, also a favourite fly of David Foster for grayling, is similar to that in Pritt's *Book of the Grayling*. It would seem to be in the nature of Bumbles that they should vary and evolve. Among those who fish them each has his favourite and has probably modified it to suit himself, the fish or simply the availability of materials at the time the fly was dressed.

In *The Art of the Wet Fly* (1979) W S R Fogg includes his 'representative' selection of Bumbles, giving the option of a double hackle.

W S R FOGG'S PATTERNS (from *The Art of the Wet Fly*)

ORANGE BUMBLE

Hook: 14-10
Body: Orange floss silk, rubbed with a strand of peacock's sword feather and naropw gold tinsel.
Hackle: Honey dun hen tied in palmer style. A double-hackle may be formed with the addition of a red-brown hackle.

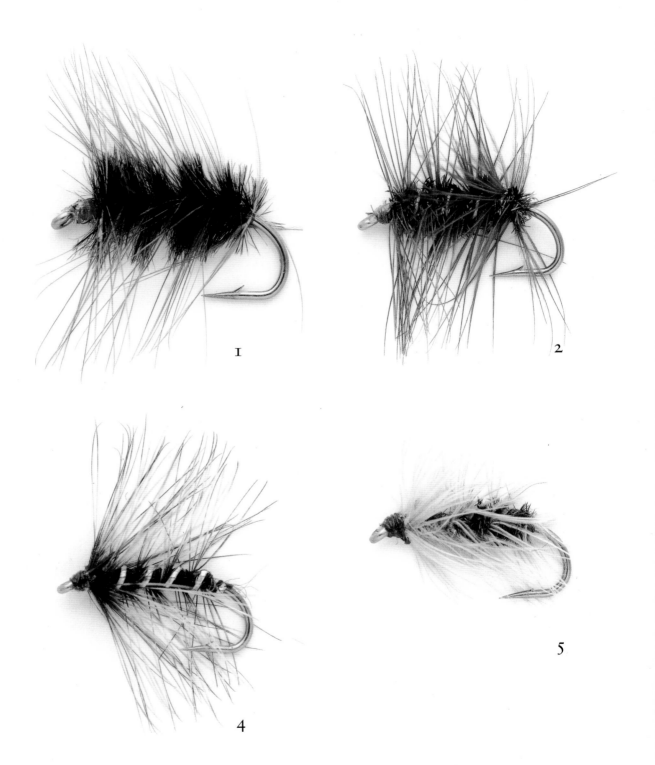

3

PLATE 2
DAVID FOSTER'S BUMBLES
AND PALMERED FLIES

1   Palmer/Plain
    (Cotton/Shipley)

2   Red Bumble or Earwig

3   Honey Dun Bumble

6

4   Grey Palmer
    (Foster)

5   Ordinary Bumble

6   Furnace Bumble

1

2

4

5

PLATE 3
ROGER WOOLLEY'S BUMBLES
AND PALMERED FLIES

1   Golden Earwig

2   Rough Bumble
    (Woolley)

3   Honey Dun Bumble

3

4   Steel Blue

5   Yellow Bumble
    (Woolley)

6   Mulberry Bumble

6

HONEY DUN BUMBLE
Hook: 14-10
Body: Salmon pink floss silk ribbed with a strand of peacock's sword feather.
Hackle: Honey dun hen tied in palmer style. A double hackle may be formed with the addition of a red-brown hackle.

CLARET BUMBLE
Hook: 14-10
Body: Claret floss silk ribbed with a strand of peacock's sword feather.
Hackle: Medium blue dun hen hackle tied in palmer style. A double-hackle may be formed with t the addition of a claret hackle.

STEEL-BLUE BUMBLE
Hook: 14-10
Body: Light orange, dark orange and dark red floss silk twisted together and laid on in alternate ribs with peacock herl between them.
Hackle: Steel-blue hen hackle tied in palmer style. A double-hackle may be formed with the addition of a hackle of any of the principal body colours.

When tied, these Bumbles are brightened and enhanced by the second hackle.

Modern materials are now incorporated in Bumble patterns. John Roberts in *Fly Fishing for Grayling* (1999), Excellent Press, Ludlow, gives this pattern naming Adrian Jones as its originator.

PEARLY BUMBLE
Hook: 12-14
Thread: Brown or Olive.
Tail: Olive hackle fibres.
Body: Pearl lurex ribbed with olive-dyed grizzle hackle.
Rib: Silver wire.
Collar Hackle: Slightly longer body hackle.

A further dressing from *Fly Fishing For Grayling* is the Orange Bumble. This is palmered only over the front half of the body.

ORANGE BUMBLE
Hook: 14-16
Body: Orange floss.
Rib: Peacock sword herl and fine gold wire or tinsel.
Hackle: Palmered honey-dun over front half of the body.
Collar Hackle: Slightly longer body hackle.

Both have acquired a collar hackle and tail. Still the Bumble evolves! Bumbles dressed by T C Kingsmill-Moore are quite probably nothing to do with those of Derbyshire, and in any case move the series far from the trout and grayling of Dove and Derwent. The final patterns I have chosen to end these notes are, I think, very appropriate. They are the dressings of a well-known Derbyshire angler and include modern materials. Here are the Flumble and Grumble, the Bumbles of John Neville of Eckington:

FLUMBLE		GRUMBLE
Hook:	14	
Body:	Fluorescent orange floss	Fluorescent green floss
Body Hackle:	Honey Cock	Honey Cock
Collar Hackle:	Honey Cock	Honey Cock
Tail:	Hackle fibres	Hackle fibres
Rib:	Round gold tinsel	Round gold tinsel

These are the flies to fish dry after the mayfly has finished.

W H Aldam mentions Bumbles in his editorial comments on the Little Chap, a beetle representation, in *A Quaint Treatise*. He remarks that from various hackles and peacock herl...

> *'...may be produced a somewhat fashionable series of flies used in Derbyshire, called 'bumbles,' a name I very much object to. This bumble tribe was first introduced by a very worthy and clever Yorkshire Fly Fisherman, but pirated by an unprincipled fellow in Derbyshire'.*

Aldam does seem to have been very sensitive on the subject of 'pirated' flies. Another incident involved the Indian Yellow which appeared in Ronalds's fifth edition dressed as an alternative Derbyshire tie of the Red Spinner. Those responsible for divulging this dressing to Ronalds's editor were two 'friends' of Aldam. Perhaps they were from Derbyshire.

Roger Woolley includes Bumbles in his catalogue list compiled for use in rivers, '...from Kashmir to Burma...and in the Central Provinces and the Nilgiris.' The client for whom the flies were initially produced was Lieutenant Colonel Alban Wilson who had almost thirty years experience with the Gurkhas.

The Bumble has travelled long and far. Its origins are the subject of surmise. Derbyshire, Staffordshire, Hampshire, Devon, Indian and even American fish have succumbed to its charms. It has changed its coat oftener than the Vicar of Bray. It has been sized from 18 – 8. It is considered a Fancy fly, a General Purpose fly, a Trout or Grayling fly. It can be wet, dry or emerging and comes in many colours like Joseph's coat. It deserves to be used on its home waters!

TRADITIONAL FLIES

These flies have been selected from the lists of Cotton, Aldam, Ronalds, Turton, Shipley and Foster; all were practical, experienced anglers though of another age. Their tackle was less sophisticated, entomology in its infancy and they fished for wild trout and grayling. Most included dressings written about or invented by others. A number of patterns have a pedigree of being recorded time after time, probably because they were found to be successful. It is unlikely that all the flies in the lists were regularly used by the anglers who recorded them. They were businessmen, tackle makers and fly dressers. A good portfolio of dressings would be important to offer to clients, in the workshop or at the waterside.

A number of the flies have different names but very similar dressings and evidently imitate the same insect. Virtually all represent aquatic or terrestrial insects which anglers still seek to imitate today. There are some omissions from the old lists. Sedges as a group are largely unrepresented. Surface flies were difficult to imitate and use without floatants, which may account for this absence. Some dressings, Green Drake, Black Gnat and Yellow Dun, are easily matched to familiar insects. Others, Iron Blue, Alder and Red Spinner are somewhat disguised but nonetheless present under different names.

Remarks credited to Aldam are normally those taken from the 'Old Man's' manuscript unless otherwise stated.

When considering the season of the flies, it is important to bear in mind the calendar advance of eleven days, which took place in Charles Cotton's time. Otherwise, some of his timings of when flies appear would seem rather early.

ALDER   A fly which is often dismissed by modern anglers as being of little interest to fish. In the past there are reports of this fly accounting for large bags of trout, especially larger fish. It is mentioned as being very useful on the Dove. Cotton calls it the Camlet fly and, perhaps followed by Ronalds, recommends dibbling the live insect in addition to the use of artificials. 'A good fly' is Turton's remark, his name for the Alder the Orl Fly. Its season is through May and June. If dressed with peacock herl, the flue should be thinned down by rubbing to present a slimmer body. A small Black Alder was often used by A N Bromley during black gnat hatches.

BLACK GNAT   Large mating swarms of Black Gnats appear between April and September. In addition, lesser numbers are present most days. Male and female differ considerably in bulk and colour. Males are slim and black, females distinctly brown and appear larger. Cotton's dressing is listed under March. Ronalds offers a buzz tie under May and June. Shipley's Silver Twist Hackle is listed under May. The first fly W H Aldam tied and used from the 'Old Man's' manuscript was the 'Tailey Tail', an imitation of the female Black Gnat. He fished the Derwent shortly afterwards and spooned a fish, full of female black gnats. He put up the 'new' fly and took thirteen fish in as many casts. He gave two 'Tailey Tails' to his companion, a beginner, who then caught a further eleven brace. The day's total, in peaty water, was thirty seven brace while others on the river caught only five fish between them. John Turton also lists a pattern of the Tail to Tail – this under July and August. Definitely one for the corner of the fly box.

BLUE DUN   Olives are represented by the Blue Dun and its Red Spinner in various guises. Cotton has a dressing for February; Ronalds one in March. David Foster's Blue Dun is identified as the 'February and November shade' of the Olive. Aldam's Indian Yellow is thought to be a representation of the Blue Winged Olive. John Turton's Whirling Dun listed in early April is another Large Olive imitation. William Shipley gives a handful of dressings from January to March. The importance of the Olives is well recognised by all the Derbyshire writers, although the flies may be infrequent on the acidic upper reaches of some rivers.

COW DUNG Another fly which many anglers do not rate highly. It is present throughout the season from March and particularly so around 'grass day' when dairy cattle are turned out after the winter. The fly is blown onto the water in rough weather. It is of interest to fish, particularly so early in the season when there is little other surface fly activity. Cotton gives it a fleeting comment, Ronalds a buzz alternative. It is also listed by Turton, Shipley and Foster. Since these, and several other authors list the pattern, it must have been used and found somewhat successful in the past.

DUN CUT An ancient pattern first listed by Dame Juliana Berners in her *Treatise* of 1496. Long thought to be a representation of a moth or sedge, the Dun Cut was considered by J W Hills in his *History of Fly Fishing for Trout* (1921) to be a synonym for the Yellow Dun. He associates the pattern to the Yellow Dun of Ronalds and the Dotterel Dun of Aldam. In *Practical Fly Fishing* (1849), 'Arundo' mentions the fly but sheds little light on what it represents. John Beever wrote under the pseudonym of 'Arundo' and was a longtime angler on the Derbyshire rivers. The name Dun Cut disappeared when, as J W Hills has it, 'Bowlker knocked it out of the fishing books in the middle of the eighteenth century'. David Foster used the Dun Cut as a moth imitation. The fly is recorded in *The Scientific Angler* and stated to be '... much used in the Midlands since its recent introduction...'. This presumably refers to the artificials of the Dun Cut dressed by Foster. These imitations were intended to imitate the fluttering action of moths on the water. The dressing given is double hackled using dun and brown hen breast feathers, the outer feather being dun. The body is of drab fur ribbed with silver twist on a mayfly sized hook.

FEBRUARY RED In Derbyshire this fly was often known locally as the March Brown. This led to inevitable confusion with the true March Brown, which was normally known in Derbyshire as the Dun Drake. Patterns for this fly go back to the fifteenth century and perhaps beyond. In the past it has been used to represent early stoneflies found on rivers. Leslie Magee, in *Fly Fishing The North Country Tradition*, says the true February Red is '...uncommon south of a line between the Humber and Land's End and moreover, is infrequent in stony bottomed rivers...' He proposes it is taken as a general representation of the stonefly. Ronalds has it as the '...earliest fly in North Derbyshire...' finding it abundant at Bakewell and a good fly on the Derwent. Cotton provides two dressings, the Red Brown and Lesser Red Brown. Shipley gives a Red Brown Fly and a Red Fly in February. David Foster's early season cast consisted of the Red Fly, Blue Dun and Ordinary Bumble. He notes a deepening of colour in the insects as the early season progresses. Dressed as a Hackle this is a very good grayling pattern.

GRANNOM Both William Shipley and John Turton call their patterns for the Grannom the Greentail. This is on account of its green egg sac at the rear of its body. Aldam's '*Old Man*' dates its arrival as the '...twentieth of April and of a short dewration – about fourteen days...' Foster reports it as being a favourite of fishermen, but finding it better in the latter part of summer. Cotton calls it a Shellfly but the time of appearance he gives is July, whereas the Grannom is much earlier. Alfred Ronalds has the fly emerging in April but

PLATE 4

1   Blue Dun
    (Ronalds' variant)

2   Little Chap
    (Ronalds' No 7 Buzz)

3   Green Drake
    (Ronalds)

4   Brown Spider Fly
    (Turton)

5   Willow Fly
    (Turton)

6   Grannom
    (Shipley)

found it in autopsies in August. It seems probable that all these writers may be discussing two separate species of sedge.

GRAVEL BED This insect is found on comparatively few rivers but the Derbyshire Derwent is one of them. The fly is reputed to induce feeding frenzies among fish when it hatches, which takes place in May from gravel banks alongside the water and can be prolific. The insects are similar in appearance to a small Crane Fly; lead-brown coloured body, long legs and brown-mottled wings. They are blown onto the surface, wet or dry patterns being used as s uccessful imitations. Ronalds and Woolley provide ties and a small modified 'Hopper' style dressing is also useful. Shipley and Turton's Spider Fly are dressings for the Gravel Bed.

GREEN DRAKE AND GREY DRAKE The '*Old Man's*' manuscript gives a detailed and accurate description of the Mayfly's life cycle. The observations he made included egg laying, development of the larva and placing adults in a window to watch the ecdysis of the brilliantly coloured imago. The Mayfly's appearance is reported as the fourth of June or thereabouts. Cotton also gives a most accurate description of the Drake though he has its emergence around the twentieth of May. The calendar adjustment would bring this into early June. Foster's Favourite, an elaborate dressing of the Mayfly, is strongly recommended by its inventor and his acquaintances. He offers buzz dressings for both Drakes. Perhaps as would be expected, Ronalds's flyplates are superb. He too gives buzz dressings for both the Green and Grey Drakes. The patterns from William Shipley and John Turton both have wings stained appropriate colours. Several of the writers confirm the Mayfly hatch to be earlier in the quiet deeper parts of rivers than in the colder waters nearer the source. Live Mayfly dibbling, the old means of fishing the Drake, is mentioned by Charles Cotton and David Foster.

HAWTHORN Despite the early date given, Charles Cotton's Thorn Tree Fly must allude to the Hawthorn Fly. He calls it 'an admirable fly and in great repute amongst us as a killer'. Aldam's pattern is the Large Black Caterpillar. His description of it '...often fleeing over the Hawthorns...' and '...Hanging there long black leggs straight down...', make it unmistakeable. John Turton gives a dressing for March and April. His May pattern he calls the Black Caterpillar Fly, the same name given by Alfred Ronalds to his buzz dressing of the female Hawthorn. Turton advises red legs on the fly for summer. Whether fish take it for a Hawthorn at this time is debatable, but the fly certainly works. St Mark's Day is the twenty fifth of April and the Hawthorn as a consequence has acquired the additional title of St Mark's Fly.

IRON BLUE Charles Cotton, Sir Humphrey Davy and Sir John Hawkins would recognise this fly as the Violet Fly. It has the reputation of being about on cold rough days, a fact noted in Aldam's manuscript. Ronalds also gives a dressing for the Jenny Spinner, the imago of the Iron Blue. The Spinner is not mentioned by Cotton, the '*Old Man*', Turton or Shipley. David Foster makes much of the fly. He is alleged to have seen a cloud of smoke in Dovedale, which on closer examination proved to be a cloud of Iron Blue Duns in their mating flight. The fly is now, apparently, much less common on the Derbyshire and Staffordshire rivers than in past times. Cotton's Black Blue Dun, Turton's Violet Midge and Shipley's Ash Fly are perhaps imitations of the Iron Blue later in the summer. The fly appears in April and is about until September, but becoming intermittent as the year progresses. The '*Old Man's*' Little Sky Blue called by W H Aldam '...a most important fly...' is an imitation of the Small Sperwing.

LITTLE CHAP   Also known as the Smoke Fly, the Little Chap imitates a selection of beetles. Ronalds observed it from March until May and thought it best fished on a 'sultry, gloomy day...'. It is the buzz form of his Peacock Fly and he reports it as '...a great Grayling killer...much prized on the Derwent near Rowsley...'. Aldam proposes the Bumbles developed from tyings of this fly, and certainly the materials are very similar. The '*Old Man*' describes its natural origins '...bred from a grub found in the Old Cowdung... The grub creeps into the Hearth and remains all Winter – and early the next year comes into a small beetle...'. Not so fanciful as it seems, there are several beetles which frequent cow pats. Foster used the Little Chap as a precursor to the Mayfly in the morning and evening.

MARCH BROWN   Not a common fly on Derbyshire and Staffordshire rivers. The 'Derbyshire March Brown' of the '*Old Man's*' manuscript is according to Aldam, the February Red. The 'March Brown of Great Britain', as Aldam has it, is known in Derbyshire as the Dun Drake. William Shipley has a tie for the March Brown or Dun Drake under March. His next pattern is the March Brown Dun Fly. Turton too has a March Brown pattern and another for the Dun Drake or '*Old Man*'. Turton and Aldam recommend the fly for dark or gritstone waters. Foster says the fly is known in the Northern Counties as the Dun Drake, and infers, despite various names, the insect is '..characteristically the same everywhere...'. The Turkey Fly may be Charles Cotton's contribution to the discussion. Alfred Ronalds records it as the March Brown or Dun Drake. The fly, according to both Ronalds and Foster, metamorphoses into the Great Red Spinner. Foster found the fly plentiful and a great favourite of the trout. All agree on one thing; it is about on the water in March and April.

OAK FLY   Ronalds, Aldam and Foster all mention the Oak Fly as a candidate for 'live dibbling'. In his editorial remarks on the old manuscript, Aldam gives much detail of tackle, catching and storing the live flies. Turton remarks on the fly being very good in coloured water and the fact that it often takes big fish. This may suggest that he too used it live on occasion. The fly is not popular in modern times and probably achieved its historical popularity by being 'dibbled'. Alfred Ronalds also says that dressed large it is an '...excellent chub fly in the Trent...'. He has the fly on the water from May to June but other writers later still. David Foster considered the fly invaluable after Mayfly time, though it is unclear whether the artificial was used. He too says it can be dibbled in a similar style to the Drake. Called by the '*Old Man*', the 'Oringe Brown', the fly is also known as the Downlooker, Shipley renaming it as the Ash Fly. One according to its characteristic stance, the other as it is often found on ash tree boles.

1

2

4

5

118

PLATE 5

1 Little Whirling Blue Dun
   (Shipley)

2 Black Gnat (Tailey Tail)
   (Aldam No 6)

3 March Brown
   (Aldam No 1)

3

6

4 Iron Blue
   (Aldam No 4)

5 Orange Dun
   (Aldam No 11)

6 Oak Fly
   (Shipley)

ORANGE DUN A fly of '...some importance on the Dove and other Derbyshire waters...' is the opening comment of Alfred Ronalds on the Orange Dun. He rates it highly as a grayling pattern, a view shared by W H Aldam. Shipley offers a dressing for use in July, and Turton reports it as good in '...black or disturbed waters...'. It is fished from June to the end of the season and is, very probably, a representation of the Blue Winged Olive.

RED AND BLACK ANTS Few anglers seem to have experienced a large ant fall but most authorities favour carrying a pattern, 'just in case'. The 'Old Man' gives dressings and accounts of Black, Red and Small Common Ants. His observations on fish taking ants are fascinating. '...I have seen the river nearly covered over and every fish...taking them. I have seen them full up to the Gills and taken them of the points of the willows that dipped into the water...'. W H Aldam himself did not rate the ant very highly but commended the 'Old Man's' patterns. Cotton lists two ant dressings and obviously had success with them. Shipley has dressings for Black and Red Ants, whilst John Turton reports his Small Ant Fly as '...Best on bright days and in low clear water'. David Foster fished Black and Red Ants in August.

SAND FLY This with the Cinnamon Fly represents Sedges. For whatever reason there are not many sedge imitations in the old writers' lists, possibly because flies could not be made to float. Alfred Ronalds compares it to the Cinnamon Fly and has it about in April and May. He also advises its use for grayling and dace in July and August. Aldam's 'Old Man' calls it the 'Crossing Brown' and says it is an excellent fly throughout the season. The dressings of David Foster and William Shipley are practically identical. Turton's Brown Spider Fly is his offering for the Sand Fly.

SOLDIER OR SAILOR FLY These are representations of the Soldier Beetle. They are often seen near water, and presumably are blown onto the surface. Alfred Ronalds, under the Fern Fly, says they are '...much admired by fish...' and tied buzz make a very effective pattern. His Orange Fly, named as an Ichneumon imitation muddies the waters somewhat, but is probably another representation of a similar insect later in the season. The Soldier Palmer is thought by some to be an imitation of these beetles; Cotton's Orange Fly is a possible dressing. Turton has an Orange Black not unlike Cotton's pattern and his Fern Fly or Brown Gnat may be another representation. Shipley's Fern Fly is under May but gives little confidence as a beetle imitation.

STONE FLY Cotton has a dressing which, for him, is quite involved. He says the fly appears in April but is of no interest to the fish until May. Alfred Ronalds used it in rough water on windy days. He also mentions it as suitable for live dibbling. David Foster agrees with Ronalds and says it is very effective fished live. Stonefly or creeper fishing was very popular and the baits were caught, then stored, in a 'creeper horn'. Shipley and Turton both list dressings and Turton has it on the water in April and May following up again in July. He says it is good for large fish late at night and in fast water. Once more, rough windy days are favourable times to fish the Stonefly. There are many species and these imitations may well cover more than one insect.

WHIRLING BLUE DUN   This fly is said to be a standard Derbyshire pattern by Gerald Heywood in his book, *Charles Cotton and his River*. Cotton has two dressings, one in March and one in April. Heywood thinks Cotton's patterns are attempts at spinners and that he derived the name from their motion in flight. Ronalds lists the fly in September turning into a Light Red Spinner, possibly as a second edition of the Yellow Dun of April. Turton gives a tie for April, another for August and September, perhaps confirming Ronalds's opinion. Foster's Yellow Dun of April and Pale Blue Dun metamorphose into Red Spinners. '...These flies whirl in clouds a distance above the water...'. William Shipley has several Blue Duns in January and February followed by the Little Pale Blue in September.

WILLOW FLY   Another Stonefly species, along with the Needle Fly and Yellow Sally. Ronalds refers to the Willow or Withy Fly under September, saying it is extremely abundant, and present even later in the year. He ties it buzz and recommends it as a grayling pattern and a good fly on the Derwent. The '*Old Man's*' dressing is thought by W H Aldam to be a representation of the Yellow Sally, another Stonefly species. David Foster fished both Willow and Needle flies for grayling in September and October. His dressing for the Yellow Sally is not winged, enabling the fly to drop on the water as would a heavy beetle. It is recommended to palmer the hackle on the dressing. John Turton's Yellow Spider Fly may be his imitation of the Yellow Sally.

WREN TAIL   A representation of the froghopper, the insect which creates 'cuckoo spit' on herbage. Ronalds records them being very active in hot weather, making flights of up to twenty yards, when they are best used by the angler. William Shipley names it the Wren Hackle, fishing it in July. Foster has it about with ants, seen on the water in bright weather around the middle of the day in August. Another pattern rarely used by anglers, the dressing for the hackle is not obtainable but could be easily substituted. It is perhaps worth a try, given the enthusiasm of Ronalds and Foster for the fly.

YELLOW DUN   Charles Cotton mentions a dressing for a Yellow Dun in April as does Alfred Ronalds. He names it as '...one of our best flies...'. Buzz versions are given, one of which is the Dotterel Dun. The '*Old Man*' has the 'Spring or Dottrill Dun' which he says comes from the end of March to the end of May. William Shipley has a similar pattern, though not with a Dotterel hackle. Two Yellow Duns of April are provided by David Foster who considers them '...of great importance... as being the most useful to the angler through the whole season...'. Surprisingly John Turton's comprehensive list does not provide a named pattern. The Cock-up or Upwinged Dun receives the highest praise, 'This fly is the surest killer that is thrown on to the water...' and is perhaps his substitute. Maybe the dark gritstone waters he fished did not breed Olives in large numbers. The Yellow Dun was a fly well used by George Eaton of Matlock. On this pattern he caught his huge trout from the Derwent beneath High Tor. James Ogden says the Yellow Dun was a favourite fly of his father. Frank Ogden even had a special yellow dun game cock which was his pride and joy, supplying him with feathers for his own use. The fly pattern he used had a yellow silk body, waxed with cobbler's wax, a wing of young starling feather tied upright and the hackle as aforementioned.

The names given to flies by different writers vary enormously. Often the same name is given to different insects, making the process of tracking a given insect to a given pattern very difficult. These notes are a basic guide. The fly names titled are the most frequently recorded patterns from the lists of six Derbyshire 'Angler-Authors'.

SPECIALITY FLIES

The 'Speciality Flies' are those patterns invented, adapted or adopted by local anglers for Derbyshire and Staffordshire rivers. Where a hook size is given it is as the originator's pattern.

Hook size conversion chart

OLD	18	17	16	15	14	12	10
NEW	000	00	0	1	2	3	4

APPLE GREEN DUN   The Apple Green is usually used, wet or dry, as an Autumn grayling pattern. Grayling are thought to be attracted to green flies. W M Gallichan and the Marquess of Granby rated the pattern highly. Considered a 'Fancy Fly' it may represent small olive duns, and is a good rough water pattern.

Roger Woolley's dressing –

Hook:	0
Body:	Pale apple green floss silk
Hackle and Whisks:	Ginger cock
Wings:	Starling

BADGERS   There are a number of variations of Badgers as anglers adapt the patterns to their own liking. Some tie a hackle at head and tail, others prefer a palmered hackle with another as a collar. Commonly accepted are the use of two Badger hackles and a peacock herl or floss silk body.

The Double Badger is a great favourite on the Derbyshire and Staffordshire streams. The fly is often attributed to Roger Woolley as being its originator yet, strangely, is not listed in his *Modern Trout Fly Dressing*, nor any of his catalogues I have seen. Further research in August 2006 has resulted in correspondence from Noel Smith who knew Roger Woolley, and also the waterkeeper who devised the Double Badger, Donald McCleahy-Mackenzie. D M Mackenzie advised that when supplies of the Double Badger he had given to Noel Smith were exhausted, application should be made to Roger Woolley for more. When Woolley was contacted he sent a catalogue in which there was no mention of the pattern. He did know D M Mackenzie but he had not heard of the Double Badger. Noel's lone copy of the fly was sent to Woolley for dressing and inclusion in his lists.

In his writings for *The Grayling*, by Richard Lake, Woolley recommends the 'Mackenzie Fly' as a dry grayling pattern – it must surely be D M Mackenzie's Double Badger.

THE DOUBLE BADGER   *Donald MacLeahy-Mackenzie* as provided by his friend,
                           Noel Smith.

Hook:	Down-eyed round bend or similar, sizes 14, 15, 16, 17, & 18.
Tying Silk:	Pearsall's Gossamer, Black or Purple
Tail Hackle:	(Smaller than shoulder hackle): Early season: Silver Badger cock.
	Mid Summer/Autumn season: Golden Badger cock
Body:	Bronze Peacock herl wound "quite bushy".
Shoulder Hackle:	(Slightly longer than tail hackle) Silver or Golden Badger, as above. The hackles when taken from the cape, should be an elongated oval in shape, with a black root, gold/white centre and black list.

BLUE BADGER: *R Woolley*

Hook:	00 – 1
Body:	Blue floss, ribbed silver wire and silver tipped
Hackle:	Badger Cock from shoulder to tail

The Red Badger as above but with red floss body

SILVER BADGER: *R Woolley*

Hook:	0 – 1
Body:	Silver tinsel with a red tag at head and tail
Hackle:	Badger hen

BAETIS EMERGER: *Tony Bridgett*

Hook:	Emerger 14 – 20
Body:	Dubbed black material combining some glitter
Wing post:	White material of choice
Hackle:	Black or brown, wound parachute style

The fly to be fished in the surface film

BLOWN-OVER-DUN   *Philip White*

Hook:	12 T M C 100
Thread:	Primrose
Tail and Butt:	Natural cock pheasant tail
Body:	Lathkill Superfine shade no 12
Wings:	Grey or natural elkhair
Thorax:	Hare's fur
Hackle:	Olive dyed grizzle

Having tied the elk hair pointing over the eye pull it back and divide it in two. Leave one wing upright and one lying flat with a ninety degree angle between the two. Cut the hackle flush on the underside.

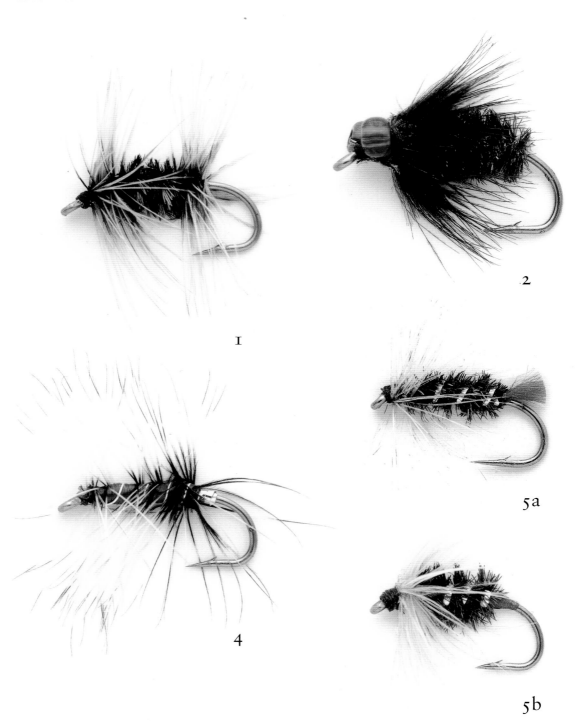

2

1

5a

4

5b

PLATE 6

1   Double Badger
     (Mackenzie))

2   Derby Beetle

3   Winter Dun
     (Foster)

4   Blue Badger
     (Woolley)

5a   Grayling Witch
     (Woolley)

5b   Grayling Witch var.

6   Whistler Fly
     (Foster)

3

6

THE BRAILSFORD

In a fly case which belonged to Roger Woolley is a mayfly labelled 'The Brailsford'. The dressing does not appear in Woolley's writings, and is presumably named for Brailsford Brook between Derby and Ashbourne.

Hook:	10-12 (4-3 New Scale)
Body:	White floss silk
Body Hackle:	Short cream or pale blue dun cock
Rib:	Peacock herl
Hackle:	Grizzle cock or grey speckled mallard breast
Wing:	Four blue dun cock hackles tied spent

The fly in Roger Woolley's fly case has been badly damaged by moth and the wings are almost totally absent but identifiable.

COCK WING DUN

Notes by A K Bridgett.

'Today it seems there are few local patterns; the town or village fishing tackle shop is a thing of the past. Most successful flies are internationally known, through the huge range of books and magazines that cover the art of fly fishing and tying. So the following might be of interest to those interested in the history of how fishing flies became popular, giving an insight into that process.

The first fly-caught trout that I took was on a Cock Wing Dun, on the Manifold river. A fly, in the first part of the century, that was well known in West Derbyshire and North Staffordshire. A fly not to be without on the rivers Dove, Manifold and Hamps. It was very often the only pattern that local rods fished.

In the late 40s and 50s there was an Ironmongers shop in Derby Street, Leek, Staffordshire, that attended to the needs of the local fishing and shooting community. As one entered the shop on the wall on the right, at the bottom of the stairs were several small display cases containing trout flies. Bearing in mind the end of the war, most boxes were empty, but in the middle four boxes were Cock Winged Duns, always full, and in brackets the name 'Moss's' Cock Winged Dun. It was with a Moss's that I had caught that trout some sixty years ago.

Several years later I became quite interested in this fly. I did find out through research that it was a favourite fly of many local and visiting rods; Sir Thomas Wardle of Swainsley Hall, on the Manifold, David Foster of Ashbourne, John Bonsall of Ecton, and my mentor and tutor James Stanmore of Leek to name but a few.

To the fly itself; its name suggests a copy of any of the up winged river flies in the dun stage. Which one the originator intended is pure guesswork. Over the years I have come across several versions of the fly itself, tied in different ways, as shown below.

Cock Wing Dun. (Moss's)

Hook size 12 or 14. Tail small bunch of Blue Dun Cock hackle fibres. Body yellow wool, more of dirty yellow colour. Blue dun hackle. Wing two slips of starling, tied pent pointing forward over the eye of the hook. Not split.

Cock Wing Dun. From David Foster's book, *The Scientific Angler.*
Same as above but with a hackle of blue dun, freckled with pale yellow. Where it was taken to be an imitation of one of the Olive Duns.

Foster's fishing tackle shop in Church Street, Ashbourne used to sell both Moss's version and another, which was:-

Cock Winged Dun.
Hook size 16. Tail, small pinch of blue dun cock hackle fibres. Body cream undyed seal's fur. Blue dun cock hackle. Wing starling wing tied pent, not split.

Following the death of the last of David Foster's male heirs, Wilfred Lou Foster in the late 60s, I was given a Cock Wing Dun by the Fosters shop manager Mr Arnold Mosley of Ashbourne from a packet he had found in the shop. It must have been an old tying as those in the packet were tied to gut. That tying was on a 12s hook. Tail dark blue dun hackle fibres, body dark mole fur, with a dark blue dun hackle, and starling wing tied pent.

SUCCESS WITH THE FLY
In 1971 on my return to the town of Leek, I was invited for a day's fishing on the river Hamps. A lovely fishing day in Spring with trout rising at every bend in the river. I could not interest the trout until I remembered the success I had had in the past with the Cock Wing Dun. From then on I did very well. It is a fly that can be counted on to catch well on the Dove, Wye, Derwent, Manifold and Hamps in the Spring.

Another feature of this fly is how well it fishes when it has been well chewed up. In fact the rougher it is, the more successful it is. I usually change flies after 15 or 20 fish, when I become too embarrassed to fish with it any more.'

The Cock Wing Dun does have a particular following on the Derbyshire and Staffordshire waters. Roger Woolley had his own pattern as did James Ogden. The latter had several variants and used it throughout the season by altering the colour of the wing. This was accomplished by judicious use of onion skin dye. Body colour was controlled by mixing in a little olive monkey neck fur or olive Berlin wool. At times only yellow silk was used as a body. His final twist was to rib the fur body with fine gold tinsel and tie in upright wings from a woodcock feather.

DERBY BEETLE Also called the Red Eyed Beetle and the Derbyshire Belle. Dressings for this pattern vary considerably. W L Foster reports it as being '...wielded by a fellow angler...' and from this point the fly was presumable developed, and included in Fosters' catalogues.

1

2

3

4

5

PLATE 7
COCK WINGED DUN PATTERNS

1 Arnold Mosley to Tony Bridgett
   from old Foster Bros. stock

2 A K Bridgett

3 Moss's Cockwing

4 Roger Woolley

5 Foster Bros.
     (A K Bridgett)

6 John Turton

7 James Ogden

8 David Foster

The dressings for these patterns
are detailed overleaf.

6

7

8

COCK WINGED DUN DRESSINGS

1 Arnold Mosley to Tony Bridgett

Hook: 3 (12 to gut)
Tail: Dark blue dun hackle fibres
Body: Dark mole fur
Hackle: Dark blue dun
Wing;   Starling tied pent

2 A K Bridgett

Hook: 2 - 3 (12 - 14)
Body: Tapered pale primrose dubbing
Hackle:
& Whisks: Pale blue dun cock hackle fibres
Wing: Paired slips of starling, tied pent over the eye

3 Moss's Cockwing

Hook: 2 - 4 (14 - 10)
Body: Yellow olive wool
Hackle:
& Whisks: Medium blue hen tied bushy
Wing: Starling, tied single upright style

4. Roger Woolley

Hook: 0 -1 (16 - 15)
Body: Blue fur on yellow tying silk
Hackle
& Whisks: Olive hen
Wings: Starling

5 Foster Bros. (A K Bridgett)

Hook: 0 (16)
Tail: Small pinch blue dun cock hackle fibres
Body: Cream undyed seal fur
Hackle: Blue dun cock
Wing: Starling tied pent

6 John Turton

Hook: Not specified
Body: Bright ash-coloured silk, having a shade of green in it
Rib: Black horse-hair and two black horns
Silk: Ash
Legs: Lightest ginger cock hackle
At times the legs may be red or yellow according to age

7 James Ogden

Hook: 2 (14)
Body: Hare's ear fur spun on fine yellow silk with golden tinsel tag
Tail: Three strands red cock hackle
Body: Starling feather fibre, broad and tied upright
After the wings are set spin on more fur and place two turns behind the wings. Pick this out to form legs.
Variations include a fine gold tinsel rib, yellow silk body; upright woodcock wing, wings and fur stained in onion dye; addition of olive Berlin wool or monkey neck fur

8 David Foster

Hook: Not specified
Body: Small portion water rat fur spun sparingly on full yellow silk
Hackle: Bluish dun hackle freckled with yellow or blue dun hackle slightly stained yellow
Wings: From an old starling's wing quill feather

Apparently, 'The glint of the red eyes is irresistible to trout, particularly after a spate...'

Hook: 12
Body: Bronze peacock herl
Hackle: Long black cock and hen hackle tied bushy
Eyes: Two red glass beads

The fly has been used as a sea trout pattern and variations are used as loch and lake flies.

FOSTER'S FAVOURITE An imitation of the Green Drake invented by David Foster of Ashbourne. As a result of the fly's success for Foster and his clients, it became known as the 'Favourite'. It is a complex pattern to dress. The wing feathers need to be dyed as does the wheat straw body. The latter has to be tied in such a manner as to leave an air-filled hollow between head and tail to ensure flotation. Partridge tail feather was used for the tail strands. Foster considered stiff whiskers prevented adequate hooking. The fly is illustrated in *The Scientific Angler* and in its time was obviously considered very effective.

Body: Wheaten straw 'rightly tinted,' ribbed with brown-red silk
Whisks: Three strands of partridge tail feather
Legs: An ample and full freckled breast feather of ginger hue, entwined with cock honey dun hackle
Wing: Mallard, Egyptian Goose or Canadian Wood Duck, dyed to a green-yellow tinge.

The Grey Drake was dressed in a similar manner.

Body: White straw ribbed with dark mulberry coloured silk
Whisks: Three strands of a black cock's saddle feather
Legs: Two dun cock hackles which may be palmered from shoulders to tail
Wings: Widgeon or dark Mallard feather dyed pale slate colour.

Foster Bros offered two series of mayflies. One pattern, the Butcher, was probably named such, as it was fished by a man called George Butcher. He was an angling guide on the rivers Wye and Derwent, taking other work in the winter. It is still used by Tony Bridgett.

Tail: Three pheasant tail fibres
Body: One third peacock herl, second third blood red silk with a gold rib, last third peacock herl
Hackle: First hackle Rhode Island Red, followed by either Partridge black and white ackle or small black and white Mallard feather dyed bright yellow
Hook: Long Shank 12.

For the sake of completion, the other patterns in Fosters series were as follows:

BUTCHER SERIES
Birdsgrove, named after the Ashbourne water on the Dove, Spent Gnat, Little Gem, Sunk Green, Grey May and Bloody Butcher. These were wet flies.

1

2

4

5

PLATE 8

1   Rough Olive

2   Gold Ribbed Hare's Ear
    (Thorpe var.)

3a Roger's Fancy
    (Woolley)

3b Roger's Fancy
    (var.)

3a

3b

4   Partridge and Hare's Lug

5   Cock Winged Dun

6   Apple Green Dun

6

IMPERIAL DRY FLY SERIES
Queen, Emperor, Black Knight, Red King, Prince and Baron.

FOSTER'S INTERMEDIATE
In *The Scientific Angler*, David Foster mentions this pattern. It is a variant of the Yellow Dun of April found in his fly lists, but no dressing is given. A little more detail is appended in the leaflet, *Foster's List of Trout Flies*, again under April. *'The fly marked as our Intermediate is intended to represent the middle or intermediate stage of all the duns whilst in the act of changing their skins, prior to their reappearance as spinners.'*

H S Hall writing in *'Fishing,'* by H Cholmondley-Pennel in 1885, also mentions 'The Intermediate'. An engraving of the fly depicts a dressing of an upwinged dun with a body detached from the beginning of the hook bend. He used the pattern to imitate the 'different gradations' of 'different duns' with particular reference to summer fishing.

The detached fly bodies were dressed with '...pale and delicate tints...' of horsehair, choosing '...shades of honey dun, light buff, or olive for legs, and varying the colour of the wings so as to suit the rest of the fly.' H S Hall took great care over the dressings to ensure a match with the observations he made of the living flies. There is no reference to David Foster but like him, H S Hall used the patterns to copy a range of developmental stages in duns.

FOX SEDGE
A pattern tied to represent a number of sedges. The guard hairs on a red fox's back vary from dark glowing red to sandy yellow. Appropriate choice of the hair and also hackle colour gives a selection of sedges, which cover most eventualities.

Hook:	Long Shank 12 or 14
Silk:	Brown
Body:	Gold lurex, leaving a gold tip palmered with two medium red cock's hackles, or colour as required.
Rib:	Dark three pound monofil - 'Maxima'.
Wing:	Glowing red hairs from the centre of a fox's back. Tie flat over the palmered hackle, cut square at the end of the hook bend.
Hackle:	Medium red cock hackle.

The under side of the fly is trimmed at an angle from the hook point to the head of the fly.

GENERAL OR SPRING BLACK
Recommended in 'Foster's List of Trout Flies' as a good pattern representing the '... whole tribe of blacks,' and '...an especial favourite in Derbyshire, Staffordshire and the North.' Roger Woolley gives a dressing under the Spring Black.

Hook:	0 (16)
Body:	Purple tying silk, dubbed thinly with magpie herl.
Hackle:	Black starling feather.

GLYMO

This is Peter Arfield's description of the Pale Watery, which he also names the *September* fly, in his own words:

'I think that I developed this fly around 1974, when, baffled by the behaviour of selectively feeding trout in late season on the Derwent and the Wye. At the time, I scarcely knew one fly from another, but I did see that some fish were targeting small pale coloured flies to the seeming exclusion of much else. When I captured a couple of these hatching flies I was struck by the succulent orange glow they seemed to have, if only for a few moments.

After a fair amount of playing around, I dropped on a description of a particular Pale Watery species that had prominent red eyes. This was to the amusement of all who heard this across the work benches of the dormer twist drill works electricians' shop. In any case, a red body was none too effective, an orange body worked on occasion, as did an amber colouring, nothing worked as well as the effect formed with a yellow dubbing applied over red silk. This internal hatching glow works well for me and continued to do so over picky late season fish. My first attempt at a parachute hackle around a crude yarn post worked well. At that time I was forming a loop of yarn as a post because it looked more wing-like and was easier to grab hold of! A lucky break, which has served me well and has continued ever since.

As the fly is not designed to be waterproofed in the conventional sense, I apply a paste type floatant on the hackle only and the soggy orange glow in the surface film seems to work pretty well. Too wet a body, and all we get is red, too dry, and the thing does not glow, just damp is the thing.

I am surprised at the interest in the fly and find it hard to believe other and more skilful hands have not fashioned something similar, but I suppose it was at least new to me at the time. Can I plead youthful ignorance and enthusiasm retrospectively?

Hook:	Dry size 18
Thread	Red
Posted yarn wing:	Antron or a poly yarn in white formed in a looped wing shape.
Parachute hackle:	Badger tied fairly small. (Dun or pale cream works too.)
Body:	Dubbed dry fly dubbing in pale yellow over the red silk underbody. Slightly prominent red head formed from the tying thread.

GOLD RIBBED HARES EAR

An old standard pattern of unknown origin but now present in most flyboxes. In its various forms and variations, the Gold Ribbed Hare's Ear is used by many Derbyshire and Staffordshire anglers. The pattern appears seven times, under various guises, in the list of current Derbyshire and Staffordshire anglers' flyboxes. Tim Thorpe lists a Goldhead Gold Ribbed Hare's Ear Nymph and another pattern without the goldhead, Steve Woolley a dry fly version.

Steve Trigg's current favoured grayling pattern dressing is as follows:

Hook: Curved heavyweight grub 10 – 16
Thread: Grey micro
Tail: Red holographic lurex
Body: Short hare's face fur, picked out
Rib: Red holographic lurex
Thorax: Long hare's face fur, picked out
Head: Gold bead to suit the size of hook

Steve also has a pink version of this fly.

GOLD RIBBED HARE'S EAR NYMPH *Tim Thorpe*

Hook: 10 - 20
Tail: Fibres from a hare's mask with a dark root
Body: Fur from a hare's ear roughly dubbed
Rib: Fine oval gold or wire to thorax
Thorax: Fur from a hare's ear dubbed on silk, then doubled and redoubled to form a thickened area so the whole fly takes on the shape of a carrot
Silk: Brown

GOLDEN EARWIG

A fly much used and probably invented by John Fosbrooke of Hartington. The pattern is a highly rated grayling catcher by W M Gallichan. Notes on this pattern featured in the *Fishing Gazette* on August 16th 1902. David Foster's Golden Palmer is very close in dressing style and William Shipley's Golden Ostrich only differs in body material. He used black ostrich. Fosbrooke's pattern may be a variation of Shipley's fly.

Body: Peacock herl, ribbed with gold wire
Hackle: A bright hackle that looks claret in the hand but against the light is a fiery red, palmered shoulder to tail.

GREATER RED SPINNER (BLANCHARD)

Walter Thorpe gives the following account regarding this fly:

'Just after starting work in 1944, I used to attend UMIST in Manchester and, at lunch time, used to visit Chamber's Fishing Tackle shop, which was on the first floor of the famous and ancient 'Shambles' Building (now relocated and still containing the Sinclair's Oyster Bar).

The tackle shop was called 'Chambers' if I remember correctly, but it was run by Mr Blanchard. He, despite some of the tales told to the contrary, was the inventor of the fly which he called his 'Greater Red Spinner.' Everyone else called it 'Blanchard's Abortion'. Despite this, it was an excellent fly. The story, from his own lips as I remember it, goes like this:

He was fishing on the river Dane one evening and there was a large hatch of sedges. He didn't have a really suitable imitation with him and tied on a large and very bushy version of a Red Spinner. It proved very effective and he had a good bag in no time. When he looked at the fly more carefully, he realised that, in tying it on, the gut had looped around the top of the hackle and pulled it down so that it faced forward. That is how he came to invent it. (Even though he knew that he was using it as a sedge imitator he still called it his 'Greater Red Spinner'. I know not why.) The one thing that I do not remember is whether he used a yellow silk body or a peacock herl body (I have seen tyings published with both alternatives). I rather think that it was the former.'

A dressing of Blanchard's Spinner is as follows:

Hook:	10
Tail:	Bunch of light red or ginger hair
Body:	Red-brown pheasant tail fibres
Rib:	Gold or silver wire
Hackle:	Very full medium red cock. Use two hackles if necessary
Wing:	Light red hair tied pent and forward of the hackle
Silk:	Dark brown

A fly simply called Blanchard's is listed under Split Wing Dry Flies in Foster Bros 1964 catalogue at 14/- per dozen

GREY DUSTER

An invaluable general purpose dry fly which probably originated in Wales. Well used on Staffordshire and Derbyshire rivers, it is a fly which is often dressed by anglers to their own pattern. A parachute version suits the writer very well in rough water as it is surprisingly easy to follow. John Neville dresses his pattern as follows:

Tail:	Badger cock hackle fibres
Body:	Dubbed mole, water vole, or best of all, coypu
Body hackle:	Palmered badger cock
Collar hackle:	Badger cock

HARE'S FACE EMERGER

Tied in 'Klinkhammer' style by Steve Trigg, this emerger pattern imitates a range of natural flies from midges to sedges.

Hook:	Curved Trigghammer 12 – 16
Thread:	Grey Micro
Body:	Fine hare's face fibres
Thorax:	Hare's face fibres
Wingpost:	Poly yarn
Hackle:	Badger cock

Greater Red Spinner or
Blanchard's Abortion
(Blanchard)

HARE'S LUG AND PLOVER

This fly, used by W S R Fogg as a representation of olive nymphs and emergers, is described in *The Art of the Wet Fly* as a personal favourite.

Silk: Brown
Body: Hare's ear fur, ribbed with fine gold wire and tapered from the thorax with a small gold tag at the tail
Hackle: Mouse coloured with yellow tips from a golden plover

John Roberts, in *Illustrated Dictionary of Trout Flies* (1986), says that the pattern has been used in Derbyshire for at least two hundred years.

HASSAM'S PET

C A Hassam was a well known angler on both the Wye and the Derwent. He was a member of the Fly Fisher's Club and considered an excellent fly dresser. He was a contemporary of both G E M Skues and R S Austin, the inventor of the 'Tups Indispensable'. Austin revealed the dressing of his creation to Skues and Hassam and it was kept secret until Austin's daughter released the details after his death.

Hassam's Pet was tied to fish the Derbyshire Wye and was named by Hassam's friend G E M Skues. The style of dressing is different from most flies.

Hassam's Pet

Hook:	15 or 16
Silk:	A few turns of primrose silk forming a platform for the hackle and also tying in whisks of pale ginger cock hackle. The latter need to be long enough to form the tail of the fly.
Body:	Pale yellow floss silk is next tied in at the shoulder. This is wound down the hook lashing down the whisks. One turn of floss is made under the whisks and the floss returned to the shoulder forming the fly body.
Hackle:	Pale ginger cock hackle is tied in, wound over the prepared platform of silk at the shoulder, finished off with a normal head and varnished.

HATCHING MAYFLY

A hatching or emerging pattern which Steve Trigg has found as one of his most productive patterns over the last few seasons.

Hook:	Straight longshank nymph, 10 – 12
Thread:	Grey Micro
Tail:	Soft red game hackle fibres
Body:	Cream seal fur
Thorax:	Dark olive and brown seal fur, mixed
Hackle:	Brown Partridge

HAWTHORN FLY

Practically every author's flylist from Charles Cotton lists a dressing for the Hawthorn. It has not always been favoured by anglers, particularly in the past when fly hatches were prolific. Tony Bridgett says the fly is now eagerly anticipated on the Dove as the numbers of river flies are falling. This is his dressing:

Hook: 12

Take black thread to a point opposite the hook barb and return to a point out one third the way from the eye. On top of the hook, tie in a strip of close cell black foam about fifteen millimetres long. Touch the tail end with a flame to form a round end. The body foam is left ten millimetres long leaving five millimetres to form the thorax. Tie in two pairs of black rubber legs, and a black cock hackle. Dub a small amount of black fur and wind to the eye. Palmer the hackle to the eye and tie in. Pull the remaining foam down to the eye, tie in to form the thorax, finishing with a whip finish.

HERON HERL OLIVE

Tony Bridgett offered this pattern as one from his 'Flybox' list.

Hook:	12 – 14
Tail:	Small pinch of Rhode Island Red cock hackle fibres
Body:	Heron herl dyed yellow, giving an olive colour. Ribbed with five turns of gold tinsel
Wing:	Starling, two strips tied upright and split
Hackle:	Blue dun cock hackle

Tony adds that heron feathers, paler blue than Canada goose, can sometimes be picked up under a heronry or at a lakeside.

INDIAN YELLOW

James Smith of Sharrow near Sheffield was the inventor of this pattern. He liaised with W H Aldam to find a silk of suitable colour for the body. The fly was used by Aldam as his standard point fly from May onward. He used the fly on all waters in Derbyshire and elsewhere with great success. It is thought to represent the Blue Winged Olive. The dressing is listed under W H Aldam and consists of virtually unobtainable materials. It may well be one for experiment with substitutes.

KILL DEVIL SPIDERS

A series of flies developed by David Foster of Ashbourne. There is no mention of the flies in *The Scientific Angler* but there is an advertisement for Fosters Perfect Kill Devil Minnow. James Ogden used a similar lure during a trip to Ireland in 1851 trolled behind his boat. Ogden referred to this as his Devil Killer. Perhaps another case of tandem development between Foster and Ogden, or is it possible one of them had the idea first? The following information included in Foster's *List of Trout Flies*, a leaflet issued by the company after David Foster's death:

"*Kill Devil Spider, Dun or Grey are the best in the early weeks, later the Olive and Fiery Brown shades are extra good, followed by the Furnace and Black, the latter especially in the evenings of a hot day when fish are sucking in smutting midges.*
...Foster's Kill Devil Spider which is a concoction intended in its various shades (there are

six varieties) represent the whole order of spider legged natural aquatic, together with many similar formed types of land bred winged insects forming food for fish. We recommend the Kill Devil Spider for use under all circumstances ... whether used wet or dry."

The Kill Devil Spider is mentioned by W L Foster in his publication *Fishing Tackle Making and Repairing* in 1929. He recommends its use in May and as a good trout and grayling pattern. Roger Woolley thought well enough of the Spider to include its dressing under Grayling Flies.

Hook:	1 - 2
Body:	Peacock herl tipped silver or gold
Hackle:	Two turns of medium bright blue cock long in the fibre

Red, Black, Olive, Furnace, Fiery Brown, Dun and Grey versions are dressed with hackles of the appropriate shade. An Olive Kill Devil is illustrated in Foster Bros catalogue of 1964 under Foster's Trout Flies. The hackle is very long – the erect fibre lengths being four times that of the hook gape.

T K Wilson's book, *Trout by all Means* (1966), contains a photograph of the Kill Devil Spider but does not elaborate on the fly other than to call it a '...killing wet fly pattern...'

My enquiries led me to believe the Kill Devil Spider was not widely used or known outside Derbyshire and Staffordshire - but I was mistaken. An article in *Trout and Salmon – Trout on a Bike* (July 2005) written by Paul McCormaic – pointed to an Irish connection. Paul described the pattern as a 'true blue Wicklow fly'. Had it, then, come from Ireland after all? Did Roger Woolley take the fly to Fermanagh from Derbyshire when he went to work for the Chetwynds? Did James Ogden use the fly on the Irish loughs in 1851?

Paul has contacted Irish experts and is satisfied there is no Fermanagh connection. However he says in both County Wicklow and County Wexford the Kill Devil Spider is very popular. Along with other peacock bodied flies such as the Black and Peacock, it is very successful in the fast acidic mountain waters. In Wexford it is the primary killer of sea trout, particularly at night.

He considers that the fly was very likely introduced by visiting English anglers, also saying that many Irish patterns came that way, especially so before independence in 1921. The fly has been modified, particularly in Wicklow. It now has a tail and a Wicklow variant has just a few sparse fibres of blue jay in front.

Paul McCormaic gives the following dressings:-

Hook:	14 - 10
Rib:	Silver wire
Body:	Rear third, flat silver; front two thirds, brown peacock herl. Proportions may vary 50/50 or even 60/40

Hackle: Furnace Greenwell or Black Cock. For slow or still water hen hackles are used. Paul's preference is for a grouse shoulder hackle.

A rather mysterious pattern, the Kill Devil Spider is probably used more in its adopted country than in its native counties, but it is a fly I have used with some success. I wonder if another Derbyshire pattern called the Bumble has an Irish connection?

MACK'S FANCY

A special pattern developed by D M Mackenzie for use on the upper stretches of 'his' water in Wolfscote Dale and Beresford Dale which he kept for members of the Manners family. The natural fly appeared only intermittently on the Dove but when present was 'mustard'. It imitates the Claret Dun, not normally seen on limestone streams. The fly was only effective on the reaches above Milldale, below where many alkaline springs feed into the river. The dressing is that given to Donald Mackenzie's friend, Noel Smith.

Hook: Size 14, Round Bend or similar.
Hackle and Tails: Very carefully selected Blue Andelusian cock hackle, as stiff as possible; by nature, Blue Andelusian tends to be a softish webby hackle, but of wonderful colour, and occasionally, quality.
Body: Claret Pearsall's Gossamer tying silk.
Wing:-   Single starling, upright, on top of the hook. (Not double split wing)

OAKDEN'S CLARET

This fly is illustrated in the 1964 edition of Foster Bros catalogue. It is a winged dry fly and is listed under the 'Gold Medal' Fly brand. The exhibition at which the gold medal was awarded took place in 1904 but obviously Oakden's Claret must have been included later. A pattern of the fly appears in Veniard's *Five Hundred Fly Dressings*, the dressing attributed to Roger Woolley. However the dressing does not appear in *Modern Trout Fly Dressing*.

The dressing given by Veniards:—

Tail: Fibres of blue dun cock hackle
Body: Claret tying silk
Wing: Single starling sloping forward
Hackle: Blue dun cock

A manuscript of T K Wilson describes the origin of Oakden's Claret:

'This popular Midland pattern is one of the youngest of our fancies, and though a floater, has a special attraction for nymphing trout; it is also a useful fly for grayling.

It dates back to 1933, and was originated by Major T H Oakden, D S O., M C., R A., of Rolleston, Burton-on-Trent.

The Major was fly fishing on the Dove one evening towards the end of June, and though there was a very good hatch of several varieties of duns, the trout refused all floating imitations steadfastly continuing with their nymphing.

Oakden's Claret

A dislike for nymphing at dusk set the unsuccessful angler pondering as to what artificial was most likely to tempt them to the surface. From experience he had learned that Dove trout preferred a pattern that was darker than the natural fly on the water, and they always came most readily at a thin bodied creation that floated 'wing up'. A suggestion of red in the body was also considered a desirable feature.

The very next morning he described to his friend Roger Woolley the fly he had in mind, and that well-known Derbyshire angler and fly dresser tied two or three specimens. Woolley suggested the name for the one selected and it was christened accordingly.

That evening, under conditions identical with those prevailing the previous evening, the new creation was tried out and proved an immediate success, ten fine trout being landed in two hours' fishing.

"Since then," writes Major Oakden, "it has been my principal 'stand-by', and from mid-May to August it has never let me down. I have also found it an excellent back-end fly for grayling, and especially so when the olive dun is on the water."

And having found a 'winner', the Major went out of his way in order that other fly fishermen might share his discovery. He made a point of keeping a good stock of the fly in his case, and gave them to those of the fraternity he met on the river who had failed to enjoy sport. Invariably they found the "Claret" successful, and as a result, and in a comparatively short time, it was being used on many other English rivers besides the Dove.

It is most deadly during warm weather, and when there is a hatch of duns it may be fished the day throughout. ...

143

Here is the dressing:-

Body:	Crimson tying silk, well waxed.
Hackle and Tail:	Dark Blue Dun Cock's.
Wings:	Hen blackbird or starling, tied as a single wing and angled to lean over the eye of the hook.
Hook:	oo or o

It is an interesting speculation that perhaps an ancestor of Major Oakden was a subscriber to William Shipley and Edward Fitzgibbon's book *On Fly Fishing* published in 1838. A 'Mr. Oakden' is listed but unfortunately no further information is given. The town of Ashbourne where William Shipley lived and had his business is only a dozen or so miles from Rolleston-on-Dove where Major Oakden lived.

Another pattern dressed by Woolley and this time included in *Modern Trout Fly Dressing* is Tommy's Favourite, or as some would have it, Tommy's Fancy. This pattern was also dressed and named for Major Oakden, or possibly his father. With this fly Woolley and Oakden had a memorable day on the Okeover stretch of the Dove, catching over a hundred grayling.

OLIVE AND PEARL CADDIS

Steve Trigg considers this the pattern, of the many colour combinations he carries, in which he has most confidence at present.

Hook:	Curved heavyweight grub 10 – 14
Thread:	Grey micro
Body:	Olive sparkle yarn and pearl body czech
Thorax:	Hare face fur

He also includes an Olive, dressed Paradun style.

Hook:	Standard straight shank 12 – 18
Thread:	Grey micro
Tail:	C D C fibres
Body:	C D C fibres
Wing:	Two whole C D C feathers, cut to size

PARTRIDGE SERIES

These are certainly the flies of northern anglers, probably specifically so of Yorkshiremen, but acquired, adopted or poached by rogues from Derbyshire and Staffordshire! These sparsely dressed hackles are important patterns on the rough waters of the Peak, being dressed in a number of different colours. Silver, orange, yellow, red, green and hare's lug are among them. The body is short and thin, the hackle wound only two or three turns to leave the fibres of hook length. Often used as droppers they are popular patterns on all rivers of the area.

PARTRIDGE AND HARE'S LUG

A favourite fly of the writer as a dropper in the early season.

Hook: 12 – 16
Silk: Orange dubbed lightly with hare's poll fur and wound to allow the silk to 'grin' through the body.
Hackle: Two turns of speckled partridge hackle of hook length.

PARTRIDGE AND ORANGE

This fly is a close representation, along with the Partridge and Red, of early stoneflies. Highly considered in Yorkshire it even catches fish in Derbyshire and Staffordshire! Leslie Magee matches the Partridge and Orange to the Blue Winged Olive.

Tony Bridgett's dressings are:

PARTRIDGE AND ORANGE
Body: Orange silk with no rib
Hook: 12 or 14
Hackle: A brown and black partridge neck feather, sparse, no more than three turns

PARTRIDGE AND RED
Body: Red wool put on thinly
Hook: 14
Hackle as the Partridge and Orange. The Partridge and Red is often locally used in coloured water.

PARTRIDGE AND YELLOW

Steve Trigg presently lists this pattern as his 'favourite dropper fly during the spring and summer months when pale or light olives are on the water'.

Hook: Standard straight shank 14 – 18
Thread: Yellow micro
Body: Yellow floss
Hackle: Grey partridge

SILVER PARTRIDGE

Tony Bridgett's final Partridge dressing

Hook: 14
Body: Silver tinsel with no rib
Hackle: Black and brown neck feather, sparse, no more than three turns

The '*Old Man*' of W H Aldam's *Quaint Treatise* has a fly called the Partridge Rump, his version of the Derbyshire March Brown and listed with the other patterns from the old manuscript.

Rabbit Fly

RABBIT FLY

This fly was made to imitate small brown midges which appeared in the evening on a reservoir. One May afternoon I saw similar flies on the surface of the Derwent at Willersley, and having caught little that day, I decided to try the fly. The result was an afternoon to remember.

Hook: 16
Body: Sandy fur from a rabbit's neck dubbed thinly on brown silk
Hackle: Red cock, short in the barb, tied with two turns. Dress well with floatant. The fly also works very well with grayling, especially under trees and close under banks.

RED CATERPILLAR

Widely advertised as a trout and grayling pattern by Fosters: '...particularly useful when tied large, cast and allowed to sink...'. It is said to be good both at noon and in the evening. David Foster explains in *The Scientific Angler* how the dressing came to light and the details of its publication. A well-known Dove angler made much use of the pattern but kept the dressing to himself. Whilst fishing one day he lost the fly in a tree. This was later retrieved by Foster. From him, Alfred Ronalds and the general public, '...obtained the secret of the mid water fly...'. The fly is a representation of the Tiger Moth Caterpillar, but tied on a hook as large as a six I imagine there is little use for it on the Dove these days.

RED TAG

The fly originated in Worcestershire as a trout pattern called the Worcester Gem around 1850. Francis Walbran is credited with its introduction to Yorkshire. Here it gained a reputation as a grayling catcher. It acquired a new name and has now become a standard in the waters of the Peak. Steve Trigg has developed his own version of this pattern:

Hook:	Standard straight shank 14 – 18
Thread:	Black micro
Tail:	Red holographic lurex
Body:	Peacock herl
Rib:	Red holographic lurex
Hackle:	Red game hen

He also ties it with a three millimetre copper bead at the front end.

The original dressing itself varies from tier to tier. Some use green peacock herl, others, as Roger Woolley, tie it with a bronze peacock body.

Hook:	00 – 1
Body:	Bronze peacock herl with a tip of gold or silver under tag of red floss
Hackle:	Red cock or hen

John Neville prefers the somewhat similar Sturdy's Fancy. This, tied by Tom Sturdy of Masham, has an 'off white' hackle. Sturdy's Fancy, as the Red Tag, can be fished wet or dry.

ROUGH OLIVE

An imitation of the Early Olive Dun or Blue Dun, a favourite Derbyshire and Staffordshire standard. Roger Woolley ties this pattern.

Hook:	1 – 2
Body:	Heron's herl dyed olive. (Picric acid was once used to colour this feather, but as it is somewhat explosive, it is no longer readily available.) A suitable substitute feather is dyed swan or white goose.
Rib:	Gold wire
Hackle and whisks:	Dark olive cock
Wings:	Dark starling or hen blackbird

I have found turmeric a very satisfactory dye for colouring Canada goose or heron herl olive.

ROUGH WATER DRY

A general pattern to represent sedges and mayflies, depending on the size tied, from Steve Trigg. It is designed for use in fast water and able to ride the waves.

Hook:	Standard straight shank 10 - 14

Thread:	Black micro
Tail:	Natural grey C D C fibres
Body:	Natural grey C D C fibres
Hackle:	One whole natural grey C D C feather
Wing:	Elk hair

SUMMER DUN

W H Aldam saw an ephemeral on Bakewell meadows and copied the insect. With the fly he hooked a trout of about six pounds. '...looking the size of a big Dublin Bay Haddock...'. James Smith attempted to net the fish but the dropper caught in the meshes and the hook straightened '...the fish gradually sinking out of sight, going down broadside...'. The materials unobtainable but could be easily substituted with a little ingenuity.

Hook:	2 or 3 Kendal sneck
Wings:	the lightest part of a young Starling's wing quill feather.
Body:	gold coloured silk with buff Berlin wool dubbing or fur from the buff spot on the throat of a foreign Marten, or as it is called, Sable's gill.
Legs:	rich buff Cochin China hackle,
Tail:	from the Bittern of buff Cochin China cock or hen.

TUPS INDISPENSABLE

As already mentioned, this fly was invented by R S Austin and the pattern confided to C A Hassam, giving the pattern an extremely tenuous Derbyshire link. That aside, a number of anglers use modified versions of the 'Tups'. Richard Ward's fly variant has a body of sunrise pink fluorescent seal fur. A normal Tups is much used on the Derwent.

WARD'S APHID. CHATSWORTH APHID

To quote from John Neville in *Trials and Triumphs of an Angler* (1991) 'One good pattern which imitates both the greenfly appearing in hot weather at Chatsworth and the olive bodied midges of the Wye'. Richard Ward was the originator of this dressing.

Body:	Sparse fluorescent bright green floss
Hackle:	Sparse honey hackle
Hook:	'Tiny'

WHISTLER FLY

David Foster relates an occasion when he caught a large number of fish on the Whistler when others did not attempt to fish the coloured water with worm. This fancy fly is a Derbyshire standard for use in coloured, even rising, water. Its name is derived from the hackle feather used, this being from the neck or breast of the Whistling or Golden Plover. Foster recommends a feather from the breast of a red-brown pigeon as a substitute.

Foster's dressing for the Whistler:–

Body:	Flat gold tinsel
Hackle:	Red-brown pigeon's breast feather or Whistling Plover

WINTER DUN

A Derbyshire pattern and a favourite of David Foster. This was the point fly on his grayling cast, along with the Steel Blue Bumble and Cock Winged Dun. It is also known as the Silver Dun.

The dressing given by T E Pritt in *The Book of the Grayling*:–
Body: Flat silver tinsel, evenly laid on
Wings: The light part of a fieldfare's quill feather
Legs: Light blue dun hen hackle. Tying silk, mulberry or dark claret, leaving a sombre reddish head.

Dressed with a gold body it is a good pattern for trout in coloured water.

Richard Ward itemises four flies of his own invention. These are an Ethafoam Bodied Mayfly, a Non Descript Sedge, a Poly Prop Sherry and a Poly Prop Spent Gnat. Each is identified by its initials.

In my research I have come across three flies which may, or may not, be Derbyshire or Staffordshire Specialities. Lack of information is the reason for doubt. The details found and their dressings are included below. I would welcome any further detail relating to these flies.

ESTERHAZY DUN

William Shipley (1838) gives three dressings using 'Esterhazy coloured silk'. They are the Dun, Red Dun and Dark Dun. Esterhazy obviously refers to the colour. Esters are chemical compounds but that takes us little further. Milky? Bluish? White?
W L Foster lists the Esterhazy Dun in his list for October, suggesting the fly may be a grayling pattern. Shipley's patterns are under January, February and March respectively.

Shipley's dressing for the Esterhazy Dun:–
Hook: No 2 Kendal
Wing: Fieldfare
Body: Bright Esterhazy coloured silk
Legs: Blue Dun Cock

UPCHERS FANCY

There is a photograph of the fly in Foster Bros 1964 catalogue. From the illustration the tie would appear to be:–

Tip: Red Silk
Body: Short, of bronze peacock herl
Hackle: Bushy red-brown hen

The fly is mentioned in Robert G Diendorfer's *The Incompleat Angler* (1977). This details the travels of an American angler visiting waters fished by Izaak Walton. The author bought the fly at Foster's Sporting Services in Ashbourne and he uses it on the River Manifold. In the catalogue it is listed under Trout Flies.

149

PEVERIL OF THE PEAK

I imagine this may be a Derbyshire fly pattern. Ogden-Smith's dry fly catalogue of about 1930 has the fly illustrated. The dressing given is surmised from the illustration.

Body:	Peacock herl
Hackle:	Bushy red cock
Wing:	White tipped mallard

The fly is under the title 'Mermaid Double Wing Dry Flies'. John Norris of Penrith advertised the fly under 'New Zealand Flies'. They no longer stock the pattern nor could they help with pattern or origin.

STANDARD AND MODERN FLIES

The following flies are those standards, old and new, chosen by contributors and authors, as being regularly used by them on Derbyshire and Staffordshire rivers. It is by no means a definitive list.

ADAMS

An American general purpose fly which is said to be the most used pattern worldwide. The fly has many variations including parachute hackles, deer hair bodies and palmered bodies. The Adams can be used for trout and grayling, wet or dry to represent everything from tiny 'Curses' to mayflies. I wonder we bother with anything else.

Hook:	20 – 8
Body:	Grey rabbit or muskrat fur on black or brown silk
Tail:	Grizzle and brown cock hackle fibres
Wing:	Grizzle hackle points
Hackle:	Grizzle and brown hackles

COCH Y BONDDU

Also known as the Marlow Buzz. Anglers from Alfred Ronalds onward have used this fly on the Dove and Derwent as a beetle representation.
Ronalds tied the pattern:–

Body:	Black ostrich herl twisted with peacock herl and made with red silk
Wing and Legs:	Are made buzz with dark furnace cock's hackle

ELK HAIR SEDGE

Originated by American Al Troth, this is an excellent floater in rough water. It can be tied using various body colours and wings. Leave a tuft of deer hair protruding over the hook eye. Seal the whipping with superglue.

Hook:	10 – 14
Thread:	Brown
Body:	Hare's fur

Body hackle: Furnace cock, ribbed with fine gold wire or oval
Wing:　　　Natural elk hair or elk hock

F FLY

A good imitation to represent emerging midges and gnats. The F Fly is based on Swiss patterns, invented by Marjan Fratnik, which used the feathers from around a duck's preen glands. The fly is simple and the body colour can be varied as the angler wishes.

Steve Trigg's dressing:–
Hook:　　　Standard straight shank 14 - 18
Thread:　　Black micro
Body:　　　Black micro
Wing:　　　One whole natural grey C D C feather cut to size.

Peter Arfield's modification of the F Fly has a Hare's Ear Body.

GREY WULFF

Another American fly very popular on the Derbyshire and Staffordshire rivers at mayfly time. Most anglers vary the dressing in size and colour.
A basic dressing would be:–

Hook:　　　To suit size of the naturals
Tail:　　　Brown bucktail or grey squirrel tail
Body:　　　Grey underfur from a rabbit
Wing:　　　Bunches of grey squirrel tail
Hackle:　　Blue dun cock

Richard Ward uses a single wing of yellow dyed squirrel.

GRIFFITHS GNAT

Much used on Arizona streams, this could almost be considered an American Bumble. Several patterns sent to me by a friend in Phoenix have resulted in considerable success on the Derwent.

Hook:　　　16 – 24
Thread:　　Black
Body:　　　Peacock herl
Hackle:　　Palmered grizzle cock

A silk or pearl rib is optional as a tail. The former does help to prolong the life of the dressing.

JOHN STOREY

A pattern which has its origins on the River Rye in Yorkshire, tied by the riverkeeper John Storey in the 1850s. It is a good general pattern with no particular representation determined.

Hook:	14 – 16
Wing:	Speckled mallard breast tied forward over the eye
Body:	Bronze peacock herl
Hackle:	Dark red cock hackle

KITES IMPERIAL

Oliver Kite's well known pattern used when olives are about. Another standard with numbers of variants which are often used on Derbyshire and Staffordshire rivers.

Hook:	14 – 15
Tying silk:	Purple
Body:	Heron primary herl, doubled twice at the thorax and ribbed with fine gold wire
Whisks:	Grey-brown early in the year changing to honey dun later
Hackle:	Honey dun or light ginger

LUNN'S PARTICULAR

An imitation of an Olive Spinner devised by W J Lunn, the celebrated Test riverkeeper and a favourite fly of several local anglers

Hook: 15	
Silk:	Crimson
Body:	Stalk from a Rhode Island Red hackle
Wings:	Two blue cock hackle points tied spent
Whisks:	Fibres from a Rhode Island Red hackle
Hackle:	Rhode Island Red cock

PHEASANT TAIL

Fished as a nymph or as a dry pattern the Pheasant Tail is carried by most anglers. Frank Sawyer's nymph is very useful when olives are about and will sink rapidly to fish in deeper water. Fished dry in eddies and quiet corners it often finds the larger fish. A good pattern on the Manifold.

RUSTY SPINNER

An imitation of several *Ephemerid* spinners including Medium Olive and Blue Winged Olive. G E M Skues tied it as follows, though there is a modern American dressing:

Hook:	14 or 15
Silk:	Hot orange waxed with clear wax
Body:	Chestnut coloured seal fur, ribbed with fine gold wire
Whisks:	Fibres of honey dun cock spade feather
Hackle:	Rusty dun cock

SHADOW MAYFLY
Tony Bridgett recommends this dressing:

Two brown hackles tied in as wings at a point a third the way down a long shank size twelve hook. Continue yellow silk to a point opposite the barb. Tie in a gold tinsel rib and return the silk to the eye. Tie in a grizzle hackle by the base and palmer it down the hook in close turns. Secure with ribbing of tinsel to the eye and tie off.

SHRIMPS
There are many dressings from Richard Walker's 'Chompers' to Oliver Edwards's masterpieces. Anglers have their own favourites. Mine is as follows.

Hook:	12 – 14 longshank with eye cranked a little
Silk:	Brown
Body:	Loaded with lead strip, built into a hump. Hare body fur and partridge hackle barbs dubbed on silk and wrapped in open turns
Back:	Polythene strip ribbed with gold or red wire. Tease out dubbing at the head, tail and underside

SPIDERS
Traditional patterns but susceptible to the whims of the fly tier. Paul Procter tied some wire spiders and published them in the *Trout and Salmon* edition of March 2002. They are simple to dress and the fish of Derbyshire and Staffordshire enjoy them enormously. Coloured wire or wires tied with a sparse spider style hackle makes an excellent fly.

WILLIAMS'S FAVOURITE
Originally tied by A C Williams's father, this fly is a favourite of many anglers when a black dressing is required.

Hook:	12 – 18
Body:	Black tying silk ribbed with silver wire
Tail:	Two or three black whisks
Hackle:	Black hen. If a dry pattern, black cock

DERBYSHIRE AND STAFFORDSHIRE 'FLYBOXES'

Anglers since the days of Charles Cotton have carried numbers of fly patterns, or in the case of those in Cotton's time, the means of making them at the waterside. This, over the centuries, has resulted in vast numbers of different fly dressings being created, many of which, though carried, are seldom used. There are 'just in case' flies in most flyboxes.

I have collected together a number of 'Derbyshire Flyboxes'. Each of these comprises a box of about a dozen patterns, recommended by anglers of experience and expertise on Derbyshire rivers.

Several of the anglers who wrote the books discussed earlier advised certain patterns for specific rivers or 'Derbyshire Waters' and these patterns are included in their lists. Others have generously listed the patterns they presently use and provided dressings for their own personal local flies. Practically all those asked experienced difficulty in keeping their 'Flybox' down to the specified maximum of twelve flies. One of these anglers, some seasons ago, decided to fish with just two patterns for a season, albeit in a range of sizes. He reports the experiment as lasting two weeks. For interest, the two flies chosen were the Grey Duster and Pheasant Tail Nymph, the former in sizes 10 – 16, the latter sizes 12 – 18.

The lists created are not flies specific to either trout or grayling fishing, just a simple choice for a year's angling. Where a date is applied, it is that of the angler's publication to create a time scale in the list.

W H ALDAM *A Quaint Treatise* 1876 – 'Old Man' - 1800

Black Gnat	Little Chap	Tail to Tail
Little Sky Blue	Small Black Caterpillar	Summer Dun

Aldam refers to these as 'important flies.'

ALFRED RONALDS *The Fly Fisher's Entomology* 1836

Red Fly	Red Spinner	Peacock Fly
March Brown	July Dun	Golden Dun Midge
Cinnamon Fly	Jenny Spinner	Orange Fly
Red Palmer	Green Drake	

DAVID FOSTER *The Scientific Angler* 1882

Cock Winged Dun	Fosters Favourite (Mayfly)	Whistler Fly
Winter Dun	Red Caterpillar	Ordinary Bumble
Honey Dun Bumble	Steel Blue Bumble	Red Fly
Blue Dun	Iron Blue	July Dun

MARQUESS OF GRANBY *The Trout* 1898

Olive Dun	Mayfly	Blue Dun
Orange Bumble	Apple Green Dun	Red Quill
Black Gnat	Iron Blue	Red Spinner
Yellow Dun	Alder	Governor

W M GALLICHAN *Fishing in Derbyshire and Around* 1905

Blue Dun	Olive Dun	Iron Blue
Black Gnat	Yellow Dun	Golden Earwig
Mayfly	Apple Green Dun	Claret Bumble
Hackles	Cock Winged Dun	Fiery Bumble

GERALD G P HEYWOOD *Charles Cotton and His River* 1928

Olive Quill	Ginger Quill	March Brown
Alder	Mayfly	Black Midge
Golden Dun	Pink Wickham	Whistler Fly
G R H E (Wet)	Coch Y Bonddu	Honey Dun Bumble

WILFRED L FOSTER *Fishing Tackle* 1929

Cock Winged Dun	Double Badger	Foster's Fancy
Honey Dun Bumble	Furnace Bumble	Steel Blue Bumble
Kill Devil Spider	Derby Beetle	White Witch
'Foster Nymphs'	Oakden's Claret	Upcher's Fancy

A NELSON BROMLEY *A Fly Fisher's Recollections* 1860 - 1930

Olive Dun (two shades)	Coachman	Gold Ribbed Hare's Ear
Orange Bumble	Iron Blue	Stewart's Black Spider
Red Quill	Wickham	Tup's Indispensable
Greenwell's Glory	Little Marryat	Black Alder

ROGER WOOLLEY (Advice to W Carter Platts) *Grayling Fishing* 1939

Grayling Steel Blue	Grayling Witch	Tommy's Favourite
Grey Palmer	Mulberry Bumble	Rough Bumble
Silver Twist	Waterhen Quill	Willow Fly
Needle Fly	Silver Badger	Blue or Red Badger

CHATSWORTH FISHERY 1942 – 1943 *Chatsworth Archive*

Black Gnat	Blue Dun	Butcher Mayfly
Grouse and Purple	Iron Blue	March Brown
Peter Ross	Wickham's Fancy	Yellow Dun

J N W / C R H 2005

Wire Spider (Procter)	Grey Duster	Snipe and Purple
Shrimp	Greenwell's Glory	Black and Peacock
G R H E	Rabbit Fly	Waterhen Bloa
Partridge and Hare's Lug	C D C Mayfly	Black Spider

TIM THORPE – FLY DRESSER Derbyshire Fishing Flies, Hatton 2005

Sawyer Pheasant Tail	Adams Irresistible	Double Badger
Shrimp	Iron Blue Dun	Blue Winged Olive
G R H E Nymph	John Storey	Greenwell's Glory
Goldhead GRHE Nymph	Steel Blue	Lunn's Particular

SMALL RIVER DRY FLIES 2007

Black Klinkhammer	Moss's Cockwing	Blue Mayfly
Black Beetle	Hassam's Pet	Parachute Adams
Black Midge	Wickham's Var.	Cream Cracker
Hawthorn	Iron Blue	Oakden's Claret

PEACOCK HOTEL Rowsley 2005

Sherry Spinner	Black Spinner	Rusty Spinner
Saville Super Dark Brown	Real Daddy	Red Spinner
Grey Duster	Tup's Variant	Pale Olive Spinner
Cut Wing Para	Mayfly Parachute	Spent Mayfly

PETER ARFIELD Derwent Fly Fishing School 2005

Peeping Caddis	Olive F Fly	Double Badger
Sherry Spinner	Red Spinner	Glymo
Pale Watery	Iron Blue	Light Paradun
Dark Paradun	B W O	Pale Olive

PEAK FOREST ANGLING CLUB *River Noe Fly Fishing Guide* 2005

Black Gnat	Grey Duster	Gold Head
Griffith's Gnat	Adams	F Fly
G R H E Dry	Pheasant Tail Nymph	Iron Blue
G R H E Nymph	Shrimp	Greenwell's Glory

JOHN NEVILLE *Trials and Triumphs of an Angler* 1991.

Cotton's Black Fly	Williams Favourite	Grey Duster
Double Badger	Flumble	Grumble
Lunn's Spent Gnat	Wulff Mayfly	Sturdy's Fancy
Sedges	Chatsworth Aphid	

A K BRIDGETT   Leek & District Fly Fishing Assn 2005

Cock Winged Dun	Iron Blue Dun	Hawthorn Fly
Shadow Mayfly	Butcher Mayfly (Foster)	Baetis Emerger
Elk Hair Sedge	Heron Herl Olive	Partridge and Red
Partridge and Orange	Silver Partridge	

RICHARD WARD   Contributor 'Waterlines', Haddon Estate Fishing 2005

Grey Duster Variant	Kite's Imperial	Dry Pheasant Tail
Cotton's Black Fly	Red Hackle (Cotton)	Double Badger
Sturdy's Fancy	Tup's Variant	Red Tag
Grey Wulff Variant	Chatsworth Aphid	Sedge
Poly Prop Sherry	Poly Prop Spent Gnat	Ethafoam Body Mayfly

DERWENT, Darley Dale   2004

Greenwell's Glory	Kite's Imperial	Grey Duster
Adams	Pheasant Tail Nymph	G R H E
Mayfly	Olives	Sedges
Black Klinkhammer		

STEVE WOOLLEY   Rodmaker, Ashbourne 2005

Double Badger	Derby Beetle	G R H E
Steel Blue	Adams	Grey Wulff
Black Gnat	Gold Head G R H E	Grey Duster
Black Klinkhammer	Dry Pheasant Tail	Dry G R H E

STEVE TRIGG   Steve Parton's Fishing Tackle 2005

Grey Duster	Olive Paradun	F Fly
Hare's Face Emerger	Rough Water Dry	Hatching Mayfly
Red Tag	William's Favourite	Partridge & Yellow
Pheasant Tail Nymph	Olive & Pearl Caddis	Gold Headed Hare's Face Bug

JOHN PASS   Chief Bailiff Cromford Fly Fishers' Club   2006

Gold Head G R H E	Czech Nymph	Grey Duster
Pheasant Tail Nymph	Blue Winged Olive	Iron Blue Dun
Greenwell's Glory	Sherry Spinner	Double Badger
Tup's Indispensable	Peeping Caddis	Green Drake

PLATE 9   DERBYSHIRE AND STAFFORDSHIRE FLYBOXES

Snipe and Purple

C D C Mayfly

Rabbit Fly

Gold Ribbed Hare's Ear

Partridge and Hare's Lug

Black and Peacock

Black and Red Wire Spider

Shrimp

Waterhen Bloa

Black Spider

Greenwell's Glory

Grey Duster

PLATE 10 DERBYSHIRE AND STAFFORDSHIRE FLYBOXES

Steel Blue	John Storey
Blue Winged Olive	Double Badger
Sawyer's Pheasant Tail Nymph	Greenwell's Glory

Adams Irresstible

Lunn's Particular

Iron Blue Dun

Gold Ribbed Hare's Ear Nymph

Shrimp

Gold Head Gold Ribbed Hare's
Ear Nymph

PLATE II DERBYSHIRE AND STAFFORDSHIRE FLYBOXES

Oakden's Claret

Blue Mayfly

Black Beetle

Parachute Adams

Black Klinkhammer

Hassam's Pet

Black Midge

Iron Blue

Cream Cracker

Wickham's Variant

Moss's Cockwinged Dun

Hawthorn

PLATE 12 DERBYSHIRE AND STAFFORDSHIRE FLYBOXES

Sherry Spinner

Red Spinner

Black Spinner

Saville Super Dark Brown

Spent Mayfly

Mayfly Parachute

Grey Duster

Cut Wing Para

Natural Daddy

Pale Olive Spinner

Rusty Spinner

Tups Variant

PLATE 13 DERBYSHIRE AND STAFFORDSHIRE FLYBOXES

Light Paradun

Dark Paradun

Peeping Caddis

Iron Blue

Blue Winged Olive

Pale Olive

Sherry Spinner

Glymo

Double Badger

Olive F Fly

Pale Watery

Red Spinner

PLATE 14 DERBYSHIRE AND STAFFORDSHIRE FLYBOXES

Flumble

Double Badger

Grumble

Cotton's Black Fly

Sturdy's Fancy

Grey Duster

Wulff Mayfly

Sedge

Lunn's Spent

Chatsworth Aphid

William's Favourite

PLATE 15 DERBYSHIRE AND STAFFORDSHIRE FLYBOXES

Red Eyed Derby Beetle

Dry Gold Ribbed Hare's Ear

Grey Wulff

Gold Head Gold Rubbed Hare's Ear

Dry Pheasant Tail

Black Gnat

STEVE WOOLLEY Rodmaker, Ashbourne 2005

Steel Blue

Adams

Gold Ribbed Hare's Ear

Double Badger

Black Klinkhammer

Grey Duster

PLATE 16 DERBYSHIRE AND STAFFORDSHIRE FLYBOXES

F Fly

Rough Water Dry

Grey Duster

Olive Paradun

William's Favourite

Partridge and Yellow

Hare's Face Emerger

Hatching Mayfly

Olive and Pearl Caddis

Pheasant Tail Nymph

Red Tag

Gold Headed Hare's Face Bug

rather than being identified individually. A number of patterns can be fished wet or dry. Where this is the case they have been classified in the form most often used locally. Of the total, 59% are dry or emerger patterns and 41% wet flies. Splitting the flyboxes into those nominated by historic and contemporary anglers, a comparison, though somewhat subjective in its content, may be made.

From these figures the preference of the historic anglers appears to be in favour of the wet fly. This, given the traditions, rivers and style of local angling is unsurprising. On the other hand, a number of those anglers lived and fished through the heady days of the late ninteenth and early twentieth centuries, along with the enthusiasm for the imitative dry evangelism of Marryat and Halford. John Bickerdyke (C H Cook), writing in 1880 says, 'On Derbyshire streams dry fly fishing is coming much into vogue. ...'

The flyboxes of the contemporary anglers indicate a different style with a higher proportion of dry or emerger patterns; the preference of those who contributed, at the present time, being that of fishing dry fly. This may be confirmed by considering the figures for traditional, speciality and modern patterns given in the modern flyboxes.

'Modern Flyboxes'	Total	Dry %	Wet%
Traditional Flies	33	49	51
Speciality Flies	19	84	16
Modern Flies	20	75	25

From this limited information the trend seems to be that when dry flies are used, speciality and modern patterns are chosen. When the choice is wet fly the traditional patterns figure highly against the other groups. The following list gives those flies mentioned up to 1905.

	Dressings	Dry %	Wet %
Historic Anglers	42	43	57
Contemporary Anglers	72	65	35

W J CUMMINS CATALOGUE 1881

The following patterns were advertised under the title of Derbyshire Flies. Taken as a group they would make a very adequate annual fly box for Derbyshire and Staffordshire waters.

SILVER TWIST This is a most valuable fly for a dropper in the beginning of season, and when the water is clearing after freshes throughout summer. In April and May, and again in October and November, if the rivers are as usual full and clear, never make up a cast without one of these.

FURNACE Exactly the same remarks apply to this fly as to Silver Twist; if anything, with more force.

FEBRUARY RED; OR MARCH BROWN A first-rate killer in the commencement of season;

say throughout April and, if cold, May. The best position on the cast is that of dropper nearest to the reel line. Another of this family is the Needle Fly, which is on the water all through the season. Each are the same in shape – but with soft, transparent wings – as what are called "Soldiers and Sailors"; or as "Yellow Sally," another well known fly.

HARE'S EAR DUN   General fly for Trout in April and May. Again in October and November for Grayling.

PEACOCK   Cold weather in May, June, and July. It is an imitation of a dark insect of the ear-wig family, which folds its wings – when not in use – within little shiny covers upon the shoulders. On chilly days these insects often become food for fishes.

BLUE DUN
SPANISH NEEDLE   A great Grayling fly from early February until this fish is no longer fit for the table; and again from September till end of the year, when Grayling are in the primest season. These flies are seen also throughout summer; it is no uncommon event for half-a-dozen to be running over a fisherman at the same moment.

WREN TAIL
BLACK GNAT
SMALL RED PALMER
LITTLE CHAP   One of a numerous family of hard backed, oval shaped insects, called clocks, that are bred in manure heaps and cow droppings. It is the shape of a "cow lady," but steely blue as to the body and wings, the latter being folded within the shiny black cover when at rest. It is a most excellent (all the season through) fly on sunny or very warm days, when the air is often full of these insects. Always use as a dropper, unless the fish show a decided partiality for it; when put on two, one at point the other third or fourth dropper.

YELLOW DUN
ASH COLOURED DUN   One of the many shades of "upright" or "cockup" Duns always to be found, in summer, on every pure river and brook in the kingdom. Excellent point fly.

YELLOW LEGS A favourite and very good sort. It answers for Yellow Sally and all the pale yellowish legged Duns seen in summer and on hot evenings. Commence with it, if warm, latter end of May or first week in June; and use occasionally throughout the summer months.

DOTTEREL   Yellow Body. One of the best - if not the best - in this schedule; but it is for summer only. Start it middle of July and continue to end of August; say at point, or the next fly to that.

PRIMROSE DUN   Will kill from middle of May to end of September; it is taken well by Trout, and is particularly acceptable to Grayling.

SUMMER DUN In the evenings after fine, hot days, from seven o' clock to dark, there are to be seen a great variety of upright (cockup) Duns, simultaneously with an abundance of wood or grass-bred moths. Then is the time, and this is the fly, for business.

WHIRLING BLUE DUN

GRAYLING AUTUMN DUN A capital killer; it is scarcely ever wrong for Grayling; they take it with the greatest avidity when on feed in their prime season – August to end of year.

SMOCK A grand Grayling fly. It is taken for the common house, or perhaps the wood fly, when cold, chilly weather in October and November numbs these, and they drop on the water in quantities to die. The period for using "Smock" is therefore limited.

GREY PALMER Exactly the same comments apply to this as to the last one. If Grayling take one they will take the other, and both might be on the cast together – Grey Palmer at point.

BUMBLE Use orange bodied Bumbles during summer, and the darker or purple in very early spring and throughout the autumn Grayling season. Scarcely enough can be written as to the virtues of this Palmer; it is a universal and certain killer, and is capable of infinite transformations in shade of body and of hackle. Certainly no cast is ever complete without one at point or next to.

No actual dressings are given in the catalogue for these patterns.

GRAYLING PATTERNS

The rivers of Derbyshire and Staffordshire have long been known for their populations of grayling. Two local anglers with considerable reputations as grayling fishers were David Foster and Roger Woolley. The following list of traditional grayling flies includes their recommendations. Foster's patterns were displayed in T E Pritt's *Book of the Grayling*. Woolley listed twelve Derbyshire grayling flies when asked by W Carter Platts for his book *Grayling Fishing*. The remainder have been mentioned by Alfred Ronalds, Marquess of Granby and W M Gallichan, in their writings.

Apple Green Dun	Orange Fly
Black Gnat	Ordinary Bumble
Blue Badger	Red Badger
Bradshaw's Fancy	Red Bumble
Cock Winged Dun	Red Fly
Fiery Bumble	Red Tag
Golden Earwig	Rough Bumble
Grayling Steel Blue	Sand Fly
Grayling Witch	Silver Badger
Honey Dun Bumble	Silver Twist
Iron Blue Dun	Steel Blue Bumble
Little Chap	Tommy's Favourite

Marlow Buzz Waterhen Quill
Mulberry Bumble White Witch
Needle Fly Willow Fly
Olive Dun Winter Dun
Orange Bumble Yellow Dun
Orange Dun

The dressings of many of these flies bear out the adage that grayling are attracted to flashy patterns. Also, the colours preferred are greens and reds.

EARLY DAYS OF DRY FLY FISHING IN DERBYSHIRE AND STAFFORDSHIRE

Anglers have used flies that float, deliberately or not, for hundreds if not thousands of years. The expression 'dry fly' means different things to different anglers. To some, an artificial fly which floats, to others, a carefully contrived creation as close in appearance to a defined natural insect as can be devised. Both will catch fish and, to their creators, give equal satisfaction in the process. A further consideration is the manner in which the fly is fished. Upstream, downstream, dibbled or dapped, static or with induced movement, the choice is considerable. For the study in hand it is simply an artificial fly designed to float on or in the surface of the water; in so doing, the object being to attract and hopefully deceive fish into mouthing the morsel. The rest of the process depends on the angler's skill.

Charles Cotton describes ways of '...fishing at the top...' and of 'dibbling' live mayflies. He requires their bodies and wings to be kept well away from wet fingers to sustain such flotation properties as they had inherent in their construction. It is difficult to believe the palmers and hackles tied by Cotton sank so quickly as to never be taken by a fish from the surface, nor that he was so unobservant and closed-minded not to try and catch them using a surface fly. A distinct feature of palmered flies is that they float when not required to do so. Cotton spent time studying fly life carefully. This is exemplified by his description of the Mayfly. He states that large numbers of fish are caught on comparatively few patterns, giving as examples the Green Drake and Stonefly. It is very likely that the materials used to tie these patterns would have provided enough buoyancy for the flies to float for a short time. This in turn is often enough to attract the attention of feeding fish. Coupled with a little judicious dapping this could be considered fishing a dry fly.

Alfred Ronalds discusses 'dibbling' live flies; those recommended for use being Stonefly, Oak Fly and Alder. The process of 'dibbling' can take place on the surface or beneath. When a live fly is lowered to the water surface on a hook, I imagine it makes considerable disturbance for a short time at least. A few successful forays with live insects coupled with a shortage of live bait may well have encouraged anglers to try dibbling an artificial. The way Alfred Ronalds describes the Gravel Bed 'raising' fish, the statement about the buzz form of the Grey Drake imitating a '...struggling and half drowned...'

insect suggests surface fishing. Finally, the Marlow Buzz, as illustrated, would surely float on the surface, as its inspiration the beetles tend to do. This of course is all supposition and may well be invalid, but nevertheless a thought provoking idea.

In 1838 William Shipley and Edward Fitzgibbon wrote *A True Treatise on the Art of Fly Fishing*. Shipley describes a method of angling, which is difficult to dispute as being 'upstream dry fly'.

'Let your flies float gently down the water, working them gradually towards you, and making a fresh cast every two or three yards you fish. We distinctly recommend frequent casting. A fish generally takes the fly immediately it has touched the water – provided always it be delicately and lightly flung – and the quick repetition of casting whisks the water out of your flies and line, and consequently keeps them drier and lighter than if they were left to float a longer time in the water.'

The cast is made upstream, the fly floats down, is false cast and again put upstream. This process is far beyond dibbling or dapping. Shipley goes on to warn against letting line onto the water, except for the 'casting line' or leader. The line would be held off the surface, by the long rods then used, as it would sink and drag the fly.

William Aldam speaks of 'dibbling' the Downlooker and Wood Fly live in his editorial notes on the 'Oringe Brown' of the '*Old Man*'. There is no further comment on the use of artificials for the same purpose but the possibility is there. His dibbled flies were fished on the surface. He describes a second method of sinking the impaled fly by the addition of a shot corn, with a hole drilled through it, threaded on the gut a 'sixteenth of an inch' from the hook shank.

James Ogden and David Foster were influential and probably competitive regarding dry fly angling in the region. Ogden, originally from Matlock, was based in Cheltenham. He and Foster were well known to one another. James Ogden was probably the first to describe dressings for floating duns. He, according to his book *On Fly Tying*, says he introduced dry patterns to clients 'forty years ago'. The book was published in 1879 so this statement takes dry flies back to around 1840.

Ogden normally fished three sunken flies. When faced with difficult fish he often changed patterns and observed a still, floating fly was regularly taken, even after many refusals of a wet fly. He experimented with single floating flies and shorter casts of two yards, finding both successful. The flies were made by dressing the body first, setting the upright wings next, tying the hackle close behind the wings and finally tying off behind the hackle. The fly was cast upstream and allowed to drift quietly, the angler extending his arm to avoid drag. Ogden even designed a basket to sit upon whilst awaiting the hatch.

On the Derbyshire Wye at Bakewell on June 5th 1865 an incident involving Ogden took place. Bakewell was a popular place to fish the live Mayfly in its season and anglers gathered there, staying, if necessary, at The Rutland Arms.

In October 1864, whilst grayling fishing from The Peacock at Rowsley, he met the steward of the Duke of Rutland. The latter enquired if Ogden thought his artificial mayflies would be successful on the Wye and Derwent. James assured him they would, despite the consensus of those who said artificials could not be dressed to catch the wily Derbyshire trout. The steward explained that if this was the case he intended to ban the use of live mayfly consequent to the slaughter they made on the rivers' stocks of trout.

Ogden was invited to fish the Wye during the next drake season. On June 5th, 1865, he went to Bakewell where there were numbers of anglers gathered awaiting the hatch. One, by the name of Hobson was greatly amused by Ogden's 'butterfly things'. He should have known better, having been tutored by, and fished with, Ogden's father Frank.

James saw a fish show, covered it with an artificial which was taken at once. Hobson's comment from the bridge was to the effect that a live mayfly had been used. He was shown the artificial and had to admit it had landed like a live fly. A further nine trout were caught in front of what must have been a growing audience. A final fish, which involved wading to cover, was hooked but Ogden became stranded in mud and fell over dropping his rod. Having reorganised himself James caught up his rod and the fish was landed by the head keeper. Further remarks from the bridge watchers indicated they considered if he had not fallen in he would have caught 'every fish in the water'. Here Ogden's day ended and he returned to The Peacock to dry off and change.

The next day he returned to Bakewell to meet the keeper. On the bridge he met with a number of anglers who were very irritated at the ban already imposed on the live fly. Ogden decided ' it would not do to fish there again'. The steward, evidently well pleased with the experiment and its conclusion gave James a week's ticket for the Lathkill to continue his sport with floating drakes.

The fly which did the damage was dressed :-

Body: straw, ribbed with waxed red silk
Tail: three strands of hen pheasant tail feather
Hackle: pale buff with brown centre, short in fibre
Wings: upright, from wood or summer duck

James Ogden's dry fly patterns are recommended by several anglers of the period, including the Marquess of Granby who owned the Bradford, Lathkill and much of the Wye where the ban on live fly was initially imposed. The mayfly patterns mounted in Aldam's *Quaint Treatise* are believed to be the work of Ogden and may be, says J W Hills, '...the oldest representations of floating flies now extant, and lovely flies they are...' Ogden's daughter, Mary Ogden-Smith, was responsible for dressing other patterns in the *Quaint Treatise*.

David Foster of Ashbourne was also an excellent fly dresser and angler. He too experimented with 'floating flies' and was supplying his clients with dry flies which had upright split wings in 1854. This is considerably later than Ogden's supply date, but was still at the forefront of the method at that time. He was obviously keen on fishing the dry

179

fly himself. 'The ever exciting nature of surface fishing adds zest to the sport...'. The process is described. 'The flies must be cast a few feet above the dimply indication of a rise and then allowed to float over...'. He considered dry fly to be a more 'scientific and artistic' way of catching trout or grayling than any other method of angling, though he was ambivalent about whether he chose to fish up or downstream. Perhaps he considered that the rough waters he often fished required a practical approach. Foster's work as a fly dresser was innovative. His flies were dressed in a way not previously described except by James Ogden. A body was tied first followed by upright cocked wings. Next came the hackle 'ample and full' to ensure a good float. He was quite insistent that whisks interfered with the fly's hooking ability and so tended not to include them in the dressings. When tying a fly he always considered its colour of importance from beneath since this would be the view obtained by the fish.

James Ogden is mentioned in *The Scientific Angler* as, 'The late James Ogden, an old friend of ours...'. However there does seem to have been a certain rivalry between the two over the matter of dry flies. William H Foster, David's son, wrote a chapter in *The Scientific Angler* entitled 'The Dry Fly'. Writing in the early 1880s, he confirms the use of dry flies, including mayflies and cock winged flies being in use in Derbyshire for '...the best part of half a century...'. He considered the use of paraffin and Vaseline as floatants as being the only 'new' development. He then has something to say about tackle. Built cane rods of eight to eleven feet of two or three sections are advised, the action of which should be '...stiff for a fly rod, save near the tip...'.

In the seventh edition of *The Scientific Angler*, C W Gedney, a client of Fosters and a well known angler on the Southern chalk streams and Dove wrote a chapter on 'Dry Fly Fishing'. He notes, '...a floating fly was used by our grandfathers, some of the old writers speak of allowing a fly to float downstream under bushes being a very deadly method...'. Very effective it may have been but it is hardly upstream dry.

Cotton, Ronalds, Shipley, Ogden and Foster all produced patterns which could be fished dry. Almost certainly they caught fish regularly on floating flies long before the new creed of G S Marryat and F M Halford. Their dry flies were fished in a complementary manner alongside wet flies, not as an unbending rule.

It is curious that F M Halford chose to develop Derbyshire Bumbles as dry patterns and also to change their livery from that first recorded by David Foster. An interesting speculation is which flies did these exact imitations represent?

Up to the mid nineteenth century, Derbyshire and Staffordshire anglers were among those who led the way in angling developments. After this time their influence was greatly eclipsed by the chalk stream anglers of the South. Several commentators consider the writings of both Ogden and Foster did not gain the recognition they deserved as this movement advanced, fuelled by the writings of F M Halford and others.

CHAPTER FOUR

ANGLERS OF INFLUENCE

In addition to the six authors already considered there have been, and are, others who have made their mark on the style, fly patterns and waters of the Peak. Their contribution may well have been as important but not publicised. It took the better part of a century for the manuscript of Aldam's '*Old Man*' to see the light of day. It is almost certain that there are other documents like this still in existence. It is equally certain that many local fly dressings have disappeared simply because they were never written down. A number of the waterkeepers had several 'Specialities' of which there is now no obvious record.

It is difficult to trace exactly when the weirs and dams on the Wye and Dove were begun or who decided the works may be beneficial. Certainly the owners of the waters must have acceded to the process but where the ideas or advice came from is less than obvious. Perhaps a simple rock dam created a pool in which someone caught more fish or larger fish and the idea, that one dam was good so a lot must be better, evolved. When the works of man in the dales are considered those who built them definitely thought it a good idea to invest time, labour and a great deal of money in angling for trout and grayling.

There are others who developed methods of angling. That which became sport for some was perhaps, still, a necessity for others to feed families. There are styles of catching fish which are, to say the least, surreptitious. Bushing, shade fishing and dibbing with drilled bullets may well have been created by those wishing to catch fish but not to be seen doing so. These techniques seem somewhat out of place in the learned tomes of angling.

Those who still fish Derbyshire and Staffordshire rivers continue to make their contributions. The preservation of angling history, care of the environment, development of innovative tackle and the creation of new fly patterns are continuous. Anglers have a tendency to be solitary and secretive in their habits, particularly when fishing. This is often masked by a sociable aspect, but try talking to one who is occupied catching fish in a good hatch. (It is even said that some fishers lie deliberately, not just about the fish caught, but even regarding the fly used to deceive them!)

Among these people are those who have spent fortunes on their sport, founded angling clubs or have written great books. Others have dressed flies, developed tackle or simply gone fishing on their local waters. These anglers of influence all have at least one thing in common; they chose the rivers of Derbyshire and Staffordshire on which to go a' fishing.

IZAAK WALTON

Walton was born in Stafford in 1593. His father, an alehouse keeper, died when Izaak was in his early years. His mother Anne remarried and, as far as is known, the family was comfortable and cared for financially. Izaak was given an apprenticeship in the drapery business by his brother-in-law, eventually setting up on his own account, dealing in quality textiles.

His business prospered and in 1626 he married Rachel Floud. Together, they had seven children, all of whom died in infancy, Rachel predeceasing the last child in 1640. Walton married a second time and a further three children were born, two of whom survived into adulthood.

From early manhood he moved in ecclesiastical circles, holding various offices and acquiring a number of influential friends. He was a staunch Anglican, eventually writing exemplary biographies of leading churchmen. With the execution of Charles I in 1649 and the establishment of the Parliament, times may have become difficult, even dangerous, for those closely attached to the established Anglican Church. Walton's writings about churchmen ceased. He had sold his business in the mid 1640s, moving to Clerkenwell. Here he lived quietly until Charles II regained the throne in 1660.

During the rule of Parliament, Izaak Walton became what would be called today a secret

Izaak Walton
Portrait from *The Compleat Angler*
1853 edition

agent. He was entrusted with the very risky delivery of the King's Garter badge from Stafford, where it had been hidden, back to London. The journey must have been an anxious time, even for a man familiar with the route. Parliamentary troops, rogues and vagabonds would be serious threats to such a traveller.

As his writings were seriously circumscribed, Walton turned to other things, one of which was angling. In 1653 *The Compleat Angler or Contemplative Man's Recreation* was published. This was a great success and was followed by a second edition and further issues. He had considerable assistance with the work, which he acknowledged in a modest and unaffected manner. As would be expected from a man of his experience, the book is of considerable literary merit. Walton was an angler of wide experience and he explored all aspects of angling. Not for him a blinkered narrow path. He used every appropriate method to pursue his sport and very obviously thoroughly enjoyed himself. In 1676 an edition of *The Compleat Angler* was produced, which included a new section on fly-fishing written by Charles Cotton.

Walton knew Cotton's father well and had formed a close friendship with the younger man. Walton's visits to Stafford and Charles Cotton's home at Beresford afforded opportunities to fish the Dove and other local rivers together. Despite a gap of some forty years in their ages the two men obviously valued each other's company.

Cotton's contribution to *The Compleat Angler* had probably been discussed a number of times but had never been written. With a very tight deadline to a publication date, Cotton, at Walton's invitation and persuasion, wrote *Part Two Being Directions how to Angle for Trout and Grayling in a Clear Stream* in about ten days. From Cotton's remarks it is obvious he wanted Walton to visit the fishing house he had constructed on the Dove at Beresford. Such was his regard for his friend, that their entwined initials are a feature of the portal. There is some doubt whether Walton made the journey to see the building. He would have been over eighty at that time and travel was arduous.

Izaak Walton's writings list a dozen flies for the year's angling. He refers to them as a 'jury'. Whilst they are not Derbyshire or Staffordshire patterns, nor of Walton's creation, they are one of the foundations of fly fishing. They were also my inspiration for the 'Flyboxes' in this current work.

'You are to note, that there are twelve kinds of artificially made flies to angle with on the top of the water. Note, by the way, that the fittest season of using these is in a blustering windy day, when the waters are so troubled that the natural fly cannot be seen, or rest upon them. The first is the dun-fly in March: the body is made of dun wool; the wings, of the partridge's feathers. The second is another dun-fly: the body of black wool; and the wings made of the black drake's feathers, and of the feathers under his tail. The third is the stone-fly, in April; the body is made of black wool; made yellow under the wings and under the tail, and so made with the wings of the drake. The fourth is the ruddy-fly, in the beginning of May: the body made of red wool, wrapt about with black silk; and the feathers are the wings of the drake, with the feathers of a red capon also, which hang dangling on his sides next to the tail. The fifth is the yellow or greenish fly (in May likewise): the body made of yellow wool: and the wings made of the red cock's hackle or tail. The sixth is the black-fly, in May also: the body made of black wool, and lapped about with the herle of a peacock's tail; the wings are made of the wings of a brown capon, with his blue feathers in his head. The seventh is the sad yellow-fly, in June: the body is made of black wool, with a yellow list on either side; and the wings taken off the wings of a buzzard, bound with black braked hemp. The eighth is the moorish-fly: made with the body of duskish wool; and the wings made of the blackish mail of the drake. The ninth is the tawny-fly, good until the middle of June: the body made of tawny wool, the wings made contrary, one against the other, made of the whitish mail of the wild drake. The tenth is the wasp-fly, in July: the body made of black wool, lapped about with yellow silk; the wings made of the feathers of the drake, or of the buzzard. The eleventh is the shell fly, good in mid-July: the body made of greenish wool, lapped about with the herle of a peacock's tail, and the wings made of the wings of the buzzard. The twelfth is the dark drake-fly, good in August: the body made with black wool, lapped about with black silk; his wings are made with the mail of the black drake, with a black head. Thus have you a jury of flies, likely to betray and condemn all the trouts in the river.'

There are remarks, next, about tackle. A rod which was light and gentle of two sections, being Walton's choice, with a line of no more than four hairs thickness. He also gives concise instructions on fly dressing and the contents of a dubbing bag to be taken to the riverside. Full instructions are given on how to make and stain a line. Anglers would not want to make more than two or three in a season!

The Compleat Angler is an encyclopaedic work of angling in Walton's time. He does not claim credit for all its aspects but must have contributed a huge amount of information himself. He was an inspiration to Charles Cotton, despite Cotton's teasing about his coarse fishing methods, and to generations of fishers since.

A modest, brave and talented man, Izaak Walton died at the age of 90 at Winchester in December 1683. The farm he bought at Shallowford near Stone is now the Izaak Walton Museum.

T C HOFLAND

T C Hofland was born in Worksop, Nottinghamshire, where his father was a cotton cloth manufacturer. In 1790 his family moved to London and there for a time they prospered. An only child, Thomas was doted on by his parents and from his early years was interested in natural history, painting and angling.

His father's business faltered and failed, leaving the family in genteel poverty. They moved to Kew where they lived quietly. One or both parents died and Thomas realised he must make his own way. He sold his horse, guns and other possessions – but not his fishing tackle – and with such money as was available, became a pupil of the artist Rathbone for three months. His ability as an artist was such that within two years he had exhibited at the Royal Academy and was acquiring both patrons and commissions for his work. He made his day to day living as an art teacher, along with selling his paintings. In 1803 he moved to Derby in the hope of finding better patrons and more commissions. Whilst here, he found teaching very lucrative and he progressed rapidly.

During this time, the rivers and streams of Derbyshire had a twofold attraction – as subjects for pictures and as water for angling. He travelled widely to fish and paint. Through a growing list of patrons, including the Dukes of Devonshire and Rutland, he acquired access to many prolific waters.

After three years in Derby, Hofland moved on to Doncaster. By this time he had become a wealthy fulltime artist, exhibiting regularly in Leeds, Yorkshire and the Lake District. He became known as a Lake artist and it was in Cumbria where he met his wife. Again, over this period he fished widely, in Yorkshire – especially on the Devonshire waters at Bolton Abbey – the Lake District, Wales and Scotland. Wherever he painted, his rod and tackle went with him. He was able to paint commercially and to prepare etchings and pictures for his book *The British Angler's Manual*. After his marriage he left Doncaster for London again, and here pursued a very successful career as an artist. The couple went to Italy and, while there, a persistent illness took hold of Hofland. He was diagnosed with stomach cancer. He returned to England, going to Leamington Spa in the hope of a cure, but it was in vain. He died in 1842.

In 1839 Hofland wrote his book. A revised and enlarged edition, with a memoir of the author, pulished by E. Jesse in 1848, infers in its preface that the publishers failed to produce the book in 1840, although Westwood & Satchell *Bibliotheca Piscatoria* quote publication as 1839. It is possible that Hofland may have never seen his completed work.

The British Angler's Manual is a detailed work on every aspect of freshwater angling; coarse and game fishing, fly dressing and patterns, British rivers and a great deal of relevant instruction and advice. It is lavishly illustrated with etchings and sketches by Hofland who was, very obviously, a skilled and enthusiastic angler. His travels had taken him countrywide in pursuit of landscape and fish. Men such as he did not seem deterred by long hours on horseback or in carriages on appalling roads in order to pursue their sport and interests.

River lists in Hofland's book wax lyrical about Dovedale but then an artistic angler would!

'Thirty years since, in company with two brother artists and anglers, I enjoyed in this enchanting valley some of the happiest days of my life.... We sallied forth every morning, carrying with us provisions for the day, and two or three bottles of Mr. Wood's brisk, light bottled ale, together with our fishing tackle and sketching apparatus, and there we spent eight successive days (Sunday excepted) in alternately sketching, painting, fishing, and rabbit-shooting. We generally broke our meal at one o'clock in the day, either at Reynard's Hall, a picturesque cave in the rocks, or under the shade of the alder trees.... At this period (circa 1809) fishing in Dove Dale was as free as it had formerly been to our father Walton and his disciples, but the water is now strictly preserved by Jesse Watts Russell, Esq., of Ilam Hall.'

The Derwent, Wye, Erewash, Trent, Blythe and Tame all attract creditable comment. He states that in Bakewell '... excellent small hackle flies...' could be bought from a saddler who was also a fly dresser. Hofland recommended these for fishing both the Wye and Derwent. He considered Derbyshire to be the equal of Hampshire as a fishing county and unrivalled for its 'wild romantic scenery'.

During his painting and angling expeditions he put up at a selection of hotels and inns; The Bowling Green at Mappleton, Dog and Partridge at Thorpe and a 'good inn' at the entrance of Dovedale – presumably the Izaak Walton. He used the Wheatsheaf in Baslow and the Rutland in Bakewell as bases to fish the Derwent and Wye. Hofland fished the Derwent at Willersley Castle – 'the magnificent seat of Richard Arkwright esq' and 'that a note to this gentleman will procure a season ticket from him'. Quite likely, if one was a nationally known artist.

T C Hofland's list has forty six fly dressings along with instructions and a list of appropriate materials. Many of the dressings include notes of where the flies are used. The hackle patterns, also referred to as Buzz flies, he reports are more in use in Devonshire, Derbyshire, Yorkshire, Cumberland and Westmoreland. In the latter two counties they are dressed on 'Kirby Sneck hooks'. The main hackles used include wren, grouse, dotterel. partridge, dun, red and black cock hackle.

In Leslie Magee's book *Fly Fishing the North Country Tradition*, he writes that such was 'Hofland's praise for the Dotteril Fly...' that the dotterel was eliminated as a breeding species in the high Pennines.

Hofland's dressings included below are his hackle patterns, and it would, perhaps, not be appropriate to leave out 'Hofland's Fancy':

Hook:	No 10
Tail:	Two or three strands of a red hackle
Body:	Reddish brown silk
Wing:	Woodcock's Tail
Legs:	Red Hackle

No 14. Brown Shiner
Small Stream – Small Hook
Large Stream, Dark Day – Larger Hook

Body:	Peacock Herl, twisted spare
Hackle:	Grouse over it (Palmered)

No 19. Wren Tail   Hook 12

Body:	Dark Orange Silk
Hackle:	Wren tail – although not a hackle in the strict sense of the word.

No 26. Grey Drake

Hofland's Fancy

No 25. Green Drake
Hofland refers to live mayfly fishing at Bakewell – something also mentioned by James Ogden who tied some of the first floating mayfly imitations.
'*When this fly (Green Drake) and the Grey Drake are on the water it is called the Drake Season, and many lovers of natural fly fishing resort to the Rutland Arms...and other places in Derbyshire to use the blow line.*'

No 27. Black Palmer '*Valuable drop fly in dark rainy or windy weather*'
Body: Ostrich Herl
Hackle: Black Cock Palmered
Rib: Silver Twist

No 28. Soldier Palmer '*In low or clear water the hackle must be spare, the hook small, the gold twist omitted and substituted with red twist.*'
Another variety uses a black hackle at the head of the fly.

187

Body:	Red Mohair or Squirrel
Hackle:	Red Cock, Palmered
Rib:	Gold Twist

No 32. For the Dee – Hackle fly

Hook:	No 9
Body:	Dull Yellow Mohair
Wings and Legs:	Hackle from neck of a Pale Dun Hen

No 33. Another fly for the Dee – Hackle Fly

Hook:	No 9
Body:	Peacock Herl
Wings and Legs:	Dark Dun Hen Hackle rather full

No 35. Coch a Bonddu
A favourite throughout the country under different names

| *Body:* | Peacock Herl |
| *Legs and Wings:* | Red and Black Hackle – Coch a Bonddu |

In the North of England on clear streams the hook size is 12 otherwise 8 or 9

No 37. Ginger Hackle

Hook:	No 8 Kendal Sneck
Body:	Yellow Silk, short and spare
Legs and Wings:	A Ginger Hackle

No 38. Grouse Hackle

Hook:	8 – 12
Body:	Varied to water and season – such as Peacock Herl, Orange Silk etc.
Legs and Wings:	A Grouse Hackle

No 39. The Dotteril Hackle
'One of the earliest flies that can be used in the North of England'

Hook:	Kirby Sneck 6 - 12
	Small Streams – Small Hook
Body:	Yellow Silk
Legs and Wings:	From Feather of a Dotteril

No 40. For the Conway

Hook:	11
Body:	Dun Orange Mohair
Legs and Wings:	A Dark Dun Hen's Hackle

No 41. A Second Conway Fly

Hook:	10
Body:	Yellow Mohair
Legs and Wings:	Bright Dun Hen's Hackle

No 42. Third Conway Fly
Hook: 9
Body: Peacock Herl
Legs and Wings: Wren Hackle (tail)

No 44. The Water Cricket
'Much commended by the North Country Angler. The fly appears in March.'
Body: Orange Floss Silk tied on with Black Silk
Legs: Best made with Peacock's Topping, if not available a Black Cock Hackle
'*Either must be wound down the body and the fibres then snapped off. This is Mr Ronalds's dressing.*'

At the end of the fly dressing chapter is the following remark. '...*that a variety of killing palmers may be dressed, by making the bodies of differently coloured peacocks' herls and by twisting over them the hackles of various kinds, such as the red, the black, the dun, the grizzle, the blue and the Coch a bonddu...*' A name for such flies is Bumble!

Hofland fished for grayling in the Dove, Wye, Derwent, and Trent. He found October to be the best month. He names yellow bodied and pale blue duns as good flies especially when fished about four inches under the surface. The Sandfly, when dressed on a size 12 hook, will be found a '*capital fly for October grayling.*'

Body: Fur from a Hare's Neck on silk of the same colour
Legs and Wings: A Ginger Hen's Hackle

Hofland declines to give fly lists for the months of the year as he feels the best flies will catch fish throughout the season. Here he concurs with Hawkins, Davy and Foster.

'*For instance the variously coloured duns serve from March to September somewhat changing their colour as the season advances...*'

Hofland used palmers as drop flies – droppers – throughout the year. The only flies he specified to a month were the Green and Grey Drake – those to be fished in June.

Thomas Hofland was an angler of very wide experience for his time. Many of his fly patterns have a distinct North Country style – particularly interesting are those which are Bumbles except in name. Whilst not formalised in Hofland's list, he obviously thought enough of the patterns to record them as effective killers.

'ARUNDO' – JOHN BEEVER

John Beever was probably not a Derbyshire man though he spent a good deal of time fishing on the Dove, Derwent and Wye. He was known to Alfred Ronalds and is the subject of favourable remarks in *The Fly-Fisher's Entomology*, later editions including quotes of Beever along with his dressing variations for Peacock Fly, July Dun and Willow Fly. In 1849, *Practical Fly Fishing* was published and it is a very practical book; though small in volume, it contains much advice on tackle and fly dressings.

189

The Derwent at Cromford
One hundred and fifty years ago John Beever –'Arundo '–
overlooked his tutor, Frank Ogden, as he fished this pool.

The rods of his early life are described as being very long, with fixed line. They may have been in two or more pieces and were often made from hazel. The line was attached to a substantial loop and was very thick at its butt. Thus the rod tip and line butt were of similar diameter. The line was of horsehair and stepped down through its length to a single hair tip. Many anglers of the day considered this too fine. Flies were tied up on the bank from a fly book, which contained the necessary materials – according to the fly on the water. Beever's comment regarding 'fine and far off' was 'never far off'. He believed most fish were caught close to the bank.

Towards the end of the book, he deals further with rod length. Those which anglers took on their travels had many sections, to make for convenient travel in carriages and coaches of earlier times. With the advent of rail travel Beever thought that each section could be as long as six feet, thus giving a rod with fewer ferrules and better action. He goes on to recommend a two or three section rod with much of its play in the top third. This would be much stiffer than the old through action rods. His proposals were aimed at providing a faster tip for casting, rapid repair of a thin tip with knife and waxed thread, better line control on the water and positive hooking of fish. All, or almost all of which, are features looked for in a modern rod. He gives detailed instructions, including measurements, to make rods at home or at least with the help of the local joiner. Again, instructions given are clear enough such that a rod could be built from them today. Beever lived at a time when fishing hooks underwent considerable changes and a short chapter informs the reader of current developments of the time and his recommendations.

Along with Derbyshire waters, John Beever travelled, probably by coach for some of his life, and fished widely in the British Isles and in France. His home for some time was at Coniston, so Cumberland and Westmoreland were well known to him. He fished the Wharfe and other Yorkshire rivers, spent time on the Herefordshire Wye and on Scottish waters including the Till, Teviot and Tweed. He fished still waters too – several flies are tied larger for lake trout.

One incident described in his book is relevant to these notes. He was fishing the pool below Cromford Bridge in which there were numbers of fish. He describes a local man, a chaise driver from Matlock called 'Frank', arriving and fishing the pool from which he took a number of fish. This was Frank Ogden, father of James Ogden the fly dresser, later of Cheltenham. Beevers describes the elder Ogden as 'one of the nicest and best fishers in England' and 'one of nature's gentlemen'.

John Beever provides dressings for thirty two patterns along with relevant comment regarding methods and waters. Sixteen of these dressings are hackle flies.

He gives a very clear piece of advice; 'On the limestone rivers of the Peak – coarse tackle and slovenly imitations WILL NOT DO!' A cast which John Beever used in Dovedale, and which was also successful on his visit to France, was made up of Spring Dun, Blue Dun and Turkey Fly.

He tells the story of a visit to the Birdsgrove water close to Hanging Bridge near

Ashbourne. Here he fished a Green Woodcock on a large hook and very thick line. The river was rough and narrow. Arriving at dusk, he fished down. Toward the 'middle of the stream' there was a splash 'as if someone had thrown into the water a large paving stone'. The broken line flew over his head and 'the sixteen hairs were staring in all directions, but the fly was gone.' This was put down to a salmon or otter.

Be careful if using this dressing!

GREEN WOODCOCK
Hackle: From a Woodcock's wing, a light coloured feather of mixed brown, dun and dirty yellow.
Body: Silk – ivy or apple green. Hare's ear dark part
Mid May – Mid July an evening fly

SPRING DUN - A Derbyshire Dressing
Hackle: Hen or Cock. The same colour as Young Starling's wing – i.e. blend of blue brown and yellow
Body: Mixed body of primrose and dandelion coloured silk

LIGHT ORANGE DUN   Good on limestone rivers of the Peak
Wings: From a light coloured Seagull or Sea Swallow, very light blue dun
Body: Silk – tawny or faded orange
Legs: Hackle, very light blue dun
Mid May – end of October

TURKEY FLY Hook: 2 – 3 (14 – 12) One from Arundo's Dove Cast
Wing: From the tail of a hen Pheasant or the quill of a Partridge
Silk: Generally primrose but sometimes chocolate
Legs: Hackle dappled, or cuckoo coloured (prevailing colours light blue dun and tawny yellow)
April – part of May

RUDDY FLY Hook: No 2 (14)   Marlo Buzz, Furnace, Coch a Bondu
Hackle: From a Ruddy Cock
Body: Silk Bright red between scarlet and crimson. Black Ostrich rather full herl
Spring and Summer beetle imitation

DARK BLUE DUN OR MERLIN Hook: 2 (14)
Hackle: Dark Blue Cock or Hen
Silk: Lead colour Dressed as a Hackle. OR –
Wing: Dark Blue part of the quill of Male Merlin Hawk
Hackle: Grey from a Jackdaw neck
Silk: Dark head with a little mole dubbing very sparse

This, Arundo says, is a good fly for a dark foggy day. In Dovedale on such a day, with the water not coloured but slightly milky, he was speaking to the keeper. During the conversation he marked several fish showing upstream. After the keeper left, Beever took 38 fish on this fly.

JAMES OGDEN

Destined to become one of the best-known fly dressers of the nineteenth century James Ogden was of Derbyshire extraction. His father, Frank Ogden, was a well-known angler and fly dresser on the county's rivers for some seventy years. Frank acted as tutor and guide to many – among them John Beever, who published *Practical Fly Fishing* in 1849 under the pen name Arundo.

James Ogden, author of *Ogden on Fly Tying*.
Formerly from Matlock, he founded his business in Cheltenham.
He was a pioneer of dry fly and many innovative tackle developments.

James and his father lived in or near Matlock and were regular visitors to the Derwent, Wye, Dove and Lathkill. It was on the Wye in 1865 he created an incident by fishing an artificial mayfly and becoming very unpopular in the process. He was a friend of Alfred Ronalds and acquaintance of both T C Hofland and David Foster.

Ogden knew the Derbyshire waters well and also fished in Ireland, Wales and Scotland, eventually moving to Cheltenham to set up in business as a tackle maker and fly dresser. From this base, his fame spread nationwide though he regularly visited Derbyshire to stay at The Peacock and fish his native streams. The area has that effect on some people. His style of angling was that of a quiet approach, using cover and following Walton's edict of 'fine and far off'.

James recommended the use of a vice when fly dressing – something very innovative in his lifetime. He was a pioneer in the development of the dry fly and was widely known for the technique he used to wing his creations. He laid great stress on matching the colour of flies, teasing out and blending dubbed bodies – the use of a magnifying glass at the waterside providing the necessary information from the natural creature. He carried a stock of tied up patterns, sometimes researched and tied long before breakfast on a fishing day, but he also carried a dubbing book to enable dressings to be created at the waterside as required. When tying flies he put on the body first, next fixed the wings followed by the hackle. The fly was finished off behind the hackle.

There was considerable rivalry between James Ogden and David Foster as to who first used and described the dry fly as a method of angling. As early as 1850 the Marquess of Granby records Mary Ogden-Smith, James's daughter, describing an incident of Ogden landing seven very large trout from the Kennet with a 'large dubbing bodied mayfly'. This probably predates David Foster's developments with dry fly.

In 1876 Aldam published *A Quaint treatise on Flees and the Art a Artyficial Flee Making*. Mounted in this book are flies tied at the time of publication. It is thought the detached bodied mayfly patterns are the work of James Ogden. This throws up an anomaly. In *Ogden on Fly Tying*, James says '*I do not approve of dressing mayflies cock-tail fashion, ...and (they) will not stand as those dressed on the hook only*'. Perhaps he changed his mind!

Sherry Spinner

Mayfly patterns from Aldam's *Quaint Treatise*.
James Ogden reputedly dressed these flies, but
in *Ogden on Fly Tying* he decries detached bodies on flies.

Detached body Mayfly pattern
from Aldam's *Quaint Treatise*

Other patterns in *Aldam's Treatise* were probably tied by Ogden's daughter and David Foster. Three years after Aldam's publication, *Ogden on Fly Tying* was published, a much smaller work but considerable in its depth and innovation.

Of Ogden's patterns the following are North Country style dressings:– Yellow Dun, Black Gnat, Marlow Buzz, Wren's Tail, Palmers cum Bumbles and Stone Midge. Others closely follow some of Alfred Ronalds's dressings: Golden Dun Midge, Sand Fly, Alder Fly, Whirling Blue Dun and Oak Fly. All are recommended for Derbyshire waters. The Yellow Dun, Alderfly and Black Gnat were used in preference to Green and Grey Drakes by Ogden's father Frank during Mayfly hatches. Another favourite was the Furnace Fly dressed thus:

Hook:	No. 2
Body:	Bright Orange Silk
Wing:	Starling tied upright
Hackle:	Two turns of good furnace

James, working from Cheltenham, had great influence on angling at a time of considerable change. In or about 1850, he introduced blue mahoe timber as a rod building material. It was considered a notable advance in flexibility and reliability. From this material, previously used to make gun ramrods, he built rods from eight to twelve feet. The shorter models were very unusual for the period. The 'Portmanteau Rod' ten feet long in five pieces, and ideal for 'Travelling Gentlemen and Commercial Travellers' was made in the 1870s by Ogden – it seems nothing is new in angling. He invented a spring folding landing net, a seat basket and the Devil Killer spinner. As the years took their toll with rheumatics James built his 'Multum in Parvo Fly Rod', an eight foot leather handled rod which enabled him to fish more comfortably, and which, no doubt, extended his commercial range.

Mary, his daughter, was trained as a fly dresser and in running a successful business. She married one of Ogden's employees, a Mr Smith, and so the company Ogden-Smith was born. This was set up in Battersea and Mary was considered a fly dresser of great skill. In turn Mary's daughter, Mrs Richardson of Kingston on Thames also worked as a professional fly dresser.

James Ogden constantly proclaimed his products, founding an important dynasty in the late nineteenth and early twentieth centuries through his daughter and son-in-law.

Most of James's life was spent outside Derbyshire but he often returned. The early influences of his home rivers and background must qualify him originally as a Derbyshire angler.

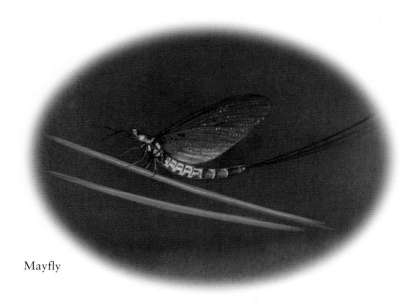

Mayfly

197

MARQUESS OF GRANBY

In 1898 the then Marquess of Granby published *The Trout*. He was the owner of the Haddon Estate and a very keen angler. Much of his angling was done on the southern chalk streams in exalted angling company, where dry fly was very much the rule. He owned much of Lathkill and Bradford dales, along with the riparian rights accorded to them, and in addition much of the river Wye. On these home rivers his attitude was slightly modified. He points out that dry fly angling can only take place under certain conditions but that '...excellent sport and capital fun are to be obtained by the other forms of fly fishing...'. On strong, rapid waters such as the Wye it was acceptable to drift a soft hackled black fly over fish in awkward lies or when they had become gut shy. He considered wet fly very much as 'chuck it and chance it'. Very aristocratic language, could he have said that?

There follows my transcription of Granby's imaginary angler through whom he informs his audience.

The angler having tackled up is given the suggestion of using an Olive Dun with a gold rib and cocked wings. The fly is anointed with a touch of paraffin oil. A short cast is made – a good fault as a bowler finds his length – and the fish is hooked, worked downstream and netted from below.

Weather conditions are bad and the angler fishes the water across and down. On the cast is a Red Quill Gnat, Alder or March Brown and movement needs to be imparted to the flies. Tailing trout are searching for underwater food and the dry fly is not for them. Palmers, Zulus and Spiders are good flies to use but do need perseverance! In addition the Partridge Hackle or Alder are often successful.

Bulging fish are taking duns just before they reach the surface and are very difficult to catch during this activity. Smutting fish also prove a problem but the angler finds they may be tempted with a Small Black Gnat or Dark Dun.

A great deal of space is occupied with the Mayfly. Granby says that size of fly is very important and that smaller rather than larger flies are the most useful. He found flies with large wings very difficult to cast in adverse winds. Paraffin oil was used to enhance floating properties of the flies but left a slick on the water surface.

Three Mayfly dressings are given –

MAYFLY 1
Body: Dubbing
Hackle: Red
Wing: Wild Duck
Tail: Mallard

Believed to be the Marquess of Granby, author of *The Trout*.
The plate, from his book, is entitled 'Waiting for a Rise'.

MAYFLY 2

Body: Straw with red silk whipping round it
Hackle: Red
Wing: Wild Duck
Tail: Mallard

MAYFLY 3

Body: Straw with Red Whipping round it
Hackle: Good amount of Bustard Hackle

Mayfly 2 is very similar to Foster's Favourite with a straw body.

Mayfly 3 is fished wet – and Granby did well fishing it downstream.

When fishing the Mayfly, Granby observed trout break all the rules '...when their mayfly feast is before them...' His advice in these circumstances, whilst not in keeping with dry fly practice, was to fish every inch of water and to 'throw over likely spots when neither fish nor natural could be observed'.

The purchase and use of suitable tackle are worthy of consideration, as are stealth and camouflage on the approach to the fish. Flies are the most important matter. Fancy flies carried by most anglers include Toppy, Hofland's Fancy, Greenwell's Glory and Zulu. Along with these is the Marquess's personal list of general utility flies.

March Brown	Red Quill Gnat	Black Gnat
Red Spinner	Olive Quill Gnat	Yellow Dun
Alder	Governor	Gold Rib Hare's Ear
Olive Dun	Wickham's Fancy	Iron Blue Dun

Bumbles, Ash Dun and Apple Green Dun are flies advised for Derbyshire waters.

An account of 'some heavy baskets of fish' is given. Among these are the following accounts. On the open water between Rowsley and Bakewell three trout were landed each over three pounds in weight. On June 8th 1897 Mr T D Croft and the Marquess killed 69 trout. Of these Mr Croft took 49 from the Bradford on Mayfly, the remaining 20 from the Lathkill by Granby on Ash and Blue Duns. Needless to say, these were heavily stocked waters. The Mayfly was rare on the Lathkill but plentiful on the Bradford. After the confluence of the two rivers the Mayfly was absent.

Grayling angling is also considered. The grayling is found in the Dove, Wye and Derwent in Derbyshire. Orange and Crimson Bumbles are widely used as are Ash Dun and Apple Green Dun. The addition of a red tag is often of advantage to any ordinary trout fly as a conversion to a grayling pattern. Other than these Autumn Duns are sufficient.

A reference is made to David Foster. '...*he knew more about the habits of grayling and the best ways of catching them than almost anybody else...*'. It is evident Granby and Foster had discussed grayling angling in detail. A pound grayling was considered a good fish in Granby's time.

Lake fishing is dealt with quite briefly. It is obvious that the Marquess had less interest in fishing still waters. He does describe, however, three patterns from Francis Francis's *A Book on Angling* 1867.

1.	*Body:*	Reddish wool with gold twist rib	(Teal and Red?)
	Hackle:	Red	
	Wing:	Teal	
2.	*Body:*	Black with silver twist rib	(Teal and Black?)
	Hackle:	Black	
	Wing:	Teal	

These last may be dressed with Mallard or Woodcock wing.

3.	*Body:*	Red wool with silver twist rib	(Heckham Peckham?)
	Hackle:	Red	
	Wing:	White tipped feather from Wild Drake's wing	

When fishing still waters Granby found the following river patterns useful: Grey Dun, Red Spinner, Red Palmer and Black Palmer, he also dapped live mayfly on lakes and rivers. The enthusiasm of the time for the Alexandra, a fly banned on many waters such was its efficacy, was shared by the Marquess. He fished it and considered the fly deadly after a spate.

The tackle he used in 1899 was sophisticated, but no doubt expensive. Waterproof plaited silk or cotton lines which were made in Manchester. Casts were of drawn tapered gut. These could be unreliable depending on type and age of the gut used. Quality brass reels from Hardy's or Foster's were in demand along with many gadgets beloved of anglers. Greenheart and other solid timber rods were still popular but subject to breakages caused by ageing and brittleness. Split cane was becoming the favoured material for those able to afford it. Granby's landing net was a folding flip up model practically identical to many of today's patterns. His wading stockings do not appear so very much different to modern 'breathables' though I suspect they were less comfortable.

SUMMARY OF RECOMMENDED DERBYSHIRE PATTERNS

Olive Dun – Cocked Wing	Black Hackle
Mayfly 1, 2 & 3	Ash Dun
Blue Dun	Apple Green Dun
Grayling Flies	Orange Bumble
Crimson Bumble	Red Tagged Flies

Almost half of Granby's publication is written by Colonel F H Custance on trout rearing. The waters controlled by the Marquess were very heavily stocked and judging by his own records, large numbers of trout were killed by comparatively few anglers. The replacement of these fish by others of suitable quality was essential to the anglers and Granby had a model fishery capable of providing the fish. Several operations at the fishery have been recorded by photographs in the book and show equipment, staff and ponds. It is obvious no expense was spared in this enterprise.

The Colonel was obviously an expert on fish rearing, detailing the process, from historical times to the transport by train of two year old fish. *The Trout*, is rounded off by a chapter entitled 'Cookery of the Trout' by Alexander Innes Shand.

His description of the trout, which is not required in the kitchen, is delightful!

'We have seen a two-pounder taken out of a drain on a rushy common, and we should have been sorry to condemn our worst enemy to eat him. Local palates profess patriotic admiration for the bloated monsters, familiar acquaintances of habitual anglers, who have eluded for years the parochial poachers. When one of them is landed at last and borne off to the village alehouse, he is made the object of a triumph, and the excuse for a carouse. But what can you expect of a fish which, like some sedentary men of letters, has never taken a yard of exercise, or swam a stroke when he could help it? He has been battening all his indolent days on newts and tadpoles and fouler garbage; and lurking, when dyspeptical and off the feed, in the slime under the tangled roots of some alder copse suggestive of a malarious mangrove swamp in the sweltering delta of the oil rivers. Test him by his shape, and he has run to head and stomach, narrow-shouldered, and pot-bellied, black and leprous – almost loathsome.'

How different from the cook's choice!

'The choicest trout have the graceful proportions of the aquatic athlete, and though the tints and speckling may be varied, they are invariably rich and lustrous.'

WILLIAM H FOSTER

W H Foster was born in 1859. He was one of David Foster's sons who compiled *The Scientific Angler* after their father's death, from his manuscript and notes. The chapter entitled 'The Dry Fly' was probably William's contribution as the initials W H F are appended. Indeed, much of the work may have been a vehicle for his views and those of the company he shared with his brother.

William was a great correspondent. *The Field* and the *Fishing Gazette* both published letters by him on a variety of subjects, some of which involved controversy. These included communications over 'Coopers Fancy', a black gnat pattern in *Fishing Gazette* 1899 and a robust discussion by letter over 'Flights Fancy' which W H Foster claimed to have been invented by his father as the Golden Dun. There is further comment on this issue by him in *The Scientific Angler*. Gerald Heywood in *Charles Cotton and his River* quotes a letter from *The Field* in 1925 which is '...over the initials W H F, well known to Dove fishermen'.

Certainly, he was a good businessman. The company exhibited in international exhibitions, becoming famed for its manufacture and retail of high quality tackle and flies. Various booklets and other publications were produced on local rivers and fishing

D. & W. H. FOSTER,
ASHBOURNE, ENGLAND,
ESTABLISHED 1833.

Publishers of the "SCIENTIFIC ANGLER." - - -

- - 7th Edition now being published.

First Prize for Lines and First Prize for Flies, Piscatorial Exhibition, 1889; Silver Medal, Cologne, 1889; Seven International Fisheries' Awards, 1883; First Prize for Rods, 1892, only times of exhibiting.

William Henry Foster took over the tackle business in Ashbourne after his father, David.

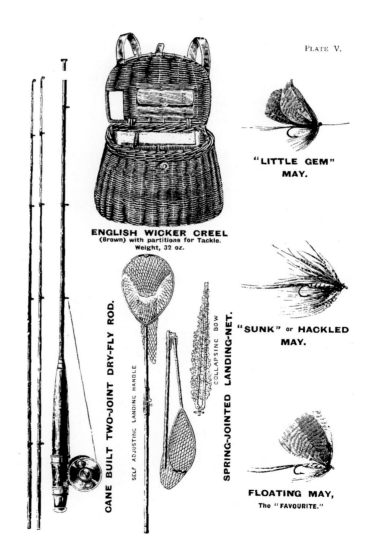

PLATE V.

ENGLISH WICKER CREEL
(Brown) with partitions for Tackle.
Weight, 32 oz.

CANE BUILT TWO-JOINT DRY-FLY ROD.

SELF ADJUSTING LANDING HANDLE

COLLAPSING BOW

SPRING-JOINTED LANDING-NET.

"LITTLE GEM" MAY.

"SUNK" or HACKLED MAY.

FLOATING MAY,
The "FAVOURITE."

Plate (reduced) from *The Scientific Angler* Illustrating tackle and flies developed by the Foster company. The net is very similar to that made by James Ogden of Cheltenham

tackle along with innovations such as the wire cored 'Acme' line and the technique of strengthening rods by wire ribbing.

The 1901 census lists him as a 'Fishing Tackle Manufacturer', aged 42 but there is no record of his brother. William's son Louis, was taken into the company and ran it until the 1960s. William died in 1947, having spent around fifty years running and developing the firm from its Church Street premises.

THE AMATEUR ANGLER   EDWARD MARSTON

Edward Marston wrote a number of books with an angling theme along with *An Amateur Angler's Days in Dovedale (1884)* and *Dovedale Revisited (1902)*. These included *An Old Man's Holidays (1900)*, *By Meadow and Stream (1896)*, *Days in Clover (1892)* and *Fishing for Pleasure and Catching It (1892)* are among them. Written in a somewhat light-hearted vein, they make entertaining reading. Whilst the detail of angling is not explained, there is much of interest. Marston was the father of R B Marston, long-time editor of *Fishing Gazette*, and so did not want for advice, should it have been needed.

He describes incidents in his angling activities familiar to every angler though recorded by few. Told to fish dry he sees no rise. Eventually, after fishing the water with a cast of three flies, he is distracted by a bird, hooks a fish and then loses it. Casting to a rise upstream the flies land in a heap and take half an hour to untangle as the rise proceeds unfished. After fishing on in heavy rain to no effect, he retires to the Izaak Walton Hotel to dry out. In *Days in Dovedale* he warns against the gradients around Reynard's Hole in the Dale and recounts a piece by William Shipley, describing a fatal fall nearby.

Marston remarks on the numbers of cascades 'scores in three miles' built to provide good conditions for trout and angling. He also compares the flavour of Dove and Manifold trout, favouring those from the Dove. He has trouble with the iron gate at Dovedale stepping stones, despite instructions about how to deal with its intricacies.

In Ilam, he meets a fellow angler 'of substance' with whom he discusses flies. He is shown patterns and asked if he would care to try them. Answering in the affirmative, he is then charged eighteen pence for a cast of three or two shillings for a dozen!

While fishing one evening, Marston's fly lands on a nettle. Having been told to 'grasp your nettle' he suffers sore fingers in the process of retrieval, and, having previously hooked a thistle, he is not too happy. The next incident described is even more fraught. This time the cast catches a twig upon which hangs a wasp's nest. The rod is abandoned and he is pursued by angry wasps. Eventually the fly is recovered by pulling at distance until the twig breaks – without the nest.

Whilst on his holiday, Marston visits the Peacock at Rowsley, but finds it full. On recommendation, he goes to the Edensor Hotel at Chatsworth, which is also full. However he visits Haddon Hall and lunches at Rowsley.

He fishes the Manifold into the evening, the next day catching a fish, finally, after

Edward Marston, author of
An Amateur-Angler's Day in Dovedale
His son was R B Marston, long time
editor of *The Fishing Gazette*.

dark. He bemoans how he envisaged fly fishing – 'a sweetly flowing stream on a Summer's evening, with trout and grayling eager to be caught'. Reality is then related:

'...soaked and sodden, torn and scratched, stung by nettles, pursued by wasps, bitten by venomous insects, my fingers lacerated and coat and trousers torn by my own hooks'.

An expedition fishing the dale down from Hartington is described, including a sojourn by Cotton's fishing house. Reaching the Izaak Walton at ten in the evening Marston's friend, the Major, has three brace of good trout. At this juncture, Marston observes that rod makers should dull the varnish of their products. The Major fishes cautiously in drab clothing, but even in the evening the flash of his rod is noticed by Marston. *Days in Dovedale* ends with a description of the Izaak Walton Hotel, and wishing the reader 'the east wind may never blow when thou goest afishing'.

Dovedale Revisited, written eighteen years later, compares places and how they have changed. Free water in Ilam, once owned by R Hanbury, is now strictly preserved by Jesse Watts Russell of Ilam Hall. Stew ponds, built in 1884 by Sir Henry Allsop, have fallen into disrepair and desolation but fish are still caught and the Dales as pleasant as ever.

There are detailed notes on the condition of Cotton's Fishing House and its various renovations at dates from 1784 to 1902. The historic building has undergone troughs and peaks since its construction in 1674 but Edward Marston records it in good order but locked, which apparently irritates him somewhat.

In 2005 the only good view available to the casual visitor is from the West at a distance. The vane and stone ball on the apex are visible as is the roof, chimney and part of a casement. The surrounding trees and shrubs shield the rest from sight.

Marston tells of his meeting with a Mr Lock. This was almost certainly Ernest Lock whose father invented Lock's Fancy. Ernest was a keeper and lived at Lode Mill, Alstonefield. He is described as '...a first rate fly fisherman and maker of the particular flies to which the Dove trout and grayling are most partial'.

On the last fishing day of his holiday, October 10th, Amateur Angler is asked by the editor of *Fishing Gazette*, his son R B Marston, to forward a Dove grayling above a pound. In this mission he fails but is rescued by his fishing companion who goes to the river and returns with a grayling of 1lb. 3 oz. This is duly dispatched to 'Mr Editor'. It is not recorded how the fish was caught!

As a very old man Edward Marston realises this will probably be his last visit to the Dove. He closes his book with lines from The Retirement by Charles Cotton and a sketch of the Dove's source.

> 'Oh, my beloved nymph, fair Dove!
> Princess of rivers! How I love
> Upon thy flow'ry banks to be;
> And view thy silver stream,
> When guided by the summer's beam!
> And in it all thy wanton fry,
> Playing at liberty;
> And with my angle, upon them
> The all of treachery
> I ever learnt, industriously to try.'

WALTER M GALLICHAN   (GEOFFREY MORTIMER)

Walter Gallichan was a well-travelled angler. He fished on the Continent and throughout Great Britain. His choice of method seemed to be whatever was appropriate and approved on the waters he fished. He enjoyed fly fishing, both wet and dry, but was also a successful and experienced bottom angler. He eventually settled in Youlgreave and, with Bradford Dale at the end of his garden, what better place could there be? He fished widely throughout the region. All the Derbyshire and Staffordshire rivers were well known to him. Contacts afforded by his writing opened up opportunities to visit closely preserved waters along with more accessible club and day ticket fishings.

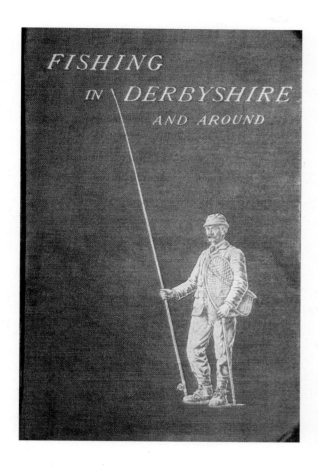

The engraving on the cover of
Fishing in Derbyshire and Around
is said to be a likeness of
W M Gallichan, who lived above
Bradford Dale.

Gallichan had written six or seven angling books when he came to Derbyshire. *Fishing in Wales* and *The Complete Fisherman* were among them. He was next persuaded to write on Derbyshire angling and in 1905 *Fishing in Derbyshire and Around* was published. The work gives details of rivers, lakes, methods, access and personalities on the Derbyshire and Staffordshire waters. He gives comprehensive tables of railway stations, licence suppliers, fly dressers and tackle dealers, along with those to contact to obtain the best advice. Comfortable hotels, especially those with angling facilities, are mentioned throughout the text. He recommends visits to waterkeepers, such as Ashton or Fosbrooke, people who could dress flies and 'guide' clients on most of the rivers mentioned in the text.

He remarks upon the effects of pollution. The mills and factories 'work some measure of mischief' along lengths of the mid and lower Derwent, the river Wye being contaminated below Buxton. The Churnet is reported as having a considerable length ruined by mill pollution. Thankfully a hundred years later the situation is much improved. One interesting observation is on the effect of crude sewage on fish at

Bakewell. The sewer outfall was analysed and pronounced 'free from elements noxious to fish'. One wonders what happened to other life in the river even if the fish were unaffected. Restocking of the Dove, Manifold, Wye, Lathkill and Bradford with trout took place regularly – several owners having their own rearing facilities. References to these waters comment on their being packed with fish even to the extent of the fishing being made too easy.

Walter Gallichan deals with each river in turn, describing suitable methods and fly patterns along with description of the waters and appropriate anecdotes.

The angler's interest in the Upper Dove begins at Crowdecote. Gallichan leased water at Pilsbury and despite a very dry season enjoyed good fishing with both trout and grayling. He tells of hooked trout boring into water vole holes in order to rub the fly out and escape. He found the water level dropped away quickly in dry weather here and fishing became very difficult. Below, down to Hartington, the river widens and deepens. Through Beresford Dale, Wolfscote Dale and Milldale the water has been adapted for trout habitat and angling. Many low dams have been constructed over a long period to create pools and runs; Mr Thomas Wardle and Mr Hall being responsible for some of the works.

Recommended fly patterns for the Upper Dove:

Iron Blue Dun	Olive Dun	Blue Dun	Golden Earwig (post spate)
Yellow Dun	Mayfly	Small Black	Gnat

Dovedale's banks are, in the main, flat and there is little rough ground for the angler to negotiate. Again, weirs and dams create pools and features to harbour fish and food species. The river retains this character to the Manifold confluence at Ilam. Angling was difficult. Educated trout and clear water meant every fish was earned – nothing changes. The water was preserved here for dry fly angling only by those who controlled and fished it. Gallichan says the Dove must be 'wooed with ardent persistence'. He does not provide a large number of flies for use – exhorting the angler to use his own discretion or otherwise approach his host for proven killers. The Dovedale fishings are considered to be at their best from April until the end of June with grayling in October. It is interesting that grayling were not pursued as vermin on the Dove.

Recommended fly patterns for Dovedale:

Pale Olive Dun	Mayfly
Dark Olive Dun	Yellow Dun

Below Dovedale, the river becomes larger and more placid. The scours on bends make for interesting angling, and fly is still successful though bait was permitted. When Gallichan fished the fly here he used a three fly cast for both trout and grayling rather than dry fly used higher upriver. In 1905 the Churnet was not fished because of pollution but Tean Brook was a water stocked with trout.

The Manifold and Dove have their sources very near to one another and for much of their length run close together. Eventually they join at Ilam, the Manifold having run underground for some distance. The Manifold carries more colour – it has more tributaries than the Dove – and is an easier river to fish as a consequence of the colour. The river at that time was also fished less then the Dove. The fish stock was smaller but the grayling tended to be larger than the trout. Gallichan thought the Manifold an earlier river than the Dove. Fish in the Manifold rose well and the river also gave good wet fly sport. Mayfly were introduced to the river by John Fosbrooke. The Manifold, says Gallichan, is a quiet, well stocked river with good fish and fly populations. It requires stealth and skill to fish the water well.

Recommended fly patterns for the Manifold:

Trout	Blue Dun	Alder	Iron Blue Dun
	Golden Earwig	Olive Dun	Bumbles
	Cock Winged Yellow Dun	Small Hackles	

Grayling	Blue Dun	Apple Green Dun
	Small Black Gnat	'Fosbrookes Specialities'

The upper waters of the Wye are dismissed by Gallichan because of pollution from Buxton. Once the river reached Ashford it became 'Ducal property' and was stocked with trout, supplementing the established population of brown and rainbow trout. The Wye is described as a 'crystal stream', which has excellent access on its banks for casting to, and stalking, fish. Its denizens are not easy to catch, a cautious approach being required and the fish very choosy. Walter Gallichan advises 'never mind tradition' in the early season. A couple of 'small hackles' will ensure sport. Casting upstream to the edges of runs, close to the bank, in holes, eddies and corners being a good approach!

The Wye is joined by the Lathkill at Wye Bridge, the conjoined rivers meeting the Derwent at Rowsley. The river keeper on the Wye in 1905 was Robert Hensburgh.

Recommended patterns for the Wye:

Olive Dun	Mayfly – Green Drake
Small Hackles – April	Bumbles – Grayling

The fly patterns need to be in small sizes and the cast kept fine.

The River Bradford ran past the end of Walter Gallichan's garden at Youlgreave and the Lathkill was close by. Both were preserved except 'to personal friends of the owners and leasees'. He was able to fish these rivers and obviously enjoyed doing so. The Lathkill, like the Dove, had weirs to create habitat for fish and features to benefit angling. The pools and runs provided high quality fly fishing. On the Bradford, weirs and the larger dams also provided water which contained large trout, as indeed they still do. Little wonder that 'the rise makes one's fingers tingle for a rod'.

At Conksbury Bridge, Mr Symington had a trout hatchery and model fishery with all the accessories thereof, and a little lower down was the Marquess of Granby's fishing pavilion. These waters were very strictly preserved and once again adapted by weirs and groynes to provide good fly water. The Marquess also had a trout hatchery and was very interested in the rearing of stock for the river. His book *The Trout* gives much of its space to trout rearing processes.

The Upper Derwent has changed much since the days of Gallichan. Howden, Derwent and Ladybower have swallowed many of the fishings enjoyed at that time by the members of the Derwent Fly Fishers. Instead, a wealth of stillwater angling has replaced that found on streams such as the Ashop, Ladybower and Abbey brooks. Trout and grayling abounded in these upper waters and Derwent Fly Fishers stocked trout for dry fly sport. Walter Gallichan speaks highly of the Rover Noe, controlled in 1905 by the six members of Peak Forest Angling Club. The Chatsworth fishery, as now, was controlled by the Duke of Devonshire and dry fly the predominant angling method, although Gallichan does mention dapping live mayfly and bluebottle. Early season wet fly angling was permitted throughout the fishery.

Recommended fly patterns for the Upper Derwent:

March Brown (coloured water)	Mayfly	Olive Dun
Ash Dun	Claret Bumble	Furnace Bumble
Apple Green Dun	Black Midge	

Darley Dale Angling Club ran the fishing from Rowsley to Matlock Bridge. Dry fly was favoured, particularly on the flats, though wet fly was used by a few anglers including Walter Gallichan, usually early season and at dusk in summer. He advises the wet fly for the runs and pools at Oaker Bends and says that between here and Matlock the river contains large barbel. May and June provided the best of the dry fly fishing, and October was the most suitable time for the good stocks of grayling.

Recommended fly patterns for the Mid Derwent:

Trout –	Gravel Bed	Green Drake	Red Spinner
	Iron Blue	Yellow Dun	Claret Bumble
	Eaton's Yellow Dun		
Grayling –	Red Tag	Apple Green Dun	
	Fiery Bumble	'Foster's Specialities'	

Around the iron bridge in Matlock was some free fishing and though not good fly water it was excellent for bait fishing. Big trout were caught here in the early twentieth century.

Downstream of Masson the river changes to streamy runs and pools. Between here and Whatstandwell fly once more provided good sport, controlled in 1905 by Matlock & Cromford Angling Club. The river thence gradually becomes a mixed fishery through to Belper, though in places still fly fished by many anglers. Pollution permitting, good coarse fishing was available above and below Derby.

Walter Gallichan caught grayling throughout the county and always gives weight to them in his writings. It seems that most owners and anglers considered them as sporting fish, when elsewhere, particularly in the South, they were systematically removed from the rivers. At Gouthwaite, in Nidderdale, Yorkshire, grayling established themselves in the reservoir, when the Nidd was dammed. This establishment in stillwater was unusual, and apparently not repeated when the Derbyshire streams were stopped for the Derwent dams.

When fishing for grayling Gallichan's advice was for green or gaudy flies or a bright lure in winter along with:

Blue Dun	Applegreen Dun	Olive
Green Drake	Coch Y Bonddu	Fiery Bumble
Golden Earwig		

In addition to the rivers described, details are given of pond, lake and reservoir angling in Derbyshire and Cheshire. He considers opportunities for Sheffield anglers who at that time travelled widely to Lincolnshire and Nottinghamshire to fish.

The list of flies, some twenty patterns, is as good a summary as any of the traditional patterns used in Derbyshire and Staffordshire during the nineteenth century. It would be interesting to know the dressings for Foster's and Fosbrooke's 'Specialities' but by their nature they were perhaps well-guarded secrets!

Walter Gallichan was considered an expert on the Welsh Border rivers. He invented a number of patterns including the Borderer and Grizzly Dun. He died in his eighties just after the Second World War.

GERALD G P HEYWOOD

The author of *Charles Cotton and his River*, Gerald Heywood was a lifelong angler on the River Dove. He began his angling career in the 1880s and his recollections go back 'to the old school of Dove fishers who, still holding the traditions of Cotton and of Ronalds, were past masters in the art of catching trout and grayling'.

Heywood tried to complete his work to coincide with the 250th year after Cotton's work was published. In this he was not quite successful, but he did produce an entertaining and very informative work with much of relevance to modern anglers.

Charles Cotton and his life form the first chapter giving a full account of the man, his family, home and times. The original format of Cotton's contribution to the *Compleat*

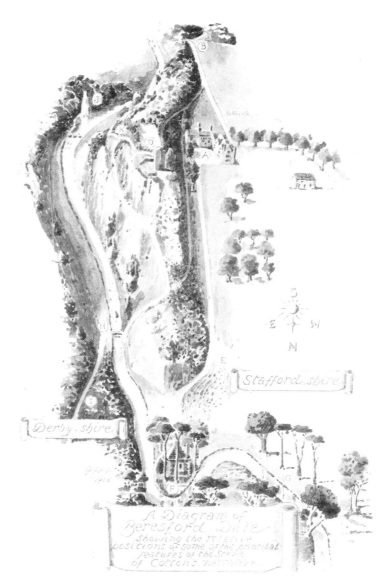

A. Beresford Hall. B. The approach from the South. C. The Avenue. D. The Tower.
E. The brink of the hill whence Viator first saw the Fishing-House. F. The Fishing-
House. G. The Walk. H. Probable site of Cotton's footbridge; a little lower down was
the great stone; below this again Viator, fishing from the Derbyshire side, caught the sixteen-
inch Grayling. I. The foot-path to Hartington. J. Pike-Pool. K. The steep path by
which Piscator and Viator returned to the House after the loss of the great Trout which
turned up a side like a Salmon.

Map of Beresford Dale drawn by Gerald Heywood for his book *Charles Cotton and his River*.

Angler follows, with Heywood's commentary interspersed. This lightens the text and informs the reader, clarifying the route taken on the journey of Viator and Piscator from Brailsford to Beresford Hall.

Beresford Hall and Cotton's Fishing House are described and illustrated with remarks on the condition of the latter in historical and modern times. Heywood then writes of the Second Day in Beresford Dale and the Third Day above the Dale. As previously, the original text is supported by the author's comments in an interesting and informative manner.

The remainder of the work compares and contrasts angling in Charles Cotton's day and Heywood's day. He raises the question about the effect of weather and temperature on the colour of flies, noting that this idea was widespread in past times, having as its adherents Charles Cotton, Sir John Hawkins and Sir Humphrey Davy. It was further elaborated by David Foster, and Heywood says it is a persuasive theory even in the face of science.

Cotton dresses April Duns with yellow silk, and Browns with red silk. In May the hackles are to be brighter and the flies smaller, perhaps showing that he thought that colours brighten and flies become smaller as the season progresses. Sir John Hawkins, who edited the fifth edition of *The Compleat Angler*, pursues a similar line on the Violet Dun:- in March and September, Violet Dun; in April, pale ash colour; in May, beautiful lemon colour; and in June and July, blue black. Sir Humphrey Davy on the Blue Dun, says '*...of the Blue Dun there is a succession of different tints...*'. In early spring, they have dark olive bodies; in April and May, yellow; in summer, cinnamon; and in winter's approach, they darken.

Charles Cotton's list of flies is next to occupy Gerald Heywood. As many others have done, he attempts to relate the old patterns to the modern. In this, he refers to a wide spectrum of authors – Bowlker, Bainbridge, Ronalds, Shipley, Blacker, Foster, Francis and Halford. The length of Cotton's fly list leads to the observation '*...a list even the courteous and attentive Viator must have found rather long and perchance a trifle tedious...*'. He adds that Cotton probably used less than half the flies he originally recorded. From the list, Heywood selects a '*team of flies which in modern dress will serve ... on the Dove today*'.

Green Drake	Grey Drake	Black Gnat
Blue Dun	Yellow Dun	

And those in 'disguise'

Iron Blue	March Brown	Alder
Red Spinner	Flying Ant	Sedge
Hawthorn		

The text notes highlight that March Brown and Blue Dun are always present in old spring fly lists. The Olive is virtually ignored or thought to be a colour variation of the Blue Dun. By 1928 the situation has reversed. Olive Dun has taken pride of place and the very existence of the Blue Dun is questioned.

The Palmer hackles, often thought to represent hairy caterpillars or 'Woolly Bears', were subjected to an experiment by Heywood. On being dropped in the water the live caterpillar used rolled up and sank. It made no further movement until removed from the water. From this he concluded that the Palmer hackles catch fish because of their hackle movement, not their resemblance to caterpillars. Further, he also notes that a few turns of gold or silver twist add greatly to their attractiveness to trout.

A discussion of Cotton's Little White Dun of July reveals the view that this is the Little Pale Blue – an old Dove standard pattern. The tie is:

Body:	Palest Primrose Yellow
Hackle:	Silvery Blue or Honey Dun Hackle
Wings:	Two feathers from the knob of a tern's wing (Sea Swallow)

Heywood suggests feathers from the knob of a pigeon's wing as substitute for the tern.

A brief chapter on Worm, Caddis and Minnow fishing is next. Cotton did not favour fishing with bait – something he chided Walton about. Nevertheless, Walton was put forward as the expert in such matters, by Cotton.

Fly fishing and its progress from the seventeenth to the twentieth century follows. Having dealt with Cotton's fishing tackle, Heywood moves on. By 1760, Sir John Hawkins's notes reveal fourteen-foot rods with ash butts, hickory middle and yew or bamboo tips. Some rods were tipped with whale bone. The reel had become commonplace and heavier lines were being used. Flies appeared with names like 'Bloa' and 'Watchett'.

At this time – mid eighteenth century – rivers were still well stocked, angling often being the preserve of those with disposable income and the time to indulge their interest. Progress had been made in communication and travel. This was important in the development of Ashbourne as the centre of a school of angling on the Dove and Manifold. The town was on a major coach road to the North West and in time became a rail terminus for the North Staffordshire Railway. Both were used by those visiting to fish the two rivers and especially the upper Dove. Hotels were available both in Ashbourne and the surrounding district close to the rivers. Flies *'infallible for Derbyshire trout and grayling and warranted to kill on every river in the kingdom...'* were available in Ashbourne. They must have been good! Messages were sent out when the Mayfly was 'up' or the grayling 'on'. Sir Humphrey Davy was a regular visitor, *'...accompanied by a noted old Dove flyfisher'*, William Shipley the elder who was a tackle maker in Ashbourne. Davy wanted to see Shipley's knowledge written up but it never happened. A pity, as Davy himself had offered to contribute. Nevertheless Shipley's son, another William, probably included much of his father's wisdom in his writings.

Rods became shorter, Shipley advising a smaller stiffer rod of eleven feet. Reels improved; though some did not, being attached to the angler's belt! Silk lines and tapered gut casts were developed and droppers became common, two being usual on the Dove. Built cane rods were invented – Blacker reports '...*the beautiful rent and glued up bamboo cane fly rods...*'.

Anglers waded more often as a result of the shorter rods and upstream method of fishing. Alfred Ronalds mentions Indian Rubber overalls used near Sheffield, breast waders of the nineteenth century, and points out the advantage of wading where fishing is not possible from the bank.

Heywood records that most of the 'old school' fished the Dove across and down. Some were, or became, out and out 'upstream men' – very much in vogue as the nineteenth century closed. He points out the advantages of both methods to reach fish lying in difficult spots. Lengths of fast water leading to deep runs under steep banks ending in shallows on the near bank, allow a downstream angler to explore the far deep and bring the flies back through midstream. Fish in this area are covered along with those in the deep and at the tail of the pool. In the 1880s flies were often still tied to gut and were very similar to those of Ronalds. However, Bumbles were widely used, having their advocates in Foster and Fosbrooke. Heywood gives no date for the advent of dry fly on the Dove, but in the 1880s '*it was not unknown at Norbury, though may have appeared earlier on the much fished Dovedale length*'. As the waters became more popular, wet fly fishing declined in favour of dry fly. Eyed hooks were used and cock winged 'Drys' sailed the waters. 'Thus the Dove flyfisher looks with a kindly and tolerant eye on all varieties of fly fishing so they be fair and sportsman like...' So says Gerald Heywood and on much of the river this is still true.

The reader is next offered some Dove patterns for dry fly and wet fly fishing. He follows an analytical approach to decide on patterns to use. Which flies are plentiful? Which flies attract fish? Which lend themselves to successful imitation? Is exact imitation necessary? Trout feeding on a hatch may require a close imitation, as may grayling in shallow water. Grayling lying deep may well be less selective. Heywood's choice of artificial flies and the naturals they emulate are recorded.

Blue and Olive Duns are imitated by Gold Ribbed Hare's Ear and the Olive Quill. G R H E is always a good pattern to begin fishing, whatever dun is present. The Blue Quill is a general pattern for the lighter duns and also for the Iron Blue. The Yellow Dun can be represented by the Ginger Quill. Suitable hook sizes for these patterns would be 17 (oo) for the Blue Quill and Yellow Dun, 16 (o) for the Iron Blue and lighter Little Pale Blue. The March Brown is not a common fly on the Dove, but Alfred Ronalds's female March Brown sparsely dressed is as good a pattern as any.

Mayfly imitations are often dressed too large, resulting in fish not taking the fly. Spent tyings of the Grey and Green Drake, again not too bulky, are recommended. Flat winged flies such as sedges, says Heywood, are of little account on the Dove. The Alder fly, when about, is appreciated by the fish but in general he considers the fly patterns available as in need of improvement. His final dry fly is the Black Gnat. His own pattern to imitate the Gnat has a gold body and black cock hackle. Along with the gnats he includes midges and small yellow flies which crawl out of the grass, but is rather dismissive of such morsels. A fly with a yellow body and silvery dun hackle on a size 18 (000) hook is his suggested representation, but Heywood prefers larger flies. Local wisdom for smutting fish was a Pink Wickham or Golden Dun and from this Gerald Heywood evolved his dressing with the gold body.

With regard to wet fly patterns, he thought winged flies were out of place and much preferred to use Hackles. Speckled or mottled insects can usefully be represented by a hackled March Brown; Beetles by a Coch-y-Bonddhu or a similar coloured Palmer with silver or gold ribbing. David Foster's Whistling Plover is a good fly in coloured water, but grouse or partridge hackles are as effective as those of golden plover. Hackled Gold Ribbed Hare's Ear, or a yellow-bodied fly with gold rib and dun hackle are effective when terrestrials, like caterpillars, drop from trees and herbage. A favourite fly of Heywood's was the Honey Dun Bumble, with either orange or bright yellow floss used in its dressing. Silver and gold-bodied flies with dun or black hackles, such as the Winter Dun, were also used by Heywood. Whereas other anglers used the Red Tag, he preferred these flies dressed with yellow or orange. He must have fished in Yorkshire!

These wet fly patterns are tied on size 16 or 15 (0 or 1) hooks. He fished a dropper three and a half feet from the stretcher or point fly, the dropper flies being no larger, and often a size less, than the point. The list of patterns concludes with the observation that no more than a dozen patterns are needed to fish the Dove. The book includes notes on road travel in Cotton's time. Having read these, one wonders that anyone went anywhere! The finale is Cotton's poem, *The Angler's Ballad*. The seventh verse seems appropriate to conclude these notes of Gerald Heywood's fine book.

> The day's not too bright,
> And the wind hits us just right,
> And all nature does seem to invite us;
> We have all things at will
> For to second our skill
> As they all did conspire to delight us.

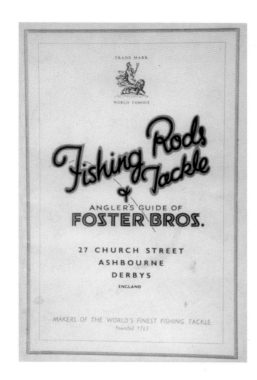

The cover of Foster Bros.
1964 catalogue. Wilfred L Foster
ran the business at this time

WILFRED LOUIS FOSTER 'WIELDER'

W L Foster was the last family member to be involved in Fosters of Ashbourne. In 1936 he took over the business of D & W H Foster from his father, William Henry Foster. He had worked in the firm since 1918, also writing two books: one in 1922, the other *Fishing Tackle Making and Repairing* in 1929. The section on repairing tackle was written by Richard Clapham. This book deals with tackle making, fly tying and the mayfly. There are pattern lists for the various months, some of which contain local specialities. Fly fishing is briefly discussed. Again Cotton's advice emerges. Keep low, fish fine and far off, where possible wade and cast upstream. Foster also writes about 'modern' lures. These include the Nailor and flies for sea trout and salmon.

FEBRUARY & MARCH

Red Fly or February Red	Light Bumble	Greenwell's Glory
Blue Dun	Cock Winged Dun	March Brown
Pale Olive	Gold Ribbed Hare's Ear	

APRIL

Needle Fly	Blue Upright	Sand Fly
Jenny Spinner	Yellow Dun of April	Red Spinner
Cow Dung	Grannom	

217

MAY

Coachman	Golden Earwig	Black Gnat
Olive Dun	Yellow Dun of May	Iron Blue
Willow Fly	Golden Dun Midge	Kill Devil Spider

JUNE

Turkey Brown	Red Palmer	Dark Mackerel
Alder	Little Dark Spinner	Midge
Black Midge	Pale Evening Dun	Little Chap

JULY

Ginger Quill	Red Ant	Red Spider
Blue Quill	Dotterel	Welshman's Button
Yellow Sally	Little Sky Blue	Orange Bumble
July Dun		

AUGUST

Whistler Fly	Wickham's Fancy	Sedge
Golden Dun	Orange Dun	Black Spider
Black Spinner	August Dun	Red Quill
Zulu		

SEPTEMBER

Whirling Blue Dun	Little Pale Blue	Red Quill
Blue Bottle	Pale Evening White	Cinnamon Fly
Dark Coachman		

OCTOBER

Grey Palmer	Esterhazy Dun	Winter Dun
October Dun	Coch y Bonddhu	Black Palmer
Hare's Ear		

W L Foster recommends Ronalds's patterns of the Green Drake and Grey Drake as Mayfly dressings. In his opinion both flies are better tied 'Buzz'. He also suggests using The Butcher – not the standard pattern but one of Foster's range of Mayflies, possibly developed from the patterns of George Butcher. In the 1964 catalogue issued by Fosters are listed 'New Hackled Floating Mays'. Two series are advertised, the 'New Imperial Series' comprising Queen, Emperor, Black Knight, Red King Prince and Baron. The second series comprises Butcher, Wet or Dry, Birdsgrove – after the water near Ashbourne, Spent Gnat and Little Gem. These flies were made by Fosters, the latter being illustrated in *The Scientific Angler*. On trout flies, Foster quotes '*...an interesting and unique fly was being wielded by a fellow angler... It consisted of an imitation beetle with two glass eyes...*' This is probably the Derby Beetle. If so, it found its way into the Foster portfolio in much the same way as the Red Caterpillar.

A series of seven 'Fosters Famous Nymphs' are illustrated, both in black and white and colour in the catalogue. They are simply named No 1 – No 7 and Mayfly Nymph. Brief descriptions taken from the catalogue photographs follow:

No 1   Bushy reddish peacock herl body; red bushy hackle; red head.

No 2   Black whisks; possible gold tag; short dark peacock herl body; black bushy hackle; black head.

No 3   White whisks; body red floss; peacock herl band; red floss; white wing over peacock herl third of body; white head.

No 4   Plump copper wire body; peacock herl wing.

No 5   Hackled creeper; Mayfly U E hook. Two peacock wing herl tails; bronze peacock herl body; G P Topping low over body; two red bead eyes.

No 6   Whisks – long partridge speckled herl; short peacock herl body; very bushy red hackle; black head.

No 7   Mayfly hook. Pheasant tail fibre whisks; yellow seal fur body; palmered brown hackle; body material picked out; peacock herl head.

The dressings are my observations and are not necessarily accurate. When and by whom they were devised is not known.

The following are flies from the Foster Catalogue, selected as being most obvious candidates for inclusion as Derbyshire specialities:

Cock Winged Dun (D Foster)	Kill Devil (Fosters)
Double Badger	Oakden's Claret
Honey Dun Bumble (D Foster)	White Witch
Furnace Bumble	Derby Beetle
Foster's Fancy (D Foster)	Foster's Nymphs
Dovedale (Foster Mayfly)	Upcher's Fancy

The Esterhazy Dun, mentioned earlier, was also listed by William Shipley.

Who Upcher was is unknown but intriguing. Was he local? Upcher's Fancy may be a grayling fly with its peacock herl body and red tip. Mention of the pattern is made in *The Incompleat Angler* by Robert D Deindorfer, an American tracing Izaak Walton's angling travels. He was recommended to use the fly on the Manifold and bought the pattern at Foster's Sporting Services in John Street, Ashbourne.

After W L Foster's death in 1968/69, his wife ran the business for several years, until about 1974. It was then sold and acquired its new name of Fosters Sporting Services. After some time this business, too, closed.

A NELSON BROMLEY

Nelson Bromley was born in Stafford in 1850. His father, a doctor, died young but the family appear to have been well provided for financially. Nelson began his angling career at the age of six, accompanied by a nurse. As he grew older, this was developed by uncles, Canon Bromley, William Bromley and Frederick Bakewell – all of them skilled anglers.

His first experiences of angling were on the River Trent at Walton near Stone. An influential aunt obtained permission for Nelson to fish the Dove below Ashbourne and Frederick Bakewell accompanied him to Shardlow. The Trent provided grayling, trout, perch, chub, dace, pike and barbel. He also writes of Bakewell losing a salmon near Cavendish Bridge at Shardlow. Nottingham style was the order of the day in the Trent but minnow spinning was much used too.

Nelson began fly fishing illicitly. He was given religious books to read on Sundays, as was often the case in strict Victorian homes. On this day he awaited the adults' siesta, stole from the house with his uncle's cane, some black thread and a roach hook. Having caught a bluebottle, he cast the fly into a trough used to store dace livebaits. A fish took and was caught, followed by a second. The fish were returned and a newly initiated fly fisher returned quietly to read his book about a bad little boy. Nelson considered this excellent sport; it was elemental fly fishing, a form of poaching and certainly involved a good deal of risk. It also taught him to keep out of sight of the fish. A second visit resulted in nothing because he showed himself.

It seems that one uncle was not so soundly asleep that day. A new fishing rod appeared soon after this event. From these early experiences he went on to fish throughout Britain, Belgium, France and Switzerland, though the Derwent, Wye and Dove feature greatly in his writings. Monsal Dale appears to have been a particular favourite haunt.

Nelson's visits to the Dove near Ashbourne with a friend, Walter Holland, were spent on a farm. Here, he was fortunate enough to be tutored by David Foster in the use of the dry fly. The boys spent time, both in the Church Street shop and on the river with him. Foster taught them to whip the fly dry, when sunk fly would not catch fish. From these days, Bromley became adept with both dry and sunk fly and adopted the style of Francis Francis:

'The judicious and perfect application of dry, wet and mid water fly fishing stamps the finished fly fisher with the hallmark of efficiency' (A Book on Angling)

Rods of ten and a half feet were preferred by Bromley; he thought they gave greater reach and control. His reel was a Nottingham style reel modified for him by Hardys. Line and gut were simply the best. He admits to being a wanton spendthrift on these items, never using less than 4x gut. He graduated from 'jack in a box' fly cases to simple tins in which to store flies. A telescopic cane rimmed net, combined creel and tackle bag and amadou to dry his flies completed his 'outfit'. Mackintoshes were an anathema to him, preferring to be wetted by clean rain rather than sweat! One final item – all anglers are tormented by insects from time to time – having tried various concoctions to prevent insect strike he used a veil. Nelson's rule with lunch – take nothing to carry home. What he did with the greaseproof paper his sandwiches were wrapped in is not recorded.

The River Wye in Monsal Dale and Bakewell were favourite places to fish for Nelson

A Nelson Bromley, angler, artist and
author of *A Fly Fisher's Reflections 1860 - 1930*

A Nelson Bromley with
R B Marston and their wives in Monsal Dale

Bromley. Here he practised, when applicable, upstream dry fly, upstream soft hackled wet fly and also a team of three across and down. He particularly seems to have enjoyed working the bob fly by the latter method. This was fixed a mere two feet from the fly line to enable it to be worked by the rod. He praises Mr F H Heald, the clerk to the Trent Fishery Board, as being a master of this method.

In Bakewell, Nelson fished for rainbows and browns while staying at the Rutland. He does not seem to have great affection for the former species, though obviously enjoying them at table. Dry fly was the order of the day and a great exponent in Bromley's time being a Mr Littlewood, then well known in Bakewell.

Monsal Dale provided enormous enjoyment for many years. Here he fished with R B Marston, caught trout and indulged his interest of watercolour painting. The manager Mr B T Dickinson and waterkeeper Raymond Lupton were advised and congratulated on the excellence of the water and stock. Observation led to a realisation of the importance of underwater trout food. He had noticed a loss of dry fly hatches caused by, in his opinion, rain washings from tarred roads. Nevertheless the fish, though not surface feeding, were in good condition and obviously obtaining good nourishment from subsurface fauna. In the flats he fished a Loch Leven cast of three flies, point Mallard and Red, middle dropper Teal and Green or Wooodcock and Yellow, bobfly always a Butcher. It may not be too popular today.

Along with the advice from David Foster, Bromley leaned toward the style of W C Stewart, author of *The Practical Angler* (1857). The use of too many flies complicates the process of angling; better to depend on a few well-tried patterns. Autopsies often contradict the exact colour or shade idea. A good mixture of aquatic and terrestrial life is quite common in a trout's intestines. Bromley considered faith in the fly pattern to be of great importance and his considerable experience led him to a fly box of a dozen or so. Dry flies were carried in a tin box:

Olive Dun (two shades), G R H E, Iron Blue, Red Quill, Wickham, Little Marryat, Coachman.

All these patterns were dressed on oo (17) hooks.

The following wet flies to gut were carried:

Orange Bumble, Stewart's Black Spider, Tups Indispensible, Greenwell's Glory, all to size oo (17) Black Alder No 1 or 2 (15 - 14).

In addition the Loch Leven cast was used at Monsal Dam.

After mayfly time the Black Spider of Stewart is recommended, as is the Little Chap of Aldam and Foster. Black gnat hatches occupied Bromley from his angling experiences on the River Greet in Nottinghamshire. He repeats Aldam's account of the Tailey Tail and its efficiency in such hatches. However, Bromley used a small Black Alder fished upstream in such conditions to great effect.

Bromley thought the grayling of the Dove better than those of the Wye. He remarks that the grayling at Bakewell seem to be disappearing – perhaps being driven out by the rainbows. It would appear that the rainbows have not yet succeeded. He does not advocate the introduction of grayling to trout waters, but where the two species are compatible, all is well and good. The Derwent grayling were, in his opinion, difficult on fly because of the leaves, and he preferred trotting with a roach rod or in the Yorkshire style.

A Nelson Bromley became an architect working in Nottingham. He was also an accomplished watercolour artist as his bookplates bear witness. In 1930 he published at the age of eighty *A Fly Fisher's Reflections 1860 – 1930*. His was a remarkable angling lifetime. He was a pupil of David Foster, friend of R B Marston, a skilled fisherman and author of a fascinating book.

ROGER WOOLLEY

Most of Roger Woolley's life was spent close to the River Dove. He was born in Tutbury in 1877. From childhood he showed considerable interest in angling and natural history, particularly aquatic entomology. He was probably encouraged in his interests by his father, it is a great advantage to be a child of parents who understand what others consider to be a misspent youth! Roger's early working days were spent locally in Tutbury where he was employed as a 'general domestic servant', probably on an estate or farm. No doubt he also spent time on the banks of the Dove, making his observations and fishing. At nineteen he went into gentleman's service in County Fermanagh with the Chetwynds. Whilst in this employ, he worked with an estate keeper who taught him much about fly dressing. In addition he was able to fish new and prolific waters. Woolley also studied, read and was taught much about natural flies and angling by his mentor.

In *Famous Flies and Their Originators*, Donald Overfield says that Woolley probably learned to be a hairdresser whilst in Ireland. When he returned to Derbyshire after two years away, he set up as a hairdresser and fly dresser in Hatton, a little distance from his birthplace. The two occupations of hairdresser and fly dresser often seem to be worked together. Overfield comments on this; and the hairdresser in many small Scottish towns is often the fishing tackle dealer and fly dresser today.

Woolley made good use of his early observations and studies in childhood. His flies were dressed without the use of a vice, to imitate natural insects of which he had first hand knowledge. He considered colour and translucence as being vital in a dressing and also favoured the Derbyshire style of lightly dressed flies. Perhaps this too was a result of personal observation, as many Irish patterns, which he would have tied during his training, are quite heavily dressed. He collected insects and continued to study them. His interest led to regular correspondence with G E M Skues, who gave particular mention to Roger Woolley in *Nymph Fishing for Chalk Stream Trout* (1939).

He served in the R A M C during the First World War, spending time in Egypt, then

Roger Woolley of Hatton
preparing to fish the Dove.

224

returning to Hatton to continue his work as a flydresser. Woolley's fly dressings and techniques are set down in his book *Modern Trout Fly Dressing*, which was published in 1932. This was the result of a series of articles he wrote for *Fishing Gazette*. In the book are clear details on the methods he used to dress his flies, along with several hundred patterns, many of which Woolley devised. In 1938 *Fly-Fisher's Flies* was published. This is an introduction to entomology and aquatic flies encountered by anglers.

Roger Woolley was considered an expert grayling angler and several angling authorities deferred to him when discussing the species. In his book *Grayling Fishing* (1939), W Carter Platts describes how he asked Roger Woolley for his opinions on gut shy grayling and appropriate patterns for the Derbyshire rivers. The advice offered regarding the former was to fish wet or dry downstream as the grayling is so sharp sighted. This method avoids the cast being seen by a taking fish. Woolley also gave an appropriate list of fly patterns as requested.

A book by Richard Lake, entitled *Grayling*, was first published in 1942, with a second edition in 1946. Four chapters of this book were written by Roger Woolley. These included notes on bait fishing, and wet and dry grayling flies. The views and advice summarised below are of considerable interest.

The use of dry fly begins in August as, before this time, the fish will not be in peak condition and few will be rising. September and October are the best months for dry fly sport though this extends into any warm November days. August flies are likely to be Olive Duns, Blue Winged Olive Duns and their spinners, along with Pale Watery Duns on some waters.

As the weather hardens, where they occur, Iron Blue Duns appear. During September and October Needle flies and Willow flies are taken and the appropriate artificials are useful. Black Gnats fly in periods of warmer weather. Artificials, which represent these flies, should be carried along with some dressings of Long Legged Gnats.

Fancy patterns are attractive to grayling on occasion, especially those with bright flashy elements. Should there be no hatch these will often interest the fish. Woolley advises small sizes 18 (000) for warm weather, increasing the size for October and November. Patterns include Grayling Steel Blue, Green Insect, Tommy's Favourite, Bradshaw's Fancy, Red Tag and Witch fished dry. On foggy days in October and November a good sized dry Bumble catches fish. Woolley considered that grayling seemed to prefer a dry fly, low in the surface so the flies need not be heavily hackled.

The grayling's underwater diet consists of nymphs, larvae and pupae along with dead and dying flies drowned in rough water. Terrestrials appear from time to time and in many waters shrimps are present.

The flybox should contain nymphs of Olives, Blue Winged Olives and Pale Wateries along with a selection of lightly dressed hackle flies. Waterhen Bloa, Greenwell Spider, Dark Watchet, Brown Owl, Olive Bloa, Dark Needle, Poult Bloa and Blue Hawk are good dressings. Grayling are partial to red tags and tinsel wrapped bodies on wet flies.

On days with no hatch, Roger Woolley states that he would always begin with a

Grayling Steel Blue and a Grayling Witch on his cast. Along with these, other good fancy patterns are Mackenzie Fly, White Witch, Tommy's Favourite, Light Bumble, Claret Bumble, Brunton's Fancy, Red and Silver Badger.

On rivers with a dark bed, Woolley always favoured his Grayling Steel Blue, whereas on chalk streams, he considered a lighter fly like the White Witch to be more successful. He often relied on fancy patterns when fishing dry fly for grayling, but when olives or other duns showed, they would be offered the appropriate artificial.

Woolley has the reputation of being very keen on the various Bumbles for use with grayling. His dressings differ in style from those of Foster, by using a silk body with herl rib. The Steel Blue, a fly for which Woolley claims the credit, was his favourite trout and grayling pattern fished wet.

In his extensive fly dressing list, Roger Woolley offers several Badger patterns. He is famed for the use of the Double Badger and this is widely fished on Derbyshire waters to this day. Strangely, it does not appear named as such in his book *Modern Trout Fly Dressing* but is almost certainly the pattern he calls the 'Mackenzie Fly' in his writings for *The Grayling*.

Woolley had a huge reputation as an angler and fly dresser. He pursued his craft for some sixty years and orders were so large that his four daughters were trained to dress flies. In later years he employed three ladies as fly dressers, all of whom gave many years of service. All the products of their work were personally inspected by Roger in order to maintain the high reputation he had gained. One of the dressers, Miss Rosa Smith, eventually took over the business after Woolley's death, re-establishing it across the River Dove in Bridge Street, Tutbury.

To make a choice of Woolley's flies, for inclusion in this brief summary of his activities, is difficult. However, the following are his nominated grayling flies for Derbyshire rivers as given to W Carter Platts:

Grayling Witch, White Witch, Red Tag, Red Badger, Bradshaw's Fancy, Needle Fly, Silver Twist, Rough Bumble, Grayling Steel Blue, Tommy's Favourite, Grey Palmer, Blue Badger, Willow Fly, Waterhen Quill, Mulberry Bumble and Silver Badger.

Half of these patterns are palmered, perhaps no coincidence from the choice of one reputed to hold Bumbles in high regard.

Such are the numbers of Roger Woolley's dressings that it would be impractical to include them all. A selection of his own designated Derbyshire patterns and those reputed to be his favourites are listed.

ROGER'S FANCY

Hook: Sizes 000 – 2 (17 – 14)
Body: Pale blue heron herl, ribbed fine flat silver with red floss tag at head & tail.
Hackle: Pale blue hen.
A favourite grayling pattern of Roger Woolley dressed by him early in his career

WITCHES

A series of flies like the Badgers, always associated with Woolley. A fly often on his cast at the beginning of a day was the Grayling Witch.

GRAYLING WITCH

Hook:	Sizes 000 – 1	(18 – 15)
Body:	Green peacock herl, ribbed flat silver.	
Tag:	Red floss.	
Hackle:	Pale or medium blue dun.	

The hackle is sometimes palmered by some dressers.

WHITE WITCH

Hook:	Sizes 00 – 3	(17 – 12)
Body:	Green peacock herl, silver tipped and ribbed silver wire.	
Tag:	Red floss.	
Hackle:	White cock from shoulder to tail.	

The White Witch is another grayling fly, probably originated by Roger Woolley and one which he recommended to W Carter Platts for Derbyshire Grayling.

RED TAG

Hook:	Sizes 00 – 1	(17 – 15)
Body:	Bronze peacock herl with a tip of gold or silver under the tag.	
Tag:	Red floss.	
Hackle:	Red cock.	

BRADSHAW'S FANCY

Hook:	Sizes 00 – 1	(17 – 15)
Body:	Bronze peacock herl, with tag of red floss at head and tail.	
Hackle:	From Norwegian crow.	

H Bradshaw was a Yorkshire man and contemporary of T E Pritt. Evidently Roger Woolley was sufficiently impressed to include this grayling pattern in his Derbyshire list. Like other grayling patterns it is probably a beetle representation.

GREY PALMER

Hook:	Sizes 0 – 2	(16 – 14)
Body:	Black floss ribbed silver wire.	
Hackle:	Badger cock from shoulder to tail.	

As with David Foster, this fly is included with Bumbles in Woolley's lists.

NEEDLE FLY

Body:	Orange silk.
Hackle:	Small dark feather from outside of a brown owl's wing.
Head:	A turn of bronze peacock herl.

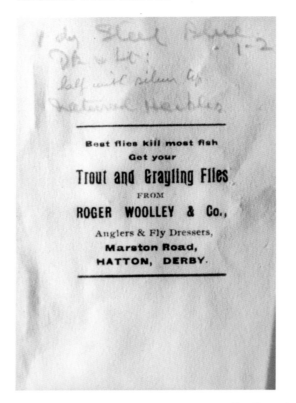

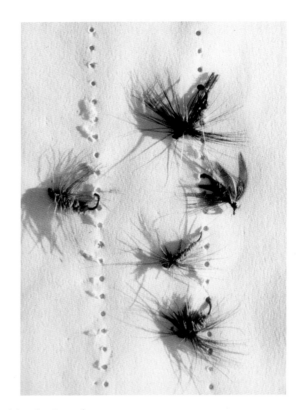

Roger Woolley fly packet with selection of patterns

WILLOW FLY

There are several patterns for this fly. The hackled dressings are:

Body: (1) Peacock quill from the eye, dyed pale orange.

             (2) Orange tying silk showing well through a dubbing of mole fur.

Hackle: Medium grizzled blue dun cock.

WATERHEN QUILL

Hook: Sizes 0 – 1   (16 – 15)

Body: Olive dyed peacock quill from the eye.

Hackle: Shiny feather from under a waterhen wing.

SILVER TWIST

Hook: Sizes 0 – 2   (16 – 14)

Body: Blue fur, ribbed silver twist.

Hackle: Medium blue dun hen from shoulder to tail.

TOMMY'S FAVOURITE or TOMMY'S FANCY

Hook:	Sizes 00 – 1 (17 – 15)
Body:	Quill from a yellow blue macaw tail feather, the yellow to show as body, the blue flue as a rib.
Tag:	Red floss, tip of silver tinsel under tag.
Hackle:	Medium blue hen.

This pattern was tied for and dedicated to a friend of Roger Woolley's, Major T H Oakden of Rolleston-on-Dove. With this pattern and the White Witch, the two anglers took 103 grayling in a day from the Okeover Club stretch of the Dove at the invitation of the then waterkeeper Gregor Mackenzie. The fly was also popular on the Manifold in the 1930s, another river fished by both men.

EARLY OLIVE DUN – Hackled Wet Patterns for Midland & Welsh Waters

1.	*Body:*	Blue fur from rabbit, mole or water rat according to shade required, unribbed or ribbed with yellow tying silk or silver wire.
	Hackle and whisks:	Dark or medium blue dun hens.
2.	*Body:*	Dark peacock quill from the stem of feather, dyed yellow, or olive waxed tying silk, ribbed gold wire.
	Hackle and whisks:	Medium blue dun hens.
3.	Rough Olive	
	Body:	Heron's herl, dyed olive, ribbed gold wire.
	Hackle and whisks:	Dark blue dun hen's.

The Rough Olive is often styled a Derbyshire fly but few writers include a dressing in their lists. It was much used by Roger Woolley and this may have been the source of its reputation.

Woolley's second book *The Fly Fisher's Flies*, published in 1938, is a concise manual with a common sense view of insect identification. The complexities of this often dissuade anglers from learning to recognise the natural fly and Woolley recognised their reticence. He recorded and illustrated the natural flies without resort to Latin names and complex drawings '...I hope to avoid all the Greek & Latin names..., and keep these notes just as a talk from one fly fisher to another, calling a March Brown a March Brown...'. In this he succeeded admirably. G E M Skues, in one of his later books, applauded Roger Woolley's knowledge of entomology – self taught – and his skill as an imitative fly dresser.

Importance is given to fly identification because it gives an angler an edge when brief hatches of fly occur. If a decision as to the appropriate pattern to be used can be made accurately, it may make the difference between catching fish or not. It also enhances the pleasure of time spent at the waterside if there is understanding of natural events unfolding over days and the season.

All the insect groups are discussed; upwings, sedges, stoneflies and terrestrials, with clear identification notes and their local names. Each group has its own chapter with stylised sketches of the important species.

Roger Woolley's concluding chapter consists of advice as to which artificial flies to try when various naturals are on the water. Included with this are suggestions for the dressing materials used on some of the artificial patterns. A summary of his list follows.

SPRING OLIVE DUN   Blue Dun; Dark Greenwell; Rough Olive; Spring Hare's Ear; Waterhen Bloa. These may be used hackled or winged, wet or dry.
MARCH BROWN   Hackled Woodcock and Hare's Ear.
IRON BLUE DUN   Dark Watchet; Infallible; Iron Blue; Snipe and Purple.
DARK OLIVE DUN   Dark Olive Dun; Greenwell's Glory; Snipe and Yellow; Waterhen Bloa (small).
MEDIUM OLIVE DUN   Gold Ribbed Hare's Ear; Greenwell's Glory; Medium Olive Dun; Olive Bloa; Olive Upright.
ALDER FLY   Tie with brown dun gamecock hackle. Good in a mayfly rise.
MAYFLY   Hackled patterns. Spent Drake; Black Drake.
BLUE WINGED OLIVE   Blue Winged Olive Dun; Hackled Blue Winged Olive; Poult Bloa.
PALE WATERY DUN   Autumn Dun; Ginger Quill; Little Marryat.
EARLY BROWN   Winter Brown; Woodcock and Orange.
WILLOW FLY   Willow Fly; Brown Owl; Orange Partridge.
NEEDLE FLY   Dark Needle; Spanish Needle.

Imitations of Turkey Dun, Claret Dun, Yellow May Dun, July Dun, August Dun and various sedges.
Winged or hackled February Red, Stonefly, Yellow Sally.

Many of Roger Woolley's dressings have become standards and are in constant use, nowhere more so than on the rivers of Derbyshire and Staffordshire. He died in 1959 at the age of 82 in Tutbury.

JOHN NEVILLE

John Neville has unique experience of Derbyshire waters. He has fished practically every pool on all the county's rivers along with many in Staffordshire. He has in the past set up and run his own small trout fishery, also being involved in a larger commercial complex. He has instructed both casting and fly dressing classes over many years. Since 1946 John has been a very regular visitor to Ladybower, and must know the water as well as any and

John Neville stalking trout on the river Dove

better than most. His angling experience includes a huge amount of coarse fishing throughout the British Isles along with game fishing in Scotland.

For a period of time he devoted himself to angling on an almost daily basis and systematically developed his skills by constant practice, planning and innovation. The fish he has caught are legion but, from his writing, he is never happier than fishing Ladybower or stalking trout in a small north Derbyshire river.

His writing, too, is comprehensive and goes back decades. He has produced a large portfolio of articles in newspapers and magazines, which are and have been, essential and entertaining reading for thousands of anglers. He has recently retired as the Derbyshire correspondent for *Trout and Salmon* magazine. His book *Trials and Triumphs of an Angler*, published in 1991, records an angling life rich in anecdote and watercraft. John is a modest and courteous man who has given a great deal of pleasure to very many people. His contribution to this current project has been of enormous value.

His angling philosophy is simple and clear. When fishing rivers, always wear drab clothes and a brimmed hat. Keep low, on all fours if necessary, be it on the bank or in the water. Fish upstream and control drag as far as possible. The fish is most likely to take the fly on the first cast so ensure this is well made. Move from pool to pool. Don't constantly target one fish or shoal. Wild fish are usually hungry and on the look out for food. In these circumstances the fly pattern is not too important but the size and colour may well be. Any fly on the water should be matched in these respects.

In the early season up to Mayfly time, the flies fished can be quite large, size twelve or even ten. After the Mayfly, size should diminish. A high floating dry fly is easily seen by the angler, often important in rough or streamy water. A bushy hackle of several turns makes the fly float well in these conditions.

For much river work, a nine-foot rod with a five or six line is a good set up. Preferably the line should be dark or drab in colour and carry a single fly. Flash is prevented by rubbing the rod down or giving it a coat of matt varnish. While not concerned about anglers, grayling particularly can be very tackle shy.

On dull days use dark coloured flies, on bright days lighter or whiteish flies. Many hatches take place later in the day as conditions warm up and light improves, so aim to be at the waterside from lunchtime onward.

Flies recommended by John Neville for Derbyshire and Staffordshire waters are as follows. Some of the dressings vary against standard patterns.

Early Season: *Black Gnat; William's Favourite; Cotton's Black Fly.*
Dry Flies: *Grey Duster; Double Badger; Bumbles; Lunn's Spent Gnat; Sedges;*
                Ward's Aphid; Cock Winged Dun; Sturdy's Fancy.
Wet Flies: *Butcher with wing and tail clipped short.*

For smutting fish, any very small offering sized 18 – 20.

Whenever angling is discussed, John Neville is able to entertain and enlighten. His stories are the result of several angling lifetimes packed into one, his generosity and humour endless.

A K BRIDGETT

Tony Bridgett is a well-known Staffordshire angler who, many years ago, was a prime mover in the foundation of the Leek and District Fly Fishing Association. Since the club's inception in 1972 he has served as Secretary for thirty two years and is now President. In addition, he is working tirelessly to keep open the Izaak Walton Cottage Museum at Shallowford near Stone. Also an active member of the Grayling Society, Tony has made radio broadcasts and features in a video recently released on Derbyshire Fly Fishing. He is an expert on the rivers of Derbyshire and Staffordshire and has unrivalled experience of angling on the Dove, Hamps and Churnet.

He is of the opinion that fly life on the Dove is diminishing and that this is having the effect of changing fly patterns in use to more fancy flies and the need for smaller sizes.

A K Bridgett, Leek and District Fly Fishing Association

233

Eighteen, twenty and twenty twos are a commonplace requirement for success. This is no mere whim. Tony is involved with the Natural History Museum in London in running courses at Ilam Hall and in Dovedale on the natural fly life of the Dove. From the practical work he has done all the anticipated species of fly are present, but not in the numbers expected. A benefit to the river from the courses has been the reintroduction of mayfly nymphs to Beresford Dale, where a pollution incident involving sheep dip had a devastating effect.

Tony has been more than generous in the information and encouragement he has provided for this project. His intimate knowledge of people and places on both the Dove and Manifold has been of great value.

Tony's favourite fly patterns for Staffordshire and Derbyshire rivers are listed below.

Wet Flies: *Silver Partridge; Partridge and Orange; Partridge and Red.*
Dry Flies: *Heron Herl Olive; Elk Hair Sedge; Baetis Emerger; Hawthorn Fly; Iron Blue Dun; Cock Wing Dun.*
Mayfly: *Butcher; Shadow Mayfly.*

Steve Trigg, angler and innovative flydresser, with more than thirty years experience on Derbyshire and Staffordshire waters.

234

STEVE TRIGG

Steve Trigg has fished on the Derbyshire rivers for over thirty years. Waters of which he has experience are the Derwent from Calver to Whatstandwell, and the Dove from Ashbourne to Tutbury, along with the rivers Ecclesbourne, Noe and Wye.

When asked for his selection of patterns for a 'Derbyshire Flybox' he found some difficulty but nominated six surface patterns and six subsurface, expressing the view that these are his current patterns and the collection may well alter in the future. Certainly, some were not in his box a few years ago.

Steve's choice of patterns, along with his comments, follows:

Grey Duster   This is the classic river fly and I cannot imagine my fly box without it but new contenders are now slowly pushing it from the number one slot. A good fly when midges and gnats are hatching.

Olive Paradun Style   A new type of fly to my box, it can be fished as a hatching dun or a returning spinner.

F Fly   Another newish fly to my box. Wonderful fly to represent emerging midges and gnats.

Hare's Face Emerger   My number one dry fly over the last few years. This fly is tied in Klinkhamen style with a hare's face body and the badger parachute hackle. This fly is a great emerger pattern for natural flies from midges up to sedges.

Rough Water Dry   When I am fishing the fast water glides I need a fly that is going to stay on the surface and ride the waves. This is my fly for that situation. Small sizes are ideal for sedge patterns, large sizes for mayflies.

Hatching Mayfly   I have chose this hatching emerging pattern because it has been my most productive over the last few seasons.

Red Tag   This fly has always been a favourite of mine. Since I added the Holographic tag and rib to the fly it has become a 'must have' grayling fly.

William's Favourite   My first choice of dropper fly to use when any black midges or gnats are hatching.

Partridge and Yellow   My favourite dropper fly during the spring and summer months when Pale or Light Olives are on the water.

Pheasant Tail Nymph   The all round river nymph for when fish are taking the nymphs of any upwinged olive flies.

Olive and Pearl Caddis   This is one of many colour combinations I carry, this being the one in which I have most confidence.

Gold Headed Hare's Face Bug   My number one grayling fly at the moment.

Steve Woolley, rodmaker, in
his Midland Works premises.

Tim Thorpe, flydresser, of
Derbyshire trout Flies, Hatton.

STEVE WOOLLEY

Steve Woolley is a rod maker and tackle dealer in Ashbourne. He began work with Foster Bros in their Church Street premises in 1973 as a Saturday boy, continuing in this role after Fosters sold the business. In 1976, Steve was employed by the new owners full time in their shop and as a rod maker. The business became Foster's Sporting Services and moved to St John's Street in Ashbourne. Steve remained with the firm until 1984.

In 1989, he opened up his own business as a rodmaker and tackle dealer. The premises are now at Midland Works, in the building originally used by Foster Bros as their workshop, being at the rear of 27 Church Street. Steve specialises in building, repairing and renovating split cane rods alongside running a comprehensive tackle shop.

Steve's Woolley's choice of flies for a 'Derbyshire Flybox,' influenced by his own considerable experience of local rivers and that of his clients, is as follows:

Dry Pheasant tail	*Adams*	*Steel Blue*
Black Ant	*Grey Wulff*	*Red Derby Beetle*
Hawthorn	*Dry G R H E*	*Gold Head G R H E*
Black Gnat	*Double Badger*	*Professor*
Mayfly		

TIM THORPE

Tim Thorpe is a professional fly dresser. He runs his business, Derbyshire Fishing Flies, at Hatton alongside the River Dove. Years ago another man dressed flies in Hatton. His name was Roger Woolley.

Tim established his business in 1990, having run night school classes on fly dressing over a period of sixteen years for the local authority. He was introduced to fishing by his father when about six years old.

Despite a diagnosis of Dermatomyositis in childhood, he developed his interest in fishing, and in the late 1960s was introduced to trout angling by John Neville, who also taught Tim to dress flies. Tim has contributed to the flyboxes in this present work and also dressed the flies illustrated under 'Derbyshire and Staffordshire Patterns'.

His choice of flies for the 'Flybox' consists of:

Gold Ribbed Hare's Ear Nymph	*Adams Irresistible*	*Steel Blue*
also a Goldhead version	*Double Badger*	*John Storey*
Shrimp	*Iron Blue Dun*	*Greenwell's Glory*
Sawyer Pheasant Tail	*Blue Winged Olive*	*Lunn's Particular*

PETER ARFIELD

Peter Arfield was brought up in the small town of Dronfield, mid way between the South Yorkshire city of Sheffield and the outskirts of Chesterfield. Early interest in fishing was

Peter Arfield, of The Derwent Fly Fishing School
and Fly Fishing Shop, Bakewell.

confined to the brooks in the valley bottom, catching small bullheads and loach by hand to take home in a jam jar and say: 'Look what I caught', a habit he continues to battle with to this day.

Having left school and being plunged into the electrical contracting industry, amid the embers of the old Sheffield steel industry, he came into contact with some 'old school' coarse fishing workmates who dragged him along to taste the joys of fishing the Lincolnshire Witham in December. There he eventually made contact with a rod caught roach, illuminated by the setting rays of the sun on a bitterly cold day. Something awoke in that moment which has stuck lifelong. Many experiences on the Yorkshire rivers in pursuit of barbel in the company of some really good friends, crammed into the back of whatever vehicle was running at the time, did not diminish an increasing appetite for fly fishing on some day ticket beats and club waters of the Derwent, Dove and Wye. Many hours were spent fishing the small streams on the edges of the Peak District and the outskirts of Sheffield. These streams, which once powered the machines of the Industrial Revolution, provided angling for tiny but perfect trout whose ancestors were sought by the 'prentice boys' of the wire mills and grinding works, now long gone. The tools of the trade, broken wheels and the like, provide some shelter from winter floods for fish on the river beds.

Influences included the *Rod and Line* works of Arthur Ransome, Bernard Venables's *Mr Crabtree*, and Brian Clarke's *The Pursuit of Stillwater Trout* (1975). The well-regarded *Angling* magazine also played a part, featuring authors such as Dick Walker and Arthur Cove.

During the 1980s Peter, part time cavern guide and itinerant thespian, was spending a large proportion of his time on the Derbyshire rivers and it was on the banks of the Dove that a pal of his, Chris Lee, hatched the idea of a tackle shop in the market town of Bakewell. Peter suggested the name of Piscatoria and a few weeks later, Chris met Peter leading a party out of one of the old lead mines of Derbyshire and asked him to manage the new shop.

All sorts of interesting adventures ensued, but by 1993, Peter had left the tackle trade, and encouraged by some existing members, Vic Knight, Lou Noble, John Hatherall and his new wife, took the APGAI examination and began passing on some of the skills he himself had scrounged from the many talented anglers he had come into contact with over the past years.

In 1997 Peter came back into the tackle trade as manager of the old shop, now renamed the Bakewell Fly Fishing Shop, and took on ownership in the spring of 2005.

CHAPTER FIVE

WATERKEEPERS AND TACKLE MAKERS

> Your rods with tops two,
> For the same will not do
> If your manner of angling you vary
> And full well you may think
> If you troll with a pink
> One too weak will apt to miscarry.

The Angler's Ballad *Charles Cotton*

The men and women who watch the rivers and make good fishing tackle were, and are, of great importance to anglers. Often in the past their work was done on a part time or seasonal basis, run alongside other employment. Their experience and contact with the rivers ensured they were prime sources of information and advice. Most were expert anglers themselves, well able to help others in their search for good sport. Most of the authors mentioned have named those to seek out for advice when fishing on the streams of the Peak.

Some of the waterkeepers had their own fly patterns or specialities. Unfortunately many of these flies have never been recorded. Others such as Moss's Cock Winged Dun, Fosbrooke's Golden Earwig and Foster's Honey Dun Bumble were successful enough to accrue fame. They found their way into reference books or at least became standard patterns on local waters. The man Edward Marston describes meeting at Ilam in *Dovedale Revisited* offered him flies certain to catch fish, though at a price.

The different styles of angling each had their season in past centuries. Mayfly time was the occasion to dap live flies and after the mayfly, minnow or upstream worm fishing was common. At other times of the year blue bottles, craneflies and alders were used to dap and dibble. Creepers or stonefly nymphs were caught and used as bait along with caddis on many upland rivers.

All of these baits had to be captured and stored; they are delicate creatures and need appropriate care and housing. W H Aldam, in his editorial notes, goes to much trouble to describe a container suitable for nymphs and flies and the means of handling them. An example of this, also quoted by others, lays great stress on handling flies with dry fingers, otherwise they sink rapidly when used.

Not too many anglers would have had time or inclination to be grubbing about in river beds after mayfly nymphs, caddises and stonefly 'creepers'. Minnows and worms may have been simpler but all needed a watchful eye regarding their condition. Waterkeepers and tackle makers would be able to provide the bait as a part of their day to day activity and have a stock to hand.

The maintenance of good angling water requires knowledge, skill, keen observation and a great deal of hard physical work; hours kept are run by seasons not the clock. Building and repairing weirs, cutting weed and clearing flood detritus are essential works which cannot be left for another day. As with all stock rearing, breeding and growing of fish is a skilled process. Encouraging appropriate wildlife and insects by providing suitable habitat on and by the sides of the rivers is essential.

Modern tackle has developed from the experience and innovation of those who made, repaired and modified equipment in the past. Once the rivers of the Peak were fished by men with rods of eighteen feet, horsehair lines and massive biceps. A tackle maker of even a hundred years ago would be able, and expected, to make or repair practically any item of tackle. Older family members or wives often dressed flies or made up various terminal tackles.

To the present day the Derwent and Dove have had more than their share of such talented and dedicated people. Waterkeeping was often a family profession. Eatons at Matlock, Hensburghs at Bakewell, Jones' at Chatsworth and Olivers' on the Dove all gave decades of service on the rivers, and such continuity of training and care resulted in the quality waters that anglers have enjoyed for over three hundred years.

JOHN EDWARD FOSBROOKE

John Fosbrooke was born in Keyworth in about 1823, and in his early life moved to Hartington on the Derbyshire/Staffordshire border. The 1901 census records him as a retired grocer and a local directory of 1887 as a shopkeeper. This was probably his profession for much of his life.

He was a distributor of fishing licences for the Trout Conservancy in 1904 and probably so for a long time previously. He acted as waterkeeper for Sir Vauncey Crewe on the upper Dove and Manifold. If not also acting for Sir Thomas Wardle, Fosbrooke certainly knew him and the two men fished together. Between them, Crewe and Wardle controlled much of the Dove and Manifold fishing rights.

W M Gallichan reports Sir Thomas Wardle and John Fosbrooke as fishing wet fly by preference and that they were able to hold their own against any of the dry fly men on the local rivers. Fosbrooke had many years of experience on both rivers. Seasonal weather did not deter him '...*pulling out grayling hand over hand whilst standing nearly up to his knees in snow...*. Visitors to the Dove and Manifold were advised to contact him for instruction and flies. '...*he ties quaint flies and killing patterns much resembling the insect as it emerges from the pupa*'.

The upper Dove was good water. Fosbrooke remarks about the water at Pilsbury '...the fish are about the best fed on the Dove...' there being much bottom food, '*harbourage*' and mayfly present.

Mayfly on the Manifold are credited to Fosbrooke. He allegedly took mayfly nymphs from the Dove and sowed the other river with them. They were supposedly transported in a milk churn – a very suitable receptacle. However ecologically unsound this may have been, it appears to have established a regular annual hatch on the Manifold. The Green Drake appeared regularly. Fly dressing was another of Fosbrooke's skills, and he tied

John E Fosbrooke fishing the Dove. He was probably the
originator of the Golden Earwig and is credited with sowing the Manifold
with mayfly larvae, thereby establishing a mayfly population on the river.

specialities which Gallichan does not identify, but the use of Fosbrooke's Golden Earwig is strongly advised after a spate. The fly was dubbed a great general pattern for the upper Dove and Manifold when fishing for trout, and especially grayling.

This dressing was given by Tony Bridgett, President of Leek and District Fly Fishing Association.

GOLDEN EARWIG
Hook: 10 – 14
Body: Gold Tinsel
Hackle: Cock hackle dyed blood red – Palmered or a few turns at the eye.

This dressing is that of Roger Woolley but not acknowledged to Fosbrooke:

Hook: 1 – 3 (15 – 12)
Body: Peacock herl, ribbed gold wire.
Hackle: Bright hackle that looks claret colour when looked down upon but when held to the light is a fiery red. Hackled shoulder to tail.

Also recommended is the Iron Blue Dun on a cold day, dressed by 'Fosbrooke of Hartington'. Fosbrooke is known to have used Bumbles, and the Golden Earwig is of a Bumble style. His other 'specialities' may well have been variations of Blue Dun, Cock Winged Dun, Alder and small hackles. Geoffrey Bucknall in *The Bright Stream of Memory* (1997) records the Golden Earwig dressing being published in Fishing Gazette and attributed to John Fosbrooke of Hartington. '*The pattern was said to be a prodigious killer of trout and grayling in the nineteenth century*'.

Writing in *Fishing in Derbyshire and Around*, Walter Gallichan describes Fosbrooke as a 'veteran' who had fished Derbyshire waters for many years. A photograph in *Dovedale Revisited* by The Amateur Angler (Edward Marston) shows Fosbrooke fishing in Wolfscote Dale. He sports a bowler hat, jacket and wading stockings, also a rather large creel. His rod appears to be about nine feet long. Lying on the bank is a circular landing net with a handle of about five and a half feet.

He fished until late in life. When, eventually, he went blind, he still fished the upper Dove with the help of friends – a very determined angler indeed! He died in the early years of the twentieth century.

ERNEST LOCK

Ernest was the son of John Lock of Andover, Hampshire. He was born in Winchester around 1871 and ultimately became a gamekeeper. His father John was a keeper on the River Itchen and well-known in angling circles.

Ernest obtained a job as a keeper on the Derbyshire/Staffordshire border and took up residence at Dove Cottage, Lode Mill, near Alstonefield. Here he rapidly gained a reputation for his Dove fly patterns along with his skill as an angler. A feature of the flies tied by both John and Ernest was their method of winging, which was kept a close secret. The flies they tied were excellent floaters by virtue of hackles cut short and the method of winging.

John Lock invented the Lock's Fancy, which is a variant of No 1 Whitchurch. The fly was dressed by Ernest. Both patterns are flies suggesting the Pale Watery during early summer. No 1 Whitchurch was a favourite of the Whitchurch Club in Hampshire and represents Pale Olives, Yellow Duns (W H Lawrie) or Whirling Blue Dun.

LOCK'S FANCY

Hook:	16 or 17
Silk:	Pale Primrose
Whisks:	Pale Honey Dun Cock
Hackle:	Pale Honey Dun Cock
Rib:	Fine Gold Wire
Wing:	Pale-medium Starling

W M Gallichan says Lock's Fancy, in a larger size, has been very successful on the Derwent in May and June. Lock is also mentioned by Gallichan as a contact for anglers to make prior to fishing.

Edward Marston: *An Amateur Angler's Days in Dovedale* and *Dovedale Revisited* reports, '*Mr Lock...is a first rate fly fisherman and maker of particular flies to which the Dove trout and grayling are most partial*'. Lock's Fancy is mentioned by Eric Taverner for use on the Derwent when Pale Olives are about. It is most unlikely the fly was tied to swim in northern waters but it certainly seems to have some good recommendations for the Derwent.

Of Lock's later life, from the early years of the twentieth century, I have found no trace. Heywood, who wrote *Charles Cotton and His River*, mentions Lode Mill but not its occupant at the time. Ernest Lock died in or about 1947.

JOSEPH COOPER   1887

Joseph Cooper was the river keeper on the Dove near Mappleton. He managed the Maple Fishing Station.

DONALD MacLEAHY-MACKENZIE

Mr. Noel Smith, organist and Master of the Music at Brechin Cathedral was a friend of D M Mackenzie. I am indebted to him for the following account of this water keeper's life, activities and fly dressings:

Donald MacLeahy-Mackenzie fishing the Dove below Shining Tor in Milldale.
He invented the 'Mackenzie Fly' - almost certainly the Double Badger.

DOVE COTTAGE,

ALSTONFIELD,

ASHBOURNE.

26. 10. 40.

Dear Friend.

I am sure that you have long ago given up hope of my answering your two long and interesting letters which I received some time ago. I have been very busy lately clearing up on the river at the end of the season & then in my garden etc. I am also a very bad correspondent it takes me a long time to make up my mind to sit down and write letters - however I've now made a start so I hope you will forgive the delay. Glad you got home safely and also pleased that you have passed your examinations -

We had a very poor fishing season the worst some I came here partly owing to the war as no one cared to come (lack of petrol etc) and the low state of the river - It is still low and not much sign of rain. I have been away on several occasions grayling fishing further down the Dove and have had some quite good catches despite the lowness of the river and the open weather. Grayling take best after a hard nights frost & a sunshine mid-day. Have you any grayling in your river. If so I would make you some grayling flies - You mentioned a fly in your last letter and gave a description of it - I think it is one of my own specials - Badger & Purple I enclose 2 specimens and if this is the one you mean let me know and I'll make you a few more - It is a very good all the season fly. With reference to the long deep flat water that you mention I also think that it ought to hold some good trout - The last half hour of daylight is usually the best time to try your luck in such places - The double badger in a small size being the best killing fly. We have Jerry over here quite a lot and he drop some bombs in the neighbourhood of Ashbourne about a week ago - I hear that Birmingham & Coventry have been getting it pretty hot just recently.

my wife and I usually take our holidays during
the first fortnight of this month, but me have not
ventured this time.
I have got a permit from Lord Swinton to fish for
Grayling on the Yore near Ripon so perhaps if
weather conditions etc are favourable my wife and
I might go for a week about the middle of next
month. I dont think I have any further news,
that would interest you so will conclude with
kindest regards & will be pleased to hear from you
again.
                Yours v. Sincerely
                  D. H. Mackenzie
                _____

P.S. Waterproof dressing for dry flies
1 oz Paraffin wax, dissolved in Benzine
      Paralene 2'' worth
         Petrol about 2 thimble fuls.

Letter from Donald Mackenzie to Noel Smith with reference
to 'one of this own specials - Badger and Purple', and
also to the Double Badger.

D M Mackenzie was born in 1873. He served with the Baden-Powell Fighting Scouts and Remington Tigers during the Boer War in South Africa between 1899 and 1902, being decorated for gallantry on several occasions. After the end of hostilities he decided to stay on in that country, becoming a security officer in the largest diamond mine in Pretoria. Here he achieved minor fame by being present with the mine manager when the immense Cullinan diamond was found in 1905. The weight of the uncut gem was huge – 3106 carats!

Later he returned home to Scotland where he was appointed Superintendent of the River Tweed Police. On retirement in 1926 Donald moved to Derbyshire and was eventually persuaded by the influential Manners family to take charge of their recently acquired stretch of the river Dove in Milldale and Wolfscote Dale. This he did, building the charming little stone weirs, planting weed, constructing the nursery out of his home-built side stream complete with hatches, opposite to and upstream of Dove Cottage in Milldale. There were no pellets in those days. He reared the fish from fingerlings to twelve inches on minced cockles, mussels and liver. The mincing was done at the kitchen table using an old fashioned vintage hand mincer. Truly, the fish were home bred from natural river Dove stock.

'Mack' and his wife 'Mairn' had four sons and one daughter.

The eldest son, Gregor, became keeper for the Okeover Club on the river Dove for nine years from 1926 until 1935. Here he began a trout hatchery, installed weirs and carried out many improvements to the benefit of angling and anglers on the water. Whilst in the employ of the Okeover Estate Gregor was permitted to invite selected anglers to fish for grayling during the trout close season. Two of these were Roger Woolley and Major T H Oakden of Rolleston-on-Dove. On a December day the pair caught over a hundred grayling from the water during a long hatch of Winter Duns. The successful patterns were the White Witch and Tommy's Fancy - the latter tied by Woolley and dedicated to Oakden.

The Okeover club, at that time, had eleven members approved by Captain Okeover and the other members. The water was dry fly only and the participants, with the exception of the local vicar, had to reside outside a fifty mile radius of the water.

Dogs and Sunday fishing were not allowed. The members visited at the beginning and end of the season, also at Mayfly time. This must have provided the waterkeeper every facility for a high level of maintenance and development on the river.

Gregor then moved to the river Quash in Rutland at the request of an Okeover Club guest for a year, before becoming head keeper for the Duke of Leeds on the Trafalgar Estate of the Wiltshire Avon. He eventually retired to Whitchurch at the head of the River Test.

Their second son, Donald, succeeded his father at Dove Cottage immediately after the 1939-45 war, but stayed only a short time before moving downstream to the Sudbury area to work for Mr. Dickie Longden on his stretch of the Dove. Regrettably,

Donald's life was short. Jim, the third son, was a postman in Ashbourne and Norman, the youngest, became superintendent of the Cam and Ouse River Board before taking up a similar post with the Eden Fishery Board in Carlisle. Jessie, their daughter, achieved considerable fame by representing the U K in the British Empire Games in the inter-war years.

Donald Mackenzie was a skilled observer and keeper. He noticed the presence of Claret Duns on the upper reaches of his water. This is an unusual fly to find on alkaline streams and its appearance in Wolfscote and Beresford Dales was intermittent. Below Milldale where springs fed the river with considerable amounts of lime rich water the fly was not in evidence. He copied this fly, producing the imitation 'Mack's Fancy'. His best known creation, the Double Badger, is often attributed to Roger Woolley though Woolley himself never claimed credit for the dressing. The two men knew one another and Mackenzie certainly recommended Woolley as a fly dresser. Roger Woolley listed a dry grayling pattern, Mackenzie's Fly, in his writings. No dressing was given but it is almost certainly the Double Badger.

Even in his later years Donald Mackenzie was of an upright military bearing, rather daunting to some though of a gentle and patient disposition. He made daily visits to Dove Holes where he maintained the pumping ram for Mrs. Prince, the proprietress of what was then the New Inn Hotel, often the base for visiting anglers. His yellow Labrador, Trixie, accompanied Donald on his rounds. This bitch had the ability to 'point' to fish which would rise to a well presented fly despite the water appearing dead!

Donald Mackenzie retired after the war, living in Ashbourne for a short time before he died in 1947. His grave is in Ashbourne Cemetery.

The dressing of the Double Badger or Mackenzie Fly as given to Noel Smith by Donald MacLeahy-Mackenzie is detailed in Chapter 3 : Derbyshire and Staffordshire Fly Patterns, page 123.

JOHN BONSALL and DORA OLIVER

In 1977 Robert Deindorfer, an American, fishing the waters used by Izaak Walton, published his book *The Incompleat Angler*. As part of his travels he visited the Dove and Manifold. Having visited Fosters' Sporting Services in Ashbourne, he met two bailiffs in the course of his fishing. Dora Oliver was the bailiff on the Dove, her advice to Robert Deindorfer being, upstream dry fly on small hooks. He reports Miss Oliver as having access to Cotton's Fishing House and using it as a base during his day's fishing of the river. Miss Oliver was a Dove bailiff for almost three decades having followed her father who preceded her in the post.

During the time Deindorfer spent on the river Manifold he encountered John Bonsall, another bailiff. Bonsall advised use of the Cock Wing Dun but does not seem to have been too impressed by his pupil's efforts. Tony Bridgett, who knew and fished with John Bonsall, passed on the following profile.

> John Bonsall lived at Ecton all his life, latterly at Ape Tor Cottage next to the Manifold. He looked after Foster's syndicate water and the Swainsley Fly Fishing Club for the Worthington family at Swainsley Hall. He did not begin to fish until he was 40, having been born about 1900. He was a bailiff for the Severn Trent Water Authority and fished the Manifold for 40 years up to his death. His favourite fish was the grayling but sadly these fish have decreased on this section of the river. The Manifold is well known for going underground just below Wetton Mill during summer. John used to tell me that the two keepers for Sir Thomas Wardle of Swainsley used to collect stranded trout and carry them upstream to where the river was still flowing. This saved about 500 fish a year which meant they did not need to restock.

This last comment confirms the collection of trout in Summer mentioned by other commentators.

> Just up the lane from John Bonsall's house at Ecton is a little pond made by the river being dammed. This is now overgrown. R B Marston (editor of the *Fishing Gazette* and son of Amateur Angler) used to visit Sir Thomas Wardle at Swainsley to fish. About 1900 Marston stated that he had caught brown trout, rainbow trout and North American Brook Trout in this pond.

Tony also mentions *William Glanville*.

> Bill Glanville lived at the keeper's cottage, Lode Mill, above Milldale. A west countryman, proud of his native dialect, he was a delight to listen to with his frequent references to you as 'Dear Boy'. He was keeper to Mrs Usher but the water is now that of a Birmingham based group.

The house, Dove Cottage, where Mr Glanville lived is probably the same occupied by Ernest Lock during his stewardship of the river many years previously.

EDWARD MOORE

Moore was recommended by Alfred Ronalds to those who needed assistance in the dressing of flies. Anglers are advised to make contact either by letter, or in person, to receive '*practical instructions by the waterside*'. Those who wrote would receive '*patterns to copy with the exact materials for each fly*'. Edward Moore lived by the Derwent at Stanton Ford, Baslow, circa 1840.

GEORGE BUTCHER

George Butcher was born in 1799. For much of his life he made a living by guiding anglers on both the Wye and the Derwent. During slack times, he also acted as guide to tourists visiting towns and villages in the Peak, becoming known as 'Old Butcher'.

A fly pattern which has cropped up several times in the research for this work is the Butcher Mayfly. This is a pattern still used on both the Dove and the Derwent and attributed to George Butcher. Foster's of Ashbourne advertised a Butcher series of Mayflies and there is a probability that these patterns originated with George Butcher. David Foster fished widely in Derbyshire and Staffordshire and he was always willing to add further patterns to his firm's portfolio of flies. Listed under 'Relics of the Past' in Foster Bros., bicentenary booklet is, '*1800: Butcher's fly book concerning the Derwent*'. I wonder where it is now? It surely must contain some original local patterns!

During my research I have been shown a slip of paper on which are written two patterns for Butcher Mayflies. This item was in Roger Woolley's personal copy of his book, *Modern Trout Fly Dressing*, the pattern details written in his own hand.

BUTCHER MAYFLY DK (dark?)
Tail: Red dyed fibres. Herl butt.
Body: Red-orange seal. Ribbed gold.
Hackle: Ginger hen's and olive dyed mallard hackles
Head: herl head

          Light
Tail: Mallard, herl butt
Body: Orange seal body
Hackle: As dark but lighter.

Woolley's dark version is very close to that still used by Tony Bridgett.

Tails: Three pheasant tail fibres
Body: One third peacock herl, one third blood red silk with a gold rib, last third peaock herl
Hackle: First hackle Rhode Island Red, followed by either partridge black and white hackle or small black and white mallard feather dyed bright yellow.

None of these appear to be patterns found in standard fly dressing manuals, a red body being very unusual; nor are the dressings present in Roger Woolley's *Modern Trout Fly Dressing*.

George Butcher died in 1876 and is buried in Calver churchyard. Inscribed on his headstone is the legend that:

'...for many years of his life, amidst the beautiful works of God's creation, (he) followed as a fisherman the humble occupation of Christ's disciples.'

Light Butcher Mayfly (Woolley)
and Roger Woolley's dressing
notes written on the reverse
of a gas ticket.

ROBERT HENSBURGH

W M Gallichan refers to 'R Hensburgh, the river keeper who lives near Haddon Hall'.

There were two men called Robert Hensburgh, or Hensburg. Robert W Hensburgh was born in 1833 at Bradwell Grove in Berkshire. His son, Robert Henry Hensburgh in, or near, Bakewell in 1873. Robert the elder became bailiff and gamekeeper to the Duke of Rutland and lived at Elliot Holme. He was well known as a fly dresser and his patterns were prized as 'killers' among Wye anglers. He later supplied his son with flies for clients.

Robert Henry Hensburgh followed in his father's footsteps, also working as a water-keeper and gamekeeper for the Duke of Rutland. His recommendations for the Wye included flies dressed on small hooks and the use of fine casts. During his time on the river 'Dry Fly' became very popular. Presumably the flies supplied by both men were, in the main, dry patterns.

A second son, Ben, was born in 1876. He became an assistant gamekeeper with his brother on the Haddon Estate.

In the foyer of the Peacock Hotel at Rowsley is a photograph of a very large trout. The fish was caught in the River Wye by 'R Hensburgh'. On the title plate of the photograph are the trout's statistics. While this must have been an exceptional catch, the Wye was very heavily stocked and the trout may have been put in from the hatchery at a good size, or have been a cannibal. The fish was caught in 1874 and weighed eight and three quarter pounds. It was 26 inches long with a girth of 17 inches.

ALFRED SMEDLEY

Alfred Smedley was a professional fisherman and fishing tackle manufacturer. He worked on the River Derwent from Matlock Bath during the mid- to late-nineteenth century, taking fishing parties to various favoured spots on this length. His father William kept Wellington House in Matlock Bath as accommodation for visiting anglers. Alfred's business was based at the Toll Bar at Rowsley, and from his advertisement, appeared to supply a comprehensive range of fly and coarse tackle, along with live and artificial baits.

ALFRED SMEDLEY,
Fishing Tackle Maker, Angler, &c.,
WELLINGTON HOUSE, MATLOCK BATH.
Flies Dressed to Pattern.
EVERY DESCRIPTION OF FISHING TACKLE MADE TO ORDER.
LIVE AND ARTIFICIAL FLIES.
A constant supply of Fishing Tackle, Flies, &c., kept at the TOLL-
BAR, ROWSLEY.

———

Excellent Apartments may be obtained at WELLINGTON HOUSE,
which, having a southern aspect and being sheltered from the cold
winds, offers excellent accommodation for Visitors to Matlock Bath.

W FLETCHER

Another tackle and rod maker who worked in Matlock Bath at the same time as Alfred Smedley was W Fletcher. He also came highly recommended as a professional angler, and worked on the same length of the Derwent. Much of the river from Matlock Bath to just above Darley Bridge was 'free water'. It held a good stock of trout, grayling, dace, barbel and even the odd sea trout - though how they got up the weirs is questionable. A seven-pound fish was taken from the river above Matlock Bridge according to a report in 1861. This stretch of water was heavily poached and local knowledge was vital to obtain good fishing. Obviously, both Fletcher and Smedley were good guides and there were sufficient visitors to keep both gainfully employed, even if they were competitors in business and on the river.

Both advertisements offer live baits, Smedley's offering live flies. Live Mayfly, alder and bluebottle were dapped or dibbled in the pool below Rowsley Bridge, these presumably being the flies supplied live. 'Creeper' fishing was also popular but the capture of all these insects or their larvae for hatching would be a time consuming process.

NORTH PARADE, MATLOCK BATH.
W. FLETCHER,
Fishing Rod & Tackle Maker.
FLY RODS AND EVERY DESCRIPTION OF
TACKLE MADE TO ORDER.
FLIES DRESSED TO PATTERN. LIVE AND ARTIFICIAL BAITS.
Gentlemen attended on Fishing Excursions.
N.B.—REPAIRS NEATLY EXECUTED.

EDWARD ALLEN

Edward Allen was waterkeeper for the Derwent length of the Darley Dale Fly Fishing Club for over forty years, being appointed when the Club was founded by W H Aldam in the early 1860s. Allen served the Club until his death around 1904. The annual general meeting of the Club is reported in the Matlock Guardian and List of Visitors, April 11th, 1905. At this meeting Edward Allen's death is reported with regret, a new keeper evidently already having been appointed. W M Gallichan lauds Allen as a good fly dresser and a man to be contacted by those intending to fish the Derwent. At this time Darley Dale Flyfishing Club had thirty five members paying four guineas a year for their sport.

As an aside – the Club Secretary also reported having 5000 trout fry in his garden pond for stocking in the river. However, the local kingfishers made considerable inroads into the stock. With regret, he shot four of the birds but was still troubled by a further two. Maybe Edward Allen was persuaded to deal with those.

254

T OUTRAM

W M Gallichan reports Thomas(?) Outram as being bailiff for the Derwent Fly-fishers Club in 1905, and presumably for some years before. The Club had their own hatchery, run by Outram. He was later assisted by a George Outram, perhaps his son. Both these men lived near Grindleford Bridge. The Club stretch ran from just above Yorkshire Bridge to Calver Weir near Baslow, with some gaps, on one bank, and twenty members fished this well stocked water at a fee of ten guineas a season. Gallichan adds that the grayling were larger than the average and most anglers fished the dry fly for preference.

George Outram was keeper to a Michael Hunter around 1900, who it appears also had a fishery. The Outram family were both gamekeepers and waterkeepers in the Grindleford and Sheffield areas.

GEORGE JAMES EATON

There were three men with the name of George James Eaton who were fishing tackle manufacturers in Matlock and district.

George James Eaton (1) was born in Great Parnham, Essex in or about 1817. At some stage he moved to Derbyshire and married a Wirksworth lady in 1840. He was, at that time, employed as a gamekeeper. In 1851 he lived in Bath Road, Matlock and had taken up the profession of fishing tackle manufacturer. At forty-three he still lived in Matlock, working in the same job. He does not appear in any census after this. Donald Overfield, in *50 Favourite Wet Flies* (1980), states that he died in 1869.

George James Eaton (2) was born at Wirksworth in 1841. By 1871 he was living at Starkholmes, near Matlock, with his wife, daughter, brother and sister. His occupation was similar to that of his father – fishing tackle manufacturer. In 1881 he was still at Starkholmes, though had moved house. At this point his wife may have died, as he was 'Head of the family' with four daughters and a son. He was still at Starkholmes in 1891, recorded as a fishing tackle manufacturer, with four daughters and two sons. He is not mentioned in the 1901 census and may well have died.

George James Eaton (3), son of George James Eaton (2), was born at Starkholmes in 1873. In 1891, aged eighteen, he was living with his father and siblings and had the occupation of fishing tackle manufacturer. By 1901 his occupation was that of professional fisherman. In 1899 he lived at Kensington Villa, Matlock Bridge. He died in the 1930s.

It would appear that the oldest George James set up in business and founded the 'dynasty'. Matlock, in his time, must have been a centre for angling, as there were at least two other men described as 'Fishing Tackle Makers' or 'Professional Fishermen' working in Matlock Bath – W Fletcher and Alfred Smedley – in the mid-1800s. In the 1861 census his wife is already absent; presumably deceased.

The Derwent in Spring above Cromford, water
well known to the Ogdens, the Eatons and Beever.

George James (2) is very probably the 'Old Eaton' whom Eric Taverner refers to in his book *Fly Tying for Trout*. A Bumble illustrated on the frontispiece of this book was said by the author to be '*...after the prescription of Old Eaton*'. Walter Gallichan, in *Fishing in Derbyshire and Around* recommends anglers to see George Eaton for flies and advice. George was keeper for the Darley Dale Club and tied flies for members and other clients. He fished both the Derwent and Wye, being credited with the capture of a two and three quarter pound grayling from the Derwent, on worm, below Matlock Bridge.

George James (3) was a 'Fly Tier' for the Derwent in 1905 according to Walter Gallichan. In 1904 'the expert' Mr Eaton caught four trout from the Derwent, weighing between two and three quarter and four and a half pounds. The largest fish of the four took a Yellow Dun. George was also fly dresser for the Matlock and Cromford Angling Association and possibly its keeper. He held the record for the largest trout on fly from the Derwent in the area. The fish weighed six pounds two ounces and was caught, under what must have been difficult casting conditions, near the iron footbridge below Matlock Bridge. Gallichan also describes him as the 'local angling correspondent'. Certainly there are some angling club reports in the Matlock Mercury and Matlock Guardian and List of Visitors from 1885 onwards.

The Eatons must have been very influential in the development of angling in the

The iron bridge over the Derwent below Matlock. Near here George James Eaton took a then record catch of trout. The largest fish, at 4³/₄lbs, took a Yellow Dun.

257

Matlock district. At least two were great advocates of the Derbyshire Bumble and the second George James perhaps devised the pattern, according to Donald Overfield. The Yellow Dun and various Bumbles were among the favourite patterns recommended by the latter two men.

An account of grayling fishing in *The Angler's Notebook* of May 31st 1880, by Nooe, includes the remark, '*Indeed with shades of Eaton's (Starkholmes, Matlock Bath) Bumbles.... You are well equipped*'. An inference to Eaton's promotion of the patterns, if not their invention.

SYD SHARROCK'S SHOP

The shop was about a third of the way up Cockpit Hill opposite Derby bus station. Lower down was a fish and chip restaurant and Burgess's agricultural merchants. A little higher were a hot dog bar and a saddlers. Over the shop was Cynthia Haslam's dancing school where, as teenagers, we learned ballroom dancing. Outside was a large triangular cobbled area where on market days 'Mad Harry' sold his goods by diminishing auction.

The whole area was a source of fascination but the central magnet was the fishing tackle shop window. Many an hour was spent gazing through the glass; often it would be partly steamed up but no matter, it was so well stocked that there was always something to covert, from rods and reels to mysterious packets with 'Veniards' stamped upon them.

In the window bottom at the front were reels of Pearsalls silks, faded and probably unusable. Propped alongside were boxes containing 'Kingfisher' lines, but at our tender years it was difficult to know what these were. Having graduated from level silk lines for coarse fishing, our own exciting purchase would be 25 yards of 'Luron 2'.

Reels hung from wire supports on the back-board of the window display. Young's Ambidex, Allcock's Felton Crosswind, Mitchel and Morrit's series fixed spools were all there; Ariel, Flick 'em, Gypsy D'Or, Avon supreme and Rapidex Centrepins, side by side with Young's and Hardy fly reels. Then there were the rods! Built cane, whole cane, Spanish reed and steel Taperflash; but these in the main were inside the shop, presumably to prevent spoiling in the sunlight.

Baskets, bags, nets, knives, catapults and small tackle items were displayed in a fascinating clutter. The place was a treasure cave of indispensable items and the choice bewildering.

Inside, the shop was long and narrow. The first part was the pet section: birds, mice, hamsters, guinea pigs and fish housed on the customer side. Behind a long counter were Mr Sharrock and his assistants. There was a pet shop smell, not unpleasant but that created by corn, bedding and sawdust. On shelves behind the counter were pet food, medicines, things in anonymous brown parcels, hay and packs of shavings.

At the end of the shop cabinets, replaced the ranks of cages. Rods stood in racks with nets, gaffs and even umbrellas! Bookshelves held *How to Catch* books, alongside tomes which are now probably sought by wealthy angling bibliophiles. One birthday, a copy of

Marshall Hardy's *Angling Ways* (1934) came from these shelves to delight a young angler. The glass topped counters displayed flies, floats, spinners, hooks, reel fittings, swivels, leads and all the essentials an angler thinks he needs. Maggots were kept in a big zinc bath, served from a pint pot for two shillings; there were small tubs of worms and ground bait in linen bags.

We always looked at the display but usually left with minor purchases. Pocket money did not go far. Mr Sharrock 'did H P' for those allowed to use it but that was not for us. On occasion, after much saving, we would buy rod making materials; cane, Spanish reed and later, when funds permitted, split cane. Building our own rods was not simply economy but something we really enjoyed. The shop was an invaluable source of ideas. We were never rushed by the staff and advice was willingly given. Mr Sharrock always watched patiently with his hands in the pockets of his brown smock whilst we decided on our purchases. He would match up ferrules with rod sections and explain the finer points of construction.

All in all, a visit to Sharrock's never palled and was an eagerly anticipated event in our angling lives.

NINETEENTH CENTURY TACKLE DEALERS

John Banks	57 Spring Gardens, Buxton Also Hardwick Square	1881
J E Booth	Bakewell	circa 1900?
	This angler is mentioned by Eric Taverner in *Trout Fishing from all Angles* (1929) as being a fisher on the River Wye. Whether or not he was a dealer is unclear. It does seem likely he may be the same man described in Foster Bros. 1964 catalogue as 'Booth of Bakewell'. No further information has become available at this time.	
F Davis and Son.	In 1887 this business was in Beetwell Street, Chesterfield. By 1900 it had moved into Lodge Lane in Derby, and was manufacturing waterproof fishing lines.	
John Hinton	42 East Street, Derby	1900
Robert Lisle	24 Derwent Street, Derby	1900
William Martin	20 Calvert Street, Derby	1881
J Peach and Sons	10 St Peters Street, Derby Makers of rods and tackle, including a patent eight plait line. The business was still operating in 1887.	1861

259

J. PEACH & SONS,

FISHING ROD

AND

TACKLE MAKERS;

MANUFACTURERS

OF THE

PATENT EIGHT PLAIT LINE,

ARTIFICIAL BAITS, ETC.,

ST. PETER'S STREET,

DERBY.

MINNOWS FOR BAIT.   FLIES DRESSED TO PATTERN.

THE TRADE SUPPLIED ON LIBERAL TERMS.

COMMISSION FOR IMPROVEMENT OF FISHERIES, HELD AT BURTON-ON-TRENT IN 1861.

TRENT AND DOVE.

Sir Oswald Mozley and Mr. Thornewell live on the Dove and have fisheries, where formerly some excellent salmon were to be found, but the weirs of the mills have of late, it is supposed, prevented them going up. It appears Clay Mills is the most difficult for salmon to pass. At one time they passed up as high as Tutbury and Rocester.

Lord Vernon also has a right of fishing of five miles on the Dove. Mr. G. W. Hay is Lord Vernon's agent. Trout and grayling may be obtained in the Dove here, but not salmon.

Mr. Hanson, a fisherman, of Burton, can give special information on the fishing in the Dove and Trent.

Messrs. J. N. Soresby have a right of fishing for about four miles between King's Mills and the junction of the Derwent. A good deal of salmon once taken, but now it is sadly diminished. Fishing for trout and grayling, however, is generally good. But we should decidedly refer the amateur angler to Mr. Peach, of Peter Street, Derby, for all particulars.

LENGTH OF THE TRENT RIVER THROUGH THE VARIOUS COUNTIES IN ITS COURSE TO THE HUMBER.

Lincolnshire, 20 miles; Nottinghamshire, 55 miles; Derbyshire, 30 miles; Staffordshire, 40 miles; entire length, 145 miles. The tributaries are the Terne, 35 miles; Erewash, 20 miles; Derwent and Wye, 70 miles; Dove and Churnet, 60 miles; Sow (Stafford), 20 miles; Tame (Warwick), 25 miles; Blythe and Anker, 30 miles; Soar and Wreck (Liecestershire), 65 miles; and Devon, 20 miles; total of river and tributaries, 575 miles.

Salmon pass over six weirs and get up to Burton, which is about 145 miles from Spurn Head, or the sea.

John Roome	58 Burton Road, Derby	1887
Charles Rosson	4 Market Head, Derby The well-known gunsmiths, who also dealt in fishing tackle.	1900
J Wallwork	Bakewell Author of *The Modern Angler* (1847). In an advertisement he is described as 'Fishing rod and Artificial Fly Maker,' opposite the churchyard, Bakewell.	1861
George Wood and Co	117 Pinstow Street, Sheffield *'Every class of rods. Flies for local dams, Yorkshire and Derbyshire rivers.'* (W M Gallichan)	1900

260

[A CARD.]

J. WALLWORK,

Author of the " Modern Angler,"

Fishing Rod & Artificial Fly Maker,

OPPOSITE THE CHURCH YARD,

BAKEWELL.

FISHING.

DERBY ANGLING ASSOCIATION.   FORMED 1899.

OFFICERS FOR 1903.—*President*, Councillor C. W. Hardy. *Hon. Solicitor*, Bendle W. Moore, Esq.   *Hon. Treasurer*, R. H. Vessey, Esq.   *Managing Committee*, Messrs. Robinson, Greensmith, A. Eyre, Vessey, Thurman, C. Hallam, Butcher, Tinker, and Lackington.   *Hon. Secretary*, Mr. Geo. Eley, Boat Tavern, Derby. *Assistant Hon. Secretary*, Mr. F. W. Cott, 22, Franchise Street.
Head-quarters of the Association.—Derwent Hotel, London Road, Derby.

List of Clubs affiliated with the Derby Angling Association, 1903.

Beaconsfield Club A.C.	Green Dragon A.C.
Bemrose and Sons' A.C.	Greyhound A.C.
Boat Tavern A.C.	Melancthon's Head A.C.
Boden's Workmen's A.C.	Midland Coach Painters' A.C.
Bridge Inn A.C.	Nottingham Arms A.C.
Castle Fields A.C.	Peel Foundry A.C.
Chaddesden Works A.C.	Perseverance A.C.
Corporation Employees' A.C.	Prince Arthur A.C.
Derby Derwent A.C.	Royal Crown A.C.
Derby Postmen's A.C.	Sir H. Wilmot Arms A.C.
Dove A.C.	Sitwell Arms A.C.
Druids' Arms A.C.	Spread Eagle A.C.
Gallant Hussar A.C.	Stork A.C.
Great Northern Inn A.C.	

TRENT BOARD OF CONSERVATORS.

SALMON ACTS, 1861 TO 1892, AND FRESHWATER FISHERIES ACTS, 1878 AND 1884.

Chairman—Sir Robert Gresley, Bart., Drakelow Hall, Burton-on-Trent.

Clerk and Solicitor to the Board—C. K. Eddowes, Esq., 2, The Strand, Derby.

Travelling Inspector—Geo. Cook, Draycott.

DERBYSHIRE CONSERVATORS FOR THE YEAR 1903.

The Most Noble The Marquis of Granby, 16, Arlington Street, London, S.W.; The Rt. Hon. Earl Loudoun, Willesley, Ashby-de-la-Zouch; Sir Robt. Gresley, Bart., Drakelow Hall, Burton-on-Trent; The Hon. F. L. Wood, Hoar Cross, Burton-on-Trent; A. F. Hurt, Esq., Alderwasley Hall, Derby; Wm. Briggs, Esq., Bleak House, Melbourne; Henry Anson-Horton, Esq., Cotton Hall, Burton-on-Trent.

SCALE OF LICENSE DUTIES.

Licenses are granted by this Board, with the approval of the Secretary of State in pursuance of the Fisheries Acts, in accordance with the following scales:—

FOR SALMON.

For each and every draft or seine net or drift or hang net, not exceeding 200 yards in length, measured along the head rope when wet	....	£5	0	0
Ditto, exceeding 200 yards in length, for every additional 40 yards or part thereof	....	1	0	0
For every stand or bow net	....	1	0	0
For each rod and line	....	0	10	0

FOR TROUT AND CHAR, EXCLUSIVELY OF SALMON.

For each and every rod and line for the season	....	0	2	6
" " for one week	....	0	1	0
For any other instrument or device not being a rod or line	....	0	10	0

NAMES AND ADDRESSES OF LICENSE DISTRIBUTORS IN DERBYSHIRE.

The following persons are authorised to issue Licenses; for any further information required, address to the Clerk of the Board, who will forward Licenses anywhere on receipt of duty.   Those marked thus (*) also issue Salmon Licenses.

Alrewas—Mr. J. Taylor, Paul Pry Inn; Chas. E. Draper, Innkeeper.
Ambergate—W. Alton, Hurt Arms.
Alfreton—Wm. Gregory, Nuttall St.
Ashbourne—Messrs. D. & W. H. Foster; W. Renshaw, Okeover Park; F. Grindey, Dovedale Hotel, Thorp; Ernest Lock, Dove Cottages, Alstonefield.
Ashover—John Taylor, Post Office.
Bakewell—T. Tyack, Rutland Arms; Mr. G. A. Hurt, Matlock Street; Mr. J. Carrington, Bridge St.
Baslow—Mr. J. Eades, Peacock Hotel.
Belper—John Lee, Nottingham Road.
Burton-on-Trent—*Mr. J. C. Perfect, Station Street.   [Gardens.
Buxton — Mr. John Banks, Spring
Chesterfield—Mr. J. Armistead, Knifesmith Gate; Mr. W. H. Urton, West Bars.   [bound Hotel.
Cromford—Mr. S. C. Cooper, Grey-
Derby—*C. K. Eddowes, Esq., 2, The Strand; *Mr. J. H. Saxton, 71, London Road; *Mr. J. Hinton, East St.; Mr. R. Lisle, 24, Derwent St.; Mr. S. Thompson, 15½, Friargate; John Kay, 95, Canal Street.
Dovedale — Mr. H. Briddon, Peveril Hotel, Thorpe; Mr. Wm. Evans, Izaak Walton Hotel.

Duffield—Mr. E. Barnes, Railway Terrace.
Etwall—Wm. Argyle.
Hartington—Mr. J. E. Fosbrooke.
Hazelwood—Mrs. W. Spalton, " Puss-in-Boots " Inn.
Hathersage—Mrs. Mary Ibbotson, Post Office.
Hope—Geo. Ashton, Jun.
Ilkeston—W. Bennett & Son, 103, Bath Street.
Miller's Dale—T. R. Holmes, Cab Proprietor.
Matlock Bridge—Mr. H. G. Hartley, Saddler, Crown Square.
Matlock Bath—Mr. W. H. Hackney, South Parade.
Pinxton—Mr. G. W. M. Taylor, Post Office.
Rowsley—Miss S. Cooper, The Peacock Hotel.
Rocester—Thos. Titley, Post Office.
Ripley—Mr. J. Warriner, Post Office.
Shirland—Mr. Robert Mason, Post Office.
South Wingfield—Mr. T. Platts, Post Office.
Sutton-on-the-Hill—D. F. Bevis, Post Office.
Wirksworth—Mrs. Allen, Post Office.

TRENT FISH CULTURE CO., LTD.

Chairman and Hon. Managing Director—Col. E. B. Hutton, Blidworth Dale, Linby, Notts.   *Directors*—C. K. Eddowes, Esq., Derby; The Hon. F. S. O'Grady, Duffield Park, near Derby; Edward Henry Pares, Esq., Hopwell, near Derby; Captain Tomasson, Woodthorpe, Nottingham; Wm. Curzon, Esq., Lockington Hall, near Derby.   *Bankers*—Crompton and Evans' Union Bank, Ltd., Derby. *Manager*—Mr. James Renshaw, The Hatchery, Milton, Burton-on-Trent.   *Secretary and Solicitor*—Mr. C. R. B. Eddowes.   *Registered Office*—2, The Strand, Derby.

From The Derbyshire
Red Book (1903)

261

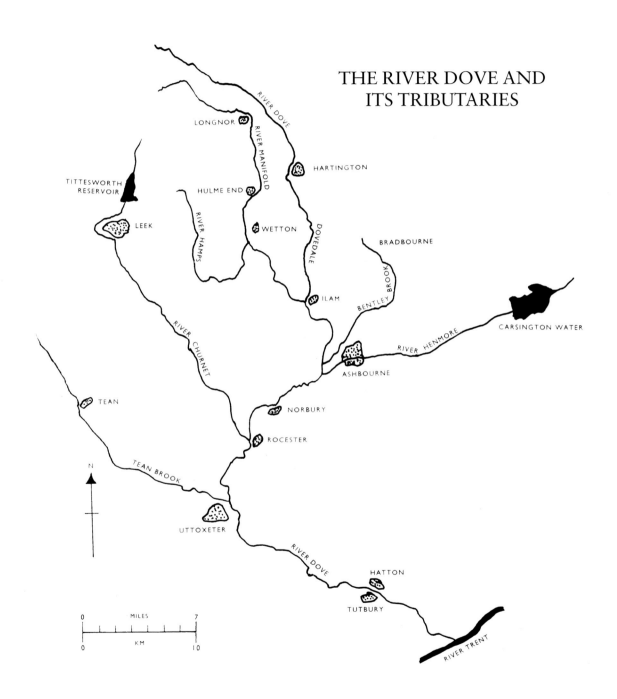

THE RIVER DOVE AND
ITS TRIBUTARIES

RIVER DOVE

LONGNOR

RIVER MANIFOLD

HARTINGTON

TITTESWORTH
RESERVOIR

HULME END

LEEK

RIVER HAMPS

WETTON

DOVEDALE

BRADBOURNE

BENTLEY BROOK

ILAM

RIVER CHURNET

CARSINGTON WATER

RIVER HENMORE

ASHBOURNE

TEAN

NORBURY

ROCESTER

N

TEAN BROOK

UTTOXETER

RIVER DOVE

HATTON

TUTBURY

MILES

0   7

KM

0   10

RIVER TRENT

CHAPTER SIX

RIVERS AND STREAMS

RIVER DOVE

The Dove has its source in Axe Edge and for much of its course forms the county boundary between Derbyshire and Staffordshire. This is an area of high moorland with heather, cotton grass and rough grazing. Soon after emerging from its spring, the infant river is joined by other small rivulets and brooks, becoming an upland stream. It exits from a steep valley and meanders through hill pastures to Crowdecote. Here, in its tree-lined bed are dubs and runs which shelter the small hill trout, resplendent in spotted red and gold livery. Angling here is much at the whim of the weather. The river shrinks in summer, making fish hard to come by. This is stalking water, cast and move on, but interesting sport.

The river has enlarged by the time it reaches Pilsbury. Here, a hundred and twenty years ago, the rod of John Fosbrooke bent to 'some of the best fish in the Dove'. Walter Gallichan fished here too, reporting hooked fish running into water vole holes in the bank to rub the hook out. Still growing, the Dove meanders on below Hartington. At the end of the nineteenth century the right bank was controlled by Sir Vauncey Crewe. He stocked the water very heavily and it was strictly preserved. The leasee of the left bank was Mr Frank Green. He stocked the river on a regular basis with rainbow trout but, unlike those on the Wye, these fish did not establish a breeding population. The Charles Cotton Hotel at Hartington has a small length of the Dove available for the use of guests.

Beresford Dale is a special place to anglers worldwide. The fishing house, built by Charles Cotton, commemorates the visits of Izaak Walton and the friendship of the two men. Situated on a meander of the Dove, it is surrounded by the river on three sides. Cotton furnished the building with anglers' comforts and had a cipher comprising his own and Walton's initials inscribed over the doorway. It is unclear whether Izaak Walton ever visited the house, being a very old man at the time of its construction; but he certainly knew of it and had expressed his desire to visit Beresford again. At that time the journey from Winchester would have been a very serious undertaking, even to go fishing.

A little way downstream is the Pike Pool, named for the rock which emerges from the depths of the river bed. It is easy to imagine Charles Cotton, accompanied by a boy with

The Pike Pool on the Dove in Beresford Dale, so named for the limestone spike emerging from the river bed.

a landing net, fishing the pool on a spring afternoon. The Dove next enters Wolfscote Dale. There are many low weirs across the river, making pools and riffles to provide improved angling water. Sir Thomas Wardle, of Swainsley Hall on the Manifold, owned the right bank of the Dove from here to Milldale during the nineteenth century. Mr John Hall, of Alsop Hall, was lessee of the left bank, and between them these two men were responsible for building and maintaining many of the weirs, and for stocking the river with Loch Leven, brown, rainbow and American brook trout, some of which were reared in stock pools. On this stretch Sir Thomas Wardle had a luncheon hut. The master anglers of the Dove knew how to enjoy their sport.

The small weirs are very much a feature of the Dove in Wolfscote Dale. The pools and

Weirs on the Dove in Milldale.

runs have created an environment, not only for fish, but also for aquatic plants, insects and birds. Here the works of man have complemented nature and created that which, for anglers, should be a 'World Heritage Site'.

Toward Milldale the Dove flows next to Lode Mill. Here, at Dove Cottage lived Ernest Lock, son of the inventor of 'Lock's Fancy'. More recently it was the home of William Glanville, keeper to Mrs Usher and Donald MacKenzie the probable originator of the Double Badger or MacKenzie Fly. At Milldale the waters pass beneath Viator's Bridge, where Piscator's pupil was alarmed by its narrow confines. Once in Dovedale, the river widens in some places, and in others is channelled by limestone features with famous names; Dove Holes, the Watchbox, Ilam Rock, and Tissington Spires. This is dry fly water. In the words of Walter Gallichan, '*It is perhaps the most tempting river in all England.*' Along here the Izaak Walton Hotel leases water for guests as it has done for a hundred and fifty years.

The Dove turns between Bunster and Thorpe Cloud, at the foot of which are the stepping stones and iron gate, a scene portrayed annually on countless postcards and calendars. In quiet times, anglers still ply their rods and skill here to speckled trout, as they have now for three and a half centuries, if not longer. The water meanders past the car park, still with fish to be caught, and a little distance further meets the Manifold. Dispute there will always be of which is the greater river in volume, but after the confluence the river is called Dove.

Now less of an upland stream, long flats appear and the first large weirs will soon hold back the river. At Mappleton, Alfred Ronalds fished and illustrated *The Fly-Fisher's Entomology* with such an accurate diagram that twenty first century anglers can fish the dubs and eddies he portrayed. Fosters named a mayfly pattern after the Birdsgrove water near here. The river pursues its course beneath Hanging Bridge, just above which the Bentley Brook enters the river. Further downstream at Church Mayfield is the confluence of the Henmore and Dove. There are big grayling to be caught in the deep water above Church Mayfield weir; the weirpool itself is an exciting place to draw a team of flies, the trout fighting hard in the rough water.

At Norbury, Gerald Heywood caught both trout and grayling of good size on the fly. The river still yields fish of high quality today. It is a noted place for grayling. Coarse fish have made their appearance by now and they, too, are of good quality and variety. The river straightens and flows to Rocester, where it is joined by the Churnet. This has suffered much from pollution in the past but is now an important water of Leek and District Fly Fishing Association. Uttoxeter is passed on the right bank and the river follows a winding course down to Hatton and Tutbury. Here Roger Woolley was born and for sixty years dressed flies for the Dove and the nation's rivers. It is very likely his first trout came from the Dove on flies of his own making. His art is still pursued in Hatton by Tim Thorpe of Derbyshire Trout Flies.

The Dove flows past Marston and Rolleston, the waters of this most evocative river

Early May on
the river Dove.

then emptying into the Trent above Burton. Once a salmon river, the Dove again plays host to migratory fish. As yet they are comparatively few in number but hopefully on the increase. They seek redds again in the gravels of the Dove.

This is an historic water. Those who have fished here include Walton, Cotton, Ronalds, Shipley, Foster, Fosbrooke, Gallichan, Granby, Skues, Halford, Woolley, Marston and Bickerdyke... Their names are the roll call of angling.

CHARLES COTTON'S FISHING HOUSE

> 'My river still through the same channel glides
> Clear from the tumult, salt and dirt of tides
> And my poor Fishing House my seats best grace,
> Stands firm and faithful in the self same place.'

> *Charles Cotton*

The house is a square stone building with a pyramidal stone tiled roof, surmounted by a sundial and ball. On top of this is a wind vane in the shape of a fish, perhaps being a comparatively modern addition. Over the rounded doorway is the legend '*Piscatoribus Sacrum 1674*' and beneath this, on the arch keystone, the cipher comprising the initials of Izaak Walton and Charles Cotton.

According to various accounts, the inside is a room about fifteen feet square. The floor was tiled in black and white marble and there was a fireplace – the chimney built at the left rear corner of the building. Spandrills on the fireplace were engraved or carved with the initials of Cotton and Walton, but there is doubt if this was original. The windows contained leaded lights – some records state stained glass – though all has by now been replaced. Wainscot covered the walls, with the ceiling divided into panels by ornamental mouldings, the panels perhaps originally bearing paintings of angling scenes and tackle. A square black marble table and various cupboards completed the furnishing. It sounds just the place for an extended lunch break before an afternoon's angling.

The fishing house has undergone many peaks and troughs since Cotton's time. John Hawkins reported in 1784 the building to be in 'indifferent condition'. In 1811 W H Pepys 'found the building going fast to decay'. Harwood's *A Survey of Staffordshire Containing The Antiquities of That County* in 1820 says the building was 'almost decayed'. By this stage the contents had long since disappeared. In 1825 the Beresford Estate was bought back by Viscount Beresford and in 1838 William Shipley and Edward Fitzgibbon reported the fishing house as being repaired 'about three years ago'. By 1844 Beresford Hall was in a very poor state and was partly occupied as a farm house. An engraving shows the fishing house in very reasonable condition. Various restorations are recorded in *Dovedale Revisited* by 'Amateur Angler' Edward Marston, up to 1902. He observed a new lock on the gate and a split cane fishing rod within the building. The said lock evidently did not prevent Marston from entering the enclosure, as it 'was not finished', and he and his companion lunched on the seats at the front of the locked building. Gerald Heywood writing in 1928 said the exterior was much as in Cotton's time. The interior had been altered and a bridge and paling fence removed.

The house is now privately owned and maintained; there being no public access.

RECOMMENDED FLY PATTERNS FOR THE DOVE

Although the Dove rises on gritstone, much of its course, particularly in the upper and middle reaches, is over limestone. This ensures that it is rich in both plant life and invertebrates. Rafts of *Ranunculus* are present, as are beds of cress and brooklime. The rocks and woods of its dales are home to a rich calicole flora with a number of rarities; Herb Paris, Lily of the Valley and several choice orchids. Ash and hazel are dominant tree species on the slopes; the whole making an ideal habitat for a wide variety of terrestrial insects which supplement the aquatic larder of the river. Hawthorn flies, beetles and crane flies all have their day and the river yields olives, iron blues, mayflies, stoneflies, sedges and shrimps.

Tony Bridgett, who has known the river for much of his life says fly numbers are far fewer now than forty years ago, particularly so the Iron Blue hatches. At that time anglers did not trouble too much with the Hawthorn fly, there were better things to imitate. At present the Hawthorn is eagerly anticipated. I saw my first mayfly hatch on the Dove in the early 1960s. At that time the flora of Dovedale was on my mind but I have never forgotten the experience. The insects were everywhere and very spectacular. They are still there, though probably in smaller numbers. It is quite possible of course that time and imagination has added to the numbers of 1963!

The following patterns are those used and recommended by Tony Bridgett, the President of Leek and District Fly Fishing Association, which controls much of the water on the upper Dove.

April:	Greenwell's Glory, February Red, Gold Ribbed Hare's Ear, Dark Olive, Cock Wing Dun, Golden Earwig, Silver Partridge, Orange Partridge and Partridge and Red.
May:	Iron Blue Dun, Olive Quill, Evening Dun, Gold Ribbed Hare's Ear, Greenwell's Glory, Cock Wing Dun, Yellow Dun of May, Pheasant Tail, Red Spinner, Black Gnat, Hawthorne Fly, Mayflies, Wickham's Fancy.
June:	Mayflies, Black Gnat, Cock Wing Dun, Elk Hair Sedge, Iron Blue Dun, Olive Quill, Pale Watery Dun, Wickham's.
July:	Iron Blue Dun, Elk Hair Sedge, Silver Sedge, Sherry Spinner, Cinnamon Sedge, Black Gnat, Partridge and Orange, Silver Partridge, Wickham's.
August and September	Olive imitations, Sedges Elk Hair type, Cinnamon Sedge, Silver Twist, Red Eyed Beetle, Iron Blue Dun, Cock Wing Dun, Soldier Beetle, Treacle Parkin, Red and Black Ant, Wickham's.

No doubt David Foster would add a Winter Dun and a Bumble or two, Alfred Ronalds a Golden Dun Midge or July Dun, Charles Cotton a Bright Brown or Hackle and there is even the chance of a stanza or two of poetry.

> 'The boxes and books
> For your lines and your hooks
> And, though not for strict need notwithstanding,
> Your scissors and your hone
> To adjust your points on,
> With a net to be sure for your landing.'

The Angler's Ballad Charles Cotton

RIVERS MANIFOLD AND HAMPS

Some two miles from the source of the Dove on Axe Edge another river rises, the Manifold. Its curious name is said to be derived from 'many folds' or meanders throughout its course. The river begins, runs and completes its course in Staffordshire, running parallel with the Dove, rarely more than two miles distant from it.

The headwaters are formed by many small tributaries and flow south east towards Longnor. The Crewe and Harpur Arms was once a popular stay for anglers and had

Springtime on the Manifold

water on the river. A hundred years ago, most of the river was owned by Sir Vauncey Crewe. Sir Thomas Wardle, a cloth manufacturer in Leek, was a lessee, and the Manifold ran past his home at Swainsley Hall near Ecton; he was able to stock and improve the sections of the river where he had riparian rights. Wardle was a friend of John Fosbrooke of Hartington, the two men often fishing the Manifold together and liaising on aspects of river management. It was Fosbrooke who seeded the Manifold with mayfly nymphs.

W M Gallichan writes that both Wardle and Fosbrooke favoured fishing wet fly against the more fashionable dry fly. Fosbrooke's Golden Earwig and the Cock Wing Dun were patterns both men regularly used on the river.

After Longnor the river turns south and flows in a tree lined course to Brund. The waters slow and the folds from which the river takes its name begin. On the bends there are deep holes, riffles and scours, all excellent holding spots for trout. It is often difficult to cast in the tree-lined tunnel but the fish are free rising and take the fly of a cautious upstream angler. Where the banks are clear it is important to keep low to avoid putting fish down.

The Manifold is considered an earlier river than the Dove. It carries more colour and there is far less in the way of aquatic flora. A good variety of fly life is available to fish both on and in the river. Where trees form tunnels, terrestrials make for interesting fishing. Spiders and beetle representations will take their share of fish and a dry hackled Greenwell or Grey Duster often selects larger trout.

Further twists and turns take the Manifold to Hulme End and Ecton where men once mined copper. At Hulme End the Leek and Manifold Railway had its terminus. Sir Thomas Wardle was financially involved with this less than successful enterprise. For many years John Bonsall who lived in Ecton was a river keeper on the Manifold who advocated the Cock Wing Dun to anglers fishing the river. He watched the water for much of his life and shared his knowledge with those who chose to listen.

W M Gallichan advises the use of Blue Dun, Olive Dun, Iron Blue Dun, Cock Winged Dun, Alder and Golden Earwig as successful flies.

The Manifold continues its southward journey to Wetton and Wetton Mill. Below here the river sinks underground in the summertime leaving an empty rocky bed. In times past Sir Thomas Wardle's keepers would catch trout stranded in the pools at this point, and transport them back upstream to save restocking the river. Here, the Manifold is joined by its tributary, the Hamps. This river sinks underground at Waterhouses. There is conjecture that the two rivers have separate underground courses as their emergent waters have different temperatures. The Manifold reappears in the grounds of Ilam Hall; the Hamps from Hamps Spring at the foot of Musden Low opposite the hall. A short distance downstream within sight of the Izaak Walton Hotel is the confluence of the Manifold and Dove.

The river Hamps rises near Mixon and flows south to Onecote and Winkhill. Its tortuous course takes it east to Waterhouses. Beyond here it sinks. The overground river bed goes north to join that of the River Manifold at Beeston Tor. The Hamps has a good stock of brown trout, which, considering the size of the water, grow to a fair size. Leek and District Fly Fishing Association have water on the river and are developing the water – running it as a catch and release fishery.

Tony Bridgett recommends similar flies for the Manifold and Hamps to those for the Dove. Add some sparsely dressed spiders for early season in the thin water. There is difficult but very rewarding angling to be had and, if you are a botanist or ornithologist, even more pleasure awaits.

BENTLEY AND BRADBOURNE BROOK

Most of the water on the brook is now, as far as I can ascertain, private; but I have a particular fondness for the upper reaches about Bradbourne. Forty five years ago, then a

The river Hamps below Winkhill.

young farm worker 'living in' on a local farm, I spent a few of my precious hours of leisure illicitly fishing and birdwatching on the brook. In fact I caught little, but the activities were an excellent diversion after long, arduous and sometimes lonely hours of work.

The brook rises near to Parwich and then runs for much of its length alongside the B5056. It crosses the road at Tissington Ford. Leek and District Fly Fishers lease the brook here from Tissington Estate. To quote Tony Bridgett once more, '*This is small stream fishing at its best. It is well stocked with trout and grayling, in particular the latter fish. However, it is difficult fishing and a stealthy approach is the only way. There are some good fly hatches including mayfly in its season.*'

Bradbourne Brook

The brook flows by Fenny Bentley. Alongside the B5056 there is much private water, which is obviously well cared for and preserved. It then passes Ashbourne to the West and joins the river Dove near Hanging Bridge.

In William Shipley's time the brook had excellent trout in its waters. He reports the best fishing between Bradbourne Mill and Woodeaves, particularly so on minnow.

RIVER CHURNET

The Churnet exits from Tittesworth reservoir, having risen on the moors two miles from Dove Head. It circles Leek to the west, then flowing south east by Cheddleton, Froghall and Oakamoor. Near Rocester it joins the river Dove.

Grayling and trout frequent the river, as do coarse fish in increasing numbers. It has produced trout of three pounds along with good sized grayling. As far back as 1838 the Churnet was considered a good water for trout, grayling and coarse angling. It has a long history of pollution incidents, many of which have been caused by dye and paper manufacture in Leek. This has been remedied and the river is now clean. The water carries some colour and bright patterns are a useful addition to the fly box when fishing here. The Yellow May Dun hatches in large numbers on the river and a large pattern will catch the attention of trout. Dark coloured flies and beetles along with those patterns recommended for the Dove are used throughout the season.

The river Churnet at Oakamoore.

TEAN BROOK

Tean Brook rises above Upper Tean and flows to the Dove via Fole and Uttoxeter. The confluence is at Dove Bridge near Doveridge.

RIVER HENMORE

In its upper reaches, the Henmore is absorbed by Carsington Water. It then travels down the valley past Atlow to Ashbourne. From here it flows south west to Clifton, emptying into the Dove at Church Mayfield. Also known as Compton Brook or the Schoo, the river was once a celebrated trout stream. Shipley praises the excellent quality of its trout in times gone by but '...*The poachers have long since taken them out. They may return when the poachers are taken out of Ashbourne – but not before*'.

David Foster reports an incident on the Henmore when a visitor, who was an expert upstream worm fisherman, made astonishing bags of trout from the clear waters of the river.

BRADLEY, BRAILSFORD, LONGFORD AND BARTON BROOKS

These streams are recorded by William Shipley as being good, if small, trout waters. He fished them with both fly and minnow advising the use of 'gaudy' flies. In the 1960s both

Hilton Brook.

Bradley and Longford brooks held good stocks of trout, looked upon by the envious eyes of budding anglers.

Brailsford Brook achieves a mention in Cotton's description of Viator and Piscator's journey from Derby to Ashbourne. Perhaps in 1676 the water had come to Cotton's notice as a trout stream. The four brooks eventually become Sutton Brook, then Hilton Brook and join the Dove below Egginton.

Cubley and Boylestone brooks are also mentioned by Shipley. As now, they were narrow and difficult to fish with the fly. They form Foston Brook, entering the Dove near Scropton.

275

THE RIVER DERWENT
AND ITS TRIBUTARIES

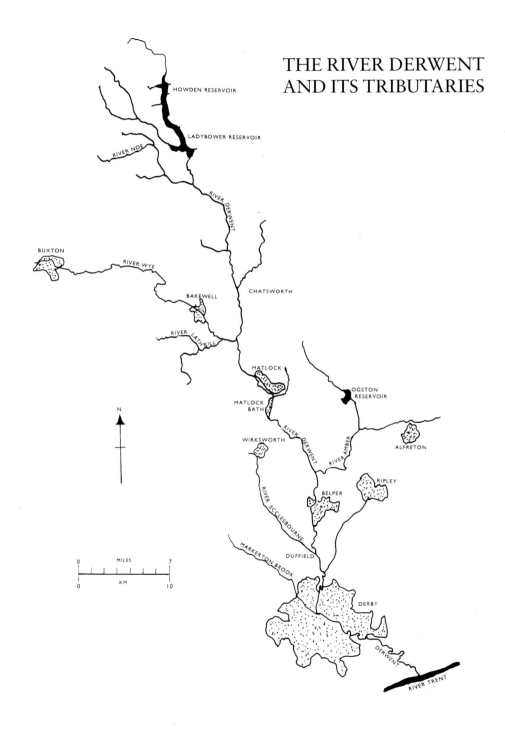

RIVER DERWENT AND ITS TRIBUTARIES

The Derwent rises high on the moors between Bleaklow and Ronksley Moor at nearly two thousand feet above sea level. In the area of Swains Greave it gathers a delta of small streams, concentrating them into a young river. From here it journeys down a V shaped course, alternating with wider flats but then once more tumbling down toward Howden and Derwent reservoirs. These were constructed to supply Manchester and Sheffield with water; Howden begun in 1901 and completed in 1912; Derwent built a little later and finished during the First World War. To this level the river has fallen about a thousand feet from its boggy moorland source.

Howden and Derwent were insufficient to supply the rising needs of the cities for water and after years of construction Ladybower was opened in 1943. This most recent inundation flooded the villages of Derwent and Ashopton along with almost a dozen farms. The lower reaches of the river Ashop and Ladybower Brook were lost to anglers but replaced by the newly stocked reservoir.

At the now submerged Ashopton Inn there was once a good cook, seven bedrooms and three miles of river available to angling guests. Half a crown a day, with a reduction for residents, bought the fishing and bait was allowed. The Derwent Fly Fishers had the rights of the Derwent from Yorkshire Bridge through Bamford to Grindleford for the river's trout and grayling.

The Derwent exits from Ladybower down a tree lined rocky bed, with good trout, to Bamford. Between here and Hathersage the river Noe joins the Derwent; its own two tributaries, Jaggers Clough and Peakeshole Water, having enlarged the stream. Some of the water from Jaggers Clough and the Noe is abstracted via an aqueduct to Ladybower. Round here drovers, the lead man being known as a 'Jagge,' drove their stock south to midland markets on the old drove roads. The waters of the Noe have been fished by members of the Peak Forest Angling Club for upward of a hundred and fifty years and the organisation still flourishes.

The Derwent now approaches Hathersage and enters a beautiful valley with streamy runs and flats, with no shortage of fish. At Padley the river is joined by Burbage Brook, which enters on the left bank, having flowed through a spectacular wooded gorge. Past Grindleford, the Derwent approaches New Bridge and the weir at Calver. The water is wide and deep here and in years past was ducted to the mill below, now converted for residential accommodation. The river is wider below Calver and the odd island has formed in the bed. At Baslow the river flows under old and new bridges and it always looks an inviting place to wet a line! For some distance from here, the angling is largely controlled by the Chatsworth Estate. There can be few better settings than Chatsworth in the autumn for a day's trout or grayling fishing. The river flows on in a wide valley past Beeley to Rowsley. Here the famed Peacock Hotel offers access to both the Wye and Derwent for its guests. It has long been a hostelry for visiting anglers and the tradition is

The upper Derwent near Hathersage, Derbyshire.

very much maintained today. In the pool below Rowsley Bridge, in the nineteenth century, live mayfly was dapped by the clients of George Eaton of Matlock.

The confluence of the Derwent and the Wye is a little distance below the bridge at Rowsley. Downstream, much of the fishing is that of the Darley Dale Club. At the turn of the nineteenth and twentieth centuries, its members had a considerable reputation as fishers of the dry fly. One of its honorary officials at the time was W H Aldam. The water alternates with deep flats and riffles down towards Darley Bridge. Beyond here the banks are very steep, dropping into deep water which is rather awkward to fish with fly. Oker Bends follow. Walter Gallichan reported big barbel being present along this stretch of river a hundred years ago. Maybe their descendants are still present. There are some good trout and grayling here, which fight hard in the current created by the narrowing course of the river. Long trotting for grayling, in the Yorkshire style, is an enjoyable activity on an autumn day on this part of the river. Here too, years ago, Eaton plied his Yellow Dun for the big browns.

Two reports from the *Matlock Guardian* and *List of Visitors* in September and October 1905 record a serious pollution incident on this stretch of the river. It was thought that lead washings caused the problem and the water was affected from Darley Bridge to below Cromford. Dead fish in large numbers were found in eddies and shallows all the way down, which included trout, grayling, perch, roach, barbel and dace. One angler was reported as saying that this was a 'blessing in disguise' as the poison got rid of the coarse fish. It also killed much of the fly life on the water at that time. The river was restocked with two thousand trout after the pollution had washed through.

Matlock has long been an angling centre. The Derwent flows beneath the bridge, loops back on itself to Matlock Dale, leaving High Tor on the left bank. The cable cars from the Heights of Abraham cross high above the river, to deposit, or collect, their excited cargo of tourists to or from the old station in Matlock Bath. Walls confine the waters on one side with high wooded banks opposite. The slalom gates of a kayak course hang where Fletcher and Smedley once fished in Matlock 'Free Water'. At Matlock Bath the river is sharply deflected by a limestone cliff to flow through the pleasure gardens. On one occasion, I saw a late night angler fishing by the light of the October illuminations at ten o' clock in the evening – some pleasure! Walls confine the river once more, but as the waters flow towards Cromford the river widens and slows as it approaches the weir at Masson. There are big chub and perch along this stretch, together with trout, grayling and barbel.

The weirpool at Masson is a lovely spot. A great brick chimney and mill dominate downstream but now have mellowed and fit the scene well. The view upstream is of High Tor, apparently rearing from the river above the weir, often with wraiths of mist obscuring the face in the early morning. The pool itself and the run from it are a delight to fish, often with dippers for company. A sweeping bend beneath the Derby Road brings the Derwent past Willersley Castle, built by Sir Richard Arkwright. T C Hofland informs

Masson Bend

the reader, in his book *The British Angler's Manual*, to write to Arkwright to obtain permission to fish here. The water is a series of runs and pools which extend down towards the old Arkwright Mill at Cromford and on toward Holmesford Cottage Inn.

Before the inn is reached the river flows under Cromford Bridge, with its so-called 'Angler's Chapel', now the property of Cromford Fly Fishers Club. The lodge was built in 1796 by Sir Richard Arkwright to house his keeper, with a view to preventing poaching on the river. The bridge is of interest – its lower arches differ from the upper. When the bridge was widened, perhaps to accommodate the Arkwright 'carriage and four', the new arches were not matched to the existing ones. Other bridges on the Derwent are similar in this respect. In the parapet of Cromford bridge there is an inscription to commemorate, '*The leap of B H Mare ...1697*'. Apparently the unfortunate survived the incident - perhaps he leaned too far to observe the grayling of a lifetime? The river creates superb angling water from here to the inn. Fast glides and streamy runs alternate with deep pools and scours. I watched Cromford members stocking the river one day and, from what I saw, there can be no shortage of quality fishing on their stretch of the Derwent.

Winter grayling fishing on the Derwent at Masson.

The Derwent at Cromford Bridge. The stone house is now the hreadquarters of
Cromford Fly Fishers Club. It was originally modelled by Sir Richard Artwright
on Charles Cotton's Fishing House in Beresford Dale.

MATLOCK & CROMFORD ANGLING ASSOCIATION.

PRESIDENT - - - CAPT. R. A. ARKWRIGHT.

VICE-PRESIDENTS :
L. H. SHORE NIGHTINGALE, ESQ.
A. S. MARSDEN SMEDLEY, ESQ.
MAJOR F. C. A. HURT.
M. DEACON, ESQ.

TREASURER :
F. L. SOMERSET, ESQ.

HON. SECRETARIES :
A. E. COATES.
B. F. PARKER.

The Fishing Hut. Cromford Bridge.

The Matlock and Cromford Angling Association was formed in 1874. It had close ties with both the Arkwright and Nightingale families who provided presidents from the association's inception until 1941. At the end of the nineteenth century the organisation had a hatchery on the Arkwright estate and also used ponds at Alderwasley for holding stock fish. In 1969 the association altered its title to Cromford Fly Fishers Club.

Here, four transport systems are compressed into little more than three hundred yards of width. Road, river, railway and canal run down the Derwent valley between Cromford Wharf and Ambergate with just a 'spit and throw' between them. Just beyond High Peak Junction, the Cromford Canal passes above the Derwent in its aqueduct next to Leawood pump. The importance of the industrial heritage of the Derwent Valley and its mills has prompted application for recognition as a World Heritage Site.

Gradually, as the river flows toward Whatstandwell, the valley sides ease and widen. Coarse fish begin to appear in greater numbers but there is still a good head of trout and grayling. Shining Cliff woods clothe the right bank down to Ambergate and Half Penny Bridge. At one time anglers stayed at the Hurt Arms, or bought their tickets at the hotel for the Derwent and Amber, which join just above the bridge. A hundred and thirty years ago, a long dead relative wrote his catches from the Amber in a book I still own. The fish were often caught at South Wingfield or near Fritchley. Long polluted, the Amber is now being brought back to its former quality.

The Derwent meanders on through fields between Ambergate and Belper and is now becoming the preserve of the coarse angler, but still well stocked with grayling and trout. The huge East Mill at Belper, surrounded by what was once a workers' village, dominates the river at Bridge Foot. A large horseshoe weir controlled the waters for use by the mill machinery. This industrial complex was the creation of the Strutts, who were contemporaries and partners of Richard Arkwright. Their mills from Belper to Derby controlled the Derwent's flow and altered, for all time, its original character. The weirs they built also blocked the passage of migratory fish, once commonly breeding on redds in the Upper Derwent Valley. The mill owners' influence did have its benefits. Schools, hospitals, good housing and bridges were provided for workers and the general population of the area.

At Milford is another of Strutt's mills, again with a spectacular weir below the A6 bridge. Near Duffield, the River Ecclesbourne, which rises close to Wirksworth, joins the Derwent. A small river, often little more than a brook, it offers excellent small stream trout fishing. Below the village is the Bridge Inn. This piece of water was always stocked with trout though my recollection is that they were very elusive when pocket money had been spent on a day ticket.

Burley bend brings the river down to Ford Lane bridge and the S bend below Allestree. Many happy days of childhood were spent along this part of the Derwent, courtesy of Jack Appleby, who had Home Farm. The river has changed much in fifty years; the rumble from the A38 now disturbs what were peaceful pastures, but a friend and I still have the occasional day on the river. Long ago we caught roach in deep water. Nowadays we meet to catch trout, grayling and dace, but mainly to reminisce and have an anglers' picnic!

In 1956, just below Ford Lane Bridge, I caught my first brown trout while minnow fishing. It was small - perhaps four ounces - but it hooked me for life on these beautiful fish.

Sluices at Darley Abbey mill once held back the water but these have now been lowered. As a consequence the river is swifter, shallower and runs over clean gravel with lush weed beds. It glides round the great S bend where the banks are protected by gritstone walls built down into the river bed. There is about a mile of these walls and they must have been a huge undertaking. Each block is dressed stone and they have been there beyond living memory.

The Derwent falls over Darley Abbey weir, constructed to supply the mill, and flows on to Derby through Darley Park. Anglers and rowers share the river here to St Mary's Bridge with its ancient chapel. In times past, the Derwent's waters drove the machines of the Old Silk Mill, much of which was lost in a fire. This site is the final mill of the Derwent Valley and it is now a museum. The river continues through Derby past the Council Offices and over the weir below.

The river now has become wider and deeper. It flows out towards Spondon and Borrowash, where there is high quality coarse fishing. Alongside the bends and curves at Draycott are meadows and gravel pits which attract a huge number of birds. Among them are the birds which anglers love to hate; the cormorants. At Shardlow, the Derwent joins the river Trent, having made its journey of some seventy miles.

The river Derwent is probably at its best for the fly fisher down to Whatstandwell. There are many lower sections of the river where it is well worth trying with fly for both coarse and game fish. Grayling and trout are well established at least to Darley Abbey weir. Both dace and chub are interesting sport to the fly.

Such is the length and diversity of the river Derwent that it is difficult to record all the natural flies and their respective imitations concisely. This list simply serves as a guide to species and artificials recommended by various authorities.

SPECIES	COMMON NAME	ARTIFICIALS
Gammarus Sp	Freshwater Shrimp	Shrimps
Protonemura meyeri	Early Brown	Winter Brown
Nemoura Sp	Small Brown Stonefly	February Red
Perlodes microcephala	Large Stonefly	Woolley's Stonefly
		Grey Duster
Leuctra fusca	Needle Fly	Needle Fly
		Dark Spanish Needle
Leuctra geniculata	Willow Fly	Willow Fly
Chloroperla torrentium	Small Yellow Sally	Yellow Sally
Hexatoma fuscipennis	Gravel Bed	Gravel Bed
		Grey Duster
Baetis rhodani	Large Dark Olive	Rough Olive
		Waterhen Bloa
		Dry G R H E
	Red Spinner	Lunns Particular
Ephemeralla ignita	Blue Winged Olive	Partridge and Orange
		B W O
		Orange Dun
	Sherry Spinner	Sherry Spinner
Baetis tenax	Medium Olive	Greenwell's Glory
		Blue Dun
Baetis muticus	Iron Blue	Snipe and Purple
		Dark Watchett
	Jenny Spinner	Jenny Spinner
Ephemera danica	Mayfly	Grey Wulff
		C D C Mayfly
	Spent Mayfly	Various patterns
Heptagenia Sulphurea	Yellow May Dun	Yellow Dun of May (Foster)
Ecdyonurus dispar	Autumn Dun	Autumn Dun (Woolley)
		March Brown (var)
Trichoptera	Sedges	Various Sedges
Diptera	Terrestrials	Hawthorn
		Black Midge
		Spiders
Coleoptera	Beetles	Red Tag
		Black and Peacock
		Little Chap
		Marlow Buzz

285

SOME NOTES FROM THE CHATSWORTH FISHERY ARCHIVE

Records of the Chatsworth Fishery and Ponds detail payments and works back to 1729. In that year Samuel Booth and John Hibbert were paid for 'Watching', which probably relates to the fishery or keeping.

More organised accounts in the early 1800s record William Stones as the waterkeeper assisted by Robert Holmes. Payments were made for puddling and liming ponds, working with the otter hounds and whelping, also netting the brooks for stock. In August 1820 Robert Holmes was paid up and dismissed for poaching. He was replaced by John Sheldon. William Stones received £51.12.0 a year, twelve guineas of that being in lieu of clothes, nets and equipment. John Sheldon received £16.0.0 per year.

There are further payments to farmers whose sheep had been worried by the otter hounds. Evidently otters were not welcome guests on the banks. Crayfish were harvested in the fishery. There are several details of payments made for working at the crayfish boxes or for repair to them. The crustaceans were caught and stored in boxes to await their fate and his Grace's pleasure. The boxes would need to be placed in running water, perhaps in a specially constructed stream, or simply in the main river, floods permitting.

Alexander Bacon was involved in these several activities with William Stones. In 1908 a record shows Alec Bacon as being recently retired, having served four Dukes. He was also mentioned by W M Gallichan as being Chief Bailiff and living at Baslow.

In 1909, Louis Jones was employed as 'Fishwatcher', assisted by Robert Hibberd. Jones served until his death in 1933. His son, L Harold Jones was then employed 'to help the family' until he joined the army as a gunner in 1940. At this juncture the fishery paid Jones's mother a pension. In 1940 James B Hulley, a helper of Jones at busy times, took over as Fishwatcher. He lived at Calton Lees, Beeley.

In 1898 the Chatsworth Fishery began just above Calver Bridge and ended at Rowsley Bridge on the east bank of the Derwent. On the west bank it began at St Mary's Wood, Bubnell, and ended at Rowsley Bridge. Trout, grayling, dace, chub and barbel were present in the river. Pike were not present, but the water was visited by otters, which were trapped by the waterkeeper. Minnow fishing was not permitted but limited bottom fishing was allowed. A membership limit of 25 was imposed along with eight honorary members and a monthly ticket for Chatsworth employees at three shillings a day. The subscription to members was five guineas, with a similar entrance fee. After the First War this was doubled. The day ticket price was not adjusted accordingly and thus caused vociferous complaints from members until it was increased. Bottom fishing was also banned at this time except for selected locals who applied to take coarse fish out of the river.

The Derwent was stocked each year to supplement natural stocks, which involved the purchase of 3000 yearling trout each season from Trent Culture at Mercaston. These were put into the river at six or seven points throughout the fishery; additional stock was provided in the form of Loch Leven trout from Howietoun Fishery near Stirling. Each

CHATSWORTH FISHERY.

Keeper's Report for Week ending _October 4th_ 194_2_

Rods seen _10_

Member's Name.	No. of Days.	Visitors.	No. of Days.
Dr _Fisher_	1	Mr _Kerr_	2
Mr _Grey_	1	" _Poachin_	1
" _Wingfield_	1	" _Tweed_	1
" _Fenton_	1	Lt Col. _Shackly_	1
" _Dixon_	1		
" _Harvey_	1		

State of Water _clear to day and normal._

Name Flies which are killing _Iron blue and claret bumble_

Is good Sport being obtained? _quite good._

Other Remarks _The River has been poluted from Aassop on 3 days during the week. Sep 29. October the 2nd and 3rd._

Signed _Jim Aulley_

Chatsworth Fishery Report, 1942.

(Devonshire MSS Chatsworth by permission of the Duke of Devonshire)

year up to and including the Second War, the tributary brooks of the main river were netted and the fish caught were turned back into the fishery. This was a major operation requiring additional labour.

The results were very impressive. The annual average of trout netted between 1920 and 1940 was 715 brace. Many of these were large fish and would have been a valuable boost to stocks. The main yield of these trout came from Barbrook, Rhymus and Beeley Brooks.

Otters were still being trapped during the Second War, a payment of ten shillings being made in 1942 with another payment to the keeper for twelve herons shot in 1946. The members brooked no competition they could control, including the two legged variety with nets, lines or rods.

The fortnightly records for the fishery compiled by James Hulley are complete for 1942 and 1943. They give details of the catch, flies and state of the river for these two years.

A notable feature of these reports is the number of pollution incidents. These normally comprised of fluorspar washing water being admitted to the river above and at the top end of the fishery. There are a number of reports where members have complained about the state of the water and on several occasions reporting it as unfishable – little wonder at ten guineas a year. The washings turned the water milky white and no doubt put fish down for some considerable time. A number of the anglers lived away, in towns such as Sheffield, Derby and Aston on Trent, and would not be pleased on arrival to find poor conditions.

Comment is made about some pollution incident on almost a monthly basis with the waterkeeper visiting the culprits, though apparently with little success.

The monthly lists of flies for the two years comprise twenty-eight patterns, allowing for variable names, and are listed below. From these I have selected a Chatsworth Fishery annual 'Flybox' comprising the nine most popular patterns.

1942

April	Blue Moth	Grouse and Purple	Sturdy's Fancy
	Butcher	March Brown	Wickham's Fancy
May	Black Gnat	Greenwell's Glory	Iron Blue
	Dark Olive	Grouse and Purple	Peter Ross
June	Blue Dun	Olive Dun	Wickham's Fancy
	Grey Dun	Peter Ross	Yellow Dun
	Hare's Ear & Gold		

July	Blue Dun	Dun Variations	Grouse and Purple
	Butcher	Furnace Brown (Bumble)	Olive Dun
August	Black Gnat	Dun Cut Moth	Pale Evening
		White	
	Blue Dun	Dun Variations	Purple Snipe
	Butcher	Grouse and Purple	Yellow Dun
September	Black Gnat	Grey Dun	Olive Dun
	Blue Dun	Iron Blue	Red Quill
	Coachman		
October	Claret Bumble	Iron Blue	

November and December: Brandling and Maggot

1943

February	Brandling Worm		
April	Blue Dun	Pale Dun	Peter Ross
	March Brown		
May	Iron Blue	Pale Blue Dun	Red Spider
	? Mallard	Pale Green (Apple Green?)	Wickham's Fancy
	Pale Blue		
June	Black Gnat	Iron Blue	Mayfly
	Grouse and Purple	March Brown	Yellow Dun
July	Black Gnat	Iron Blue	Yellow Dun
	Grouse and Purple	Red Spider	
August	Blue Dun	Gold Ribbed Hare's Ear	Iron Dun
	Butcher		
September	Blue Dun	Red Quill	Wickham's Fancy
	Grouse and Purple		
October	Iron Blue	Peter Ross	

The Grouse and Purple is one of the most popular patterns in the two lists. It is unclear whether the fly is dressed as a winged wet fly or as a hackle. Grouse hackles have been used on both the Derwent and Dove for a long time. William Shipley, T C Hofland and

John Beever 'Arundo', all gave dressings for them. Some of these had herl bodies, others silk of various colours. It is not impossible that the fly recorded in the Chatsworth lists was such a pattern, perhaps imitating aquatic stages of Iron Blues or Turkey Browns. Alternatively, the fly may be a member of the Grouse series of lake or loch flies found to be useful on the river. Roger Woolley gives several grouse hackles, the closest being the Grouse and Claret. It is a short step to a Grouse and Purple!

GROUSE AND CLARET
Hook: 0 – 1
Body: Claret tying silk, gold tipped
Hackle: Speckled brown grouse

GROUSE AND PURPLE
Hook: 8 – 14
Tail: Three or four golden pheasant tippets
Body: Purple wool or seal fur ribbed with gold though some authorities suggest silver
Wing: Brown speckled tail feather from a grouse
Hackle: Black hen

A C Williams reports this fly as being very successful on Loch Leven, the source of some of the trout stocked at Chatsworth. John Roberts suggests the fly as a representation of the Claret and Sepia Duns and their respective larvae. I believe the former does occur in small numbers in the acid waters of the upper Derwent.

Surprisingly, there is only one mention of a Mayfly in the monthly lists. However, Fosters sold a series of mayfly patterns called the 'Butchers'. Possibly the flies of that name, recorded in July and August, were mayfly dressings and not the more familiar attractors. Once more the Dun Cut reappears, this time as a moth. This is the most recent record of the fly in use I have found. A Blue Moth is also recorded, maybe an indication of late evening angling, or even night fishing. Both Claret and Furnace Bumbles are listed, possibly the Apple Green Dun in the disguise of a 'Pale Green' and 'Sturdee's Fancy'. A good chance then, that some of the fishery members were keen grayling anglers. Considering the popularity of the Iron Blue fly in the lists, the insect was probably present in high numbers on the river in 1942 and 1943.

CHATSWORTH FISHERY FLY LIST 1942 and 1943

Black Gnat
Blue Dun
Blue Moth
Butcher
Claret Bumble
Coachman
Dark Olive
Dun Cut Moth
Furness Brown
G R H E
Greenwell's Glory
Grouse and Purple
Grey Dun
Hare's Ear and Gold
Iron Blue

March Brown
Mayfly
Olive Dun
Pale Blue
Pale Blue Dun
Pale Dun
Pale Evening White
Pale Green
Peter Ross
Purple Snipe
Red Quill
Red Spider
Sturdy's Fancy
Wickham's Fancy
Yellow Dun

RIVER WYE

The Wye rises west of Buxton and flows through the town collecting, on its way, the waters of Hogshaw and Nun Brooks. It leaves Buxton alongside the A6 through Ashwood Dale toward King Sterndale. Flowing through a gorge cut into the limestone through Wye Dale, it leaves the road behind and enters Chee Dale. Here is the spectacular Chee Tor, and along the length of the gorge grow a wide variety of limestone flora. Millers Dale and the oddly named Water-cum-Jolly take the river through to Cressbrook Mill, built by Sir Richard Arkwright. From here to Ashford, through Monsal Dale, Chatsworth Estate controls the fishing. Ashford Bridge is a fine vantage point to view the inhabitants of the river. There are some large trout here – no doubt boosted in weight by a diet of bread intended for the ducks by visitors.

Below Ashford the river has been widened into a lake, at the end of which is another of Arkwright's enterprises, Lumford Mill. In the late nineteenth century the lake was stocked with rainbow trout fry. By means of floods, fish escaped into the river and found the waters to their liking – such that a breeding population developed. Few, if any, other rivers in the British Isles support a self-sustaining population of rainbows. They share the Wye, not always peacefully, with populations of brown trout and grayling, making the river a unique place to fish. Warren Slaney, the Haddon Estate waterkeeper, explains in his notes in the Haddon newsletter *Waterlines* that the rainbows are a 'different strain of trout and quite unlike every other type of rainbow in this country'. Warren notes the

291

A wet August day on the Wye near Rowsley

characteristics of the Wye fish as '*parr like marks*' on the underside, russet tip to the dorsal fin and white tips on anal and pelvic fins.

In both warm and cold conditions they rise freely to available insects and the dry flies of anglers. These are the fish Walter Gallichan called '*ghosts*' but which, he said, he never succeeded in catching. '*...though it is my ambition to secure closer inspection of these mysteries...*'. He also reported seeing brown trout from Bakewell Bridge '*as dark as tench*', along with 'normal' brown trout.

The Wye now leaves its steep gorges, flows beneath the bridge at Bakewell where Gallichan and thousands of others have watched, and enters a wide flood plain. Here it takes on the appearance in places of a chalk stream. Its course meanders in a tortuous manner, providing the highest quality fishing water. Past Haddon Hall and Park its tree lined banks, weed beds and clear water provide a rich diet for trout and grayling. A little way past the hall is the confluence with the river Lathkill, itself having already absorbed the waters of the Bradford at Alport. From the confluence, the larger river Wye creates

Anglers on the Wye in Monsal Dale, near Bakewell, 1743.
Engraved by Vivares after Thomas Smith of Derby (d.1763). From Angling in British Art, Sparrow

further meanders to Cauldwell's Mill, where it once provided the power. It is then a short journey to its own confluence with the Derwent, south of Rowsley.

The angling from north of Bakewell is controlled by Haddon Estates via the Peacock Hotel at Rowsley. The Wye is, and for a very long time has been, carefully nurtured and cared for as a trout fishery. In 1898, the then Marquess of Granby wrote *The Trout.* An angler of great experience, he owned the Lathkill, Bradford and much of the Wye and preserved the water assiduously. Some would consider he overstocked the rivers considering the 'bags' he made. In those days, Robert Hensburgh was the waterkeeper and the flies he tied were renowned as 'killers' among Wye anglers.

Today the river is looked after equally carefully, but in an ecologically friendly manner. This is best described by those directly involved in the management of the river. Warren Slaney and Gareth Pedley, the waterkeepers, and Richard Ward, a committed Wye angler, provided the pertinent detail.

River Wye near Bakewell

'The strategy is to put the rivers and their inhabitants first before any other consideration. Every action with regard to the rivers and their environs and the creatures that dwell in and around them has to be sustainable. The trout and grayling sustain their own numbers by natural breeding. This preserves the unique strains of fish that have adapted themselves to these rivers since the ice receded. To create and maintain the best possible environment for successful natural breeding, and growing on of the fish population the best conditions for food production have to be created too. This is done by careful husbandry, a combination of hard manual work linked with the modern understanding of fishery biology.

Great effort is taken to ensure sunlight can reach the riverbed so that *Ranunculus fluitans* can gain ascendancy wherever the flows are strong enough and the sun can reach. This leads to scoured gravels that make good redds for both trout and grayling and to large communities of invertebrates (including freshwater 'shrimp').

In-stream structures like living willow fences have been erected to protect banks against erosion and provide more habitat for fry, crawl-down ovipositing flies, voles, dippers and wrens. There are many examples of soft engineering with woody debris, root spreading plants and carefully positioned stones that move the current around to make more riffles and feed lanes. These disturbed surface areas attract fly-down, ovipositing flies like the Sherry Spinner, every egg laden female that is attracted to these light catching features makes one less that wastes her eggs on parked cars, shiny tarmac and puddles.

As well as in-stream structures there are buffer fences at many points along the river-banks. These prevent damage to the banks from livestock and provide strips of uncultivated land right next to the river. Flies like the Hawthorne and the Soldier Beetle abound in these areas as their larvae are safe from trampling hooves. These terrestrials are still as important here to the fly fisher as they were in the days before intensive farming, thanks to such protective measures.'

A further example taken from the Haddon Estate Fisheries Newsletter *Water-lines* No 2 involves an initiative on the river Lathkill.

'It would seem that there's a lot more to those fences and fallow banks than first meets the eye. A length of the Lathkill comes to mind that three years ago had one resident trout and about four or five more 'just passing through'. There was clearly only room for one to live there and the others only paused on their way elsewhere. Warren put the Haddon husbandry into action last year with living fences and other in-stream structures. Ten months later instead of one trout it was possible to see and count thirty resident trout and a couple of grayling!'

The natural fly life of the rivers Wye, Lathkill and Bradford is plentiful and varied. Richard Ward once more provides the following monthly lists.

'If we consider the months of the trout season and add in the grayling fishing up to December, then for the Haddon Estate's reaches of the Derbyshire Wye, the Lathkill and the Bradford, the natural flies are to be found in most years as follows:

March/April	February Red, Large Dark Olive, Hawthorn in small but regular numbers, the Blue Winged Olive and its spinner the 'Sherry Spinner'.
May	Hawthorn until mid-May. Still in small numbers but growing, the Blue Winged Olive and the 'Sherry Spinner'. From mid-May the Green Drake and its spinner, the Needle Fly and Willow Fly, various Midges, the Yellow Sally (seen a lot but usually ignored in the presence of the Drake), and the Medium Olive.
June	the Green Drake and its spinner. In greatly increasing numbers now the Blue Winged Olive and its 'Sherry Spinner'. Needle Fly, Willow Fly and Midge. Yellow Sally, mostly ignored, the Medium Olive and various Sedges now show themselves, the Caenis well worth persevering with despite the horror stories, the Pale Watery and its carroty coloured spinner.
July	the now essential Blue Winged Olive and 'Sherry Spinner'. The Needle Fly and Willow Fly, still the Midges, Reed Smuts, Medium Olives, more Sedges (various), Caenis, Pale Watery and spinner. Soldier Beetle, Daddy Long Legs if no drought.
August	the Blue Winged Olive and 'Sherry Spinner'. Midges are still important, Reed Smuts, Medium Olive, Sedges (various), Caenis, Pale Watery and spinner. Soldier Beetle, Daddy Long Legs, the now rare Iron Blue Dun (if it comes and no suitable artificial is to hand then a golden opportunity is wasted), the quite big August Dun and its spinner.
September	Blue Winged Olive and 'Sherry Spinner', Midge, Medium Olive, Sedges (various), the Large Dark Olive starts to show up in hatches of short duration, Daddy Long Legs.
October	and later the Blue Winged Olive and 'Sherry Spinner,' Midge, and and later Sedges (various), Large Dark Olive and a few Daddy Long Legs.

MATCHING THE HATCH – Patterns for the Wye.

Natural Fly	Artificial Fly
APRIL	
Large Dark Olive	Adams, Grey Duster
Olive Upright	Adams, Grey Duster
Hawthorn Fly	Hawthorn
Terrestrials	Double Badger, small sedges, Red Tag, Sturdy's Fancy

MAY

| Medium Olive Spinners | Tups Indispensible and variants, Rusty Spinners |
| Mayfly | Grey Wulff and variants |

JUNE

Mayfly	as May
Blue Winged Olive	Sherry Spinner, Rusty Spinner
Pale Watery	Sparse Tups Indispensible, Small Grey Dusters
Pale Watery Spinner	Small Rusty Spinner
Midges and Smuts	Black Gnat, Grey C D C

JULY AND AUGUST

Blue Winged Olive	Sherry Spinner, 'Moderns'
Sedges	Elk, Deer and Hare's Ear Sedges
Daddy Long Legs	Daddy Long Legs
August Dun – Olive	Large Grey Duster, Kite's Imperial, Greenwell's Glory – up to size 12

SEPTEMBER

| Large Dark Olive | As early season, Sturdy's Fancy for grayling |

RIVER LATHKILL

The Lathkill's source is above Monyash but the infant river has dissolved an underground course through the upper dale and so does not appear for about a mile. Around the end of Cales Dale, it appears as an upland brook, gradually enlarging as it wends toward Haddon. From here it becomes of real interest to the angler. There are a considerable number of high and low weirs in Lathkill, which have been constructed to improve angling there. These works took place during the nineteenth century. In Walter Gallichan's time (1905) a Mr Symington had the riparian rights on this piece of water, along with a fishing lodge on the river. The larger weirs still have the remains of buildings alongside, which presumably housed equipment connected with control of the sluices in the river.

The result of the weirs has been to widen the river and channel the flow, creating large attractive pools, parts of which appear to be of considerable depth. The banks are flat with adequate space for stalking and casting to the dark shapes which glide between the weedbeds. Towards Conksbury Bridge are large pools alongside the Lathkill. These would appear to be works of the trout hatchery and model fishery, which Gallichan mentions in *Fishing in Derbyshire and Around*.

Below Conksbury, the river flows through meadows towards Raper Lodge, the waterkeeper's home and two weirs. There are stock ponds alongside the river and

Lathkill Dale, the various works and weirs were created to improve
and preserve the water for angling.

upstream of the small bridge and horseshoe weir a lovely pool with weedbeds and some impressive trout. Notices are posted to try to persuade walkers to refrain from feeding bread to the fish, but the temptation must be great as the fish are huge. Below the bridge on the left bank is a small building, probably the Marquess of Granby's fishing pavilion, mentioned by W M Gallichan and by Raymond Hill. The Marquess of Granby owned the Lathkill fishing rights in Gallichan's time and the river is still preserved and controlled by the Haddon Estate.

The Lathkill continues its journey to Alport, backed by low limestone outcrops and woodland. Here it receives the river Bradford, passing through the village to the mill pool, which is the home of some very large trout, whose diet is supplemented by the offerings of passing visitors. The river flows parallel to the road and turns towards Bowers Hall. From here on, to its confluence with the river Wye, the course is through flat meadows with trimmed trees and buffer strips on its banks. The buffer strips are designed to protect the banks and to provide an environment for terrestrial insects. This length was once known as the Dakin River.

The water of the Lathkill has a legendary clarity. Charles Cotton, writing in 1676, says *'Lathkin is, by many degrees, the purest and most transparent stream that I ever yet saw.'* His remarks are as true today as when they were penned. The clarity is astonishing.

Lathkill Dale is an important site. The woodlands are of national botanic importance, the birdlife spectacular and, needless to say, it has a varied and numerous population of insects. Much of this is thanks to centuries of preservation, primarily for angling, but all aspects have benefited as a result.

RIVER BRADFORD

The Bradford rises near Middleton and flows first through a wooded dale, then through a series of large weirs or dams, controlled by sluices. This has a similar effect to those on the Lathkill, in that large pools are created with both shallows and then deeper water near the dam heads. There is prolific weed growth, which gives excellent cover and no doubt provides a large reservoir of aquatic food. The dams are stocked with trout. In times past, children from Youlgreave swam in these dams in the absence of the bailiffs. Walter Gallichan had some fishing here, courtesy of Miss Melland of Middleton Hall, and he was very appreciative of the privilege. The river in the lower dale reverts to the form of a smaller river, though still with low weirs and a head of fish. Here it is a series of swift runs, riffles and shallow pools.

The waters pass under a stone packhorse style footbridge beneath Youlgreave, past what Gallichan called the 'Fisherman's Cottage'. He lived in Youlgreave at Crimble Cottage and enjoyed fishing rights on several rivers in the locality. The river deepens but does not really increase in size below Youlgreave, continuing its journey until it reaches Alport where it joins the river Lathkill.

RIVER NOE

The river Noe rises on the slopes of Kinder Scout near Edale Head, flowing down to Upper Booth where it is joined by Crowden Brook. It continues through Edale, gathering the waters of Grindesbrook and then Jagger's Clough by Bagshawe Bridge. The enlarged river flows south and is next joined by the limestone impregnated Peakshole Water from Castleton. Another limestone stream, Bradwell Brook, enters the Noe at Brough, the confluence with the Derwent occurring below Bamford. Some water is abstracted from the upper reaches via an aqueduct to Ladybower Reservoir.

In 1861, the Peak Forest Angling Club was formed with six members. The club has fished the water since that time, though with a gradually increasing membership. There are now 30 members and a waiting list.

In 1905, W M Gallichan reported, '*A rather high rent is paid for the water*'. The bailiff at that time was George Ashton, who lived at the riverside near Hope. Ashton was a very experienced angler and fly dresser. The club secretary was a Mr P Rhodes, who travelled from Rotherham to fish the river.

The Noe and its tributaries are rich in insect life and contain a good stock of trout and grayling. Peak Forest Angling Club stocks the lower reaches to supplement the fish population. The club produces a comprehensive booklet for members which, along with the club rules, provides a map, advice on beats, tackle, natural fly distribution and artificial fly patterns. The Noe provides classic small freestone river fishing in lovely surroundings.

RIVER ECCLESBOURNE

Toward the other end of the Derwent is the Ecclesbourne. The river rises near Wirksworth and flows down the valley past Idridgehay, Shottle, Windley and Hazelwood to enter the Derwent near Duffield. It is a small river flowing through pastures along a tree lined course. It is a place for small rods, light lines and an ability to stalk fish. There is a good provision of both aquatic and terrestrial food for the fish in a lovely setting.

RIVER AMBER

The Amber rises above Kelstedge, flowing off the slope of East Moor to be impounded by Ogston reservoir. This is a mature and interesting stillwater trout fishery. Soon after the river is released from Ogston, it is joined by the brook carrying water from the Linacre reservoirs. The river flows south aquiring the Alfreton Brook from near Blackwell.

This, like the Amber, has had a reputation for pollution incidents. My father, who spent much time by Alfreton Brook in the first two decades of the twentieth century, remembered it as a clean stream with much birdlife, water voles and many fish in those years.

Lumbley Pool on the river Noe.

The river winds its way past the mill at South Wingfield and along the valley bottom below Pentrich. The Chatsworth Archive records trout being stocked at South Wingfield in 1939. From Wingfield Park the river runs alongside the A610 and enters the Derwent at Ambergate just above Half Penny Bridge. The Amber holds a good stock of fish including grayling.

RIVER BLYTHE

The Blythe rises on Watley Moor above Stoke-on-Trent. It follows a course through Cresswell, Newton, Church Leigh and Woodcock Heath. At Blithfield its waters are impounded by the reservoir. From here it passes near Hampstall Ridware to its confluence with the Trent at Nethertown. The river has some history of pollution incidents. In places its course has been altered somewhat, as below Cresswell Bridge, where it has been straightened and contained by walls.

The upper reaches have been fished for trout and grayling, pollution permitting, for a long period. The Blythe has acquired a permanent place in the annals of angling, for it was on this river that Alfred Ronalds fished and conducted his research on trout. The observations recorded in *The Fly-Fisher's Entomology* were conducted from the observatory he built at or on Cresswell Bridge. In Ronalds's time there was a pool below the bridge. That has now gone, but the river upstream is probably much the same.

Overlooking the bridge and the old station yard is a public house. On its gable end and sign, it bears the legend 'The Izaak Walton at Cresswell'. Perhaps another angler passed this way long before Ronalds.

William Shipley's remarks about the Blythe, written in 1838, tell that '...*the river abounded with trout and grayling*'. It was evidently widely known for the quality of its fishing in his time.

Where to Fish by H D Turing lists the river as having trout, grayling and coarse fish in 1939, but much of the water preserved angling. In more recent times Bill Tagg, a well known angler and fly dresser from Stafford, fished the Blythe. Writing in *The Art of Fly Dressing* (1970), he recalls his son taking a large trout on a Red Ant. On another occasion Bill Tagg lost a good fish on a Dry Olive imitation of his own design.

In the foreword of *The Art of Fly Dressing* is advice, which echoes that of Alfred Ronalds, Aldam's 'Old Man' and others who have tied flies for the streams of Derbyshire and Staffordshire over centuries.

'I have aimed at getting neatness first, then likeness, durability and finally life or movement into the fly...'

CHAPTER SEVEN

TRAVEL AND ACCOMMODATION FOR ANGLERS

In Charles Cotton's time, travel was limited to walking, horseback or a carriage for those with the means to hire or purchase a vehicle. As time passed, coaches became available but moving about the countryside was slow and arduous. The state of roads, especially in winter, was unreliable and at times simply impassable. Toll bars were established in the early sixteen hundreds and with them came better routes, along with more accommodation for travellers. To face such journeys, only very keen anglers would have travelled far. Izaak Walton and Charles Cotton were evidently such men.

The *Talbot Inn* (demolished in 1786) in Ashbourne market place was the anticipated resting place for 'Viator' in Cotton's account. It would have taken almost a day to travel from his previous lodging in Derby to complete the journey. Cotton persuaded him to go on to Beresford, a further seven miles or so. A long day indeed.

William Shipley praises the angling facilities of his home town. He lists all the local waters, adding that the town is within a morning's walking distance of the Wye, Derwent, Churnet, Blythe and Manifold. The *Wheatsheaf* and the *Green Man* are named as two suitable hostelries where anglers could obtain good accommodation and information:

> 'However, we think we know to whom they will direct their angling guests who either seek for local information as to fly-fishing, or for rods, tackle and flies. It may be to ourselves, or it may not - but we think the party does not live within one hundred miles from either hotel...'

It was the advent of railways which truly opened up the countryside to large numbers of people intent on business and, more importantly to anglers, pleasure. The rivers of Derbyshire and Staffordshire became far more accessible to anglers nationwide, but especially so for those from Derby, Sheffield and Manchester. Whilst many were content to travel and fish in the day, others preferred to take accommodation near the fishings. Hotels and inns furnished this accommodation, many also offering access to good private water, guides and tackle.

One of the first, and perhaps the best known, of these hotels is the *Izaak Walton*. The following item comes from David Foster's *The Scientific Angler*.

> 'For the benefit of anglers desirous of fishing the Dove and its tributaries in Derbyshire and Staffordshire, the following information is given:- Tickets for the

GREEN MAN INN

AND

BLACK'S HEAD HOTEL,

ASHBOURNE.

Robert Wallace, Proprietor.

AT this long established and first-class house parties will find every accommodation, and every attention is paid to their comfort and wants. Private Apartments and every convenience.

Commercial Gentlemen will here find an excellent and Comfortable Room always ready for them, with Good Beds, &c.

The Tourist, Angler, and Artist will find this a most excellent and convenient house, as it is near to the river DOVE and the scenery of the neighbourhood is very beautiful.

POST HORSES, FLYS, ETC.

An Omnibus meets every Train at Ashbourne Station.

"PEACOCK INN," ROWSLEY.

MR. COOPER

BEGS to return his grateful thanks to the Nobility, Gentry, and the Public in general, for the liberal patronage bestowed upon him since he took to the management of the OLD ESTABLISHED HOTEL, the "PEACOCK," at ROWSLEY; and he respectfully begs leave to solicit a continuance of the patronage so long bestowed on his predecessor. No efforts will be wanting on his part to deserve the favourable opinion and support of his Friends and the Public, by providing the best accommodation and supplying articles of the first quality.

The "PEACOCK" has long been a favourite and central resting place for the Peak Tourist, the Sketcher, the Poet, and the Angler. Roads may be said to radiate from it to several of the most interesting points in that romantic region : Haddon Hall, Chatsworth, Monsal Dale, Rowter Rocks, Buxton, Matlock, and many other places of note are, comparatively speaking, at hand ; while the facilities for reaching the more remote wonders and beauties of the district are all that the traveller, the loiterer, or the man of business could desire.

The Rowsley Railway Terminus is very near to this House.

Parties staying at this Hotel have the privilege of FREE TICKETS for FISHING in the rivers WYE and DERWENT, which run close by the Hotel and abound in Trout and Grayling of the finest quality.

As a Fishing Station, and as a centre where Visitors may enjoy the romantic beauties of the Peak of Derbyshire, the "Peacock" possesses every possible attraction and convenience.

Post Horses and Carriages

Provided for parties requiring them.

GOOD STABLING AND LOCK-UP COACH-HOUSES ON THE PREMISES.

The "Peveril of the Peak" Hotel, THORPE, DOVEDALE.

THIS Hotel, which is situated on one of the most lovely and picturesque parts of Derbyshire, near the entrance to Dovedale, and within a short distance of ILAM HALL, affords every possible convenience and comfort to the Tourist and the Angler, as well as to Families. The "PEVERIL OF THE PEAK" is situated close to DOVEDALE, and consequently is particularly convenient to Visitors to that delightful locality.

TICKETS FOR FISHING IN THE DOVE MAY BE HAD AT THE HOTEL.

MRS. WATERFALL,

PROPRIETRESS.

Dovedale length – which is some three miles in length – are issued by Mr W Prince, the host of the Izaak Walton Hotel, to his guests, price 1s 6d per diem. An additional length on the Manifold, and another shorter stretch of water on the Dove in the middle of the Okeover Club length can be fished by guests at this hotel; a ticket for all the above water being obtainable at 2s 6d per day, or 7s 6d per week.

The Dove Dale length is between four and five miles from Ashbourne Station. The new line, to be completed in Eighteen Ninety Nine, will bring Dove Dale within one mile of the L. & N.W. Railway's Thorpe Cloud Station. This new line, connecting as it is doing Ashbourne with the L. & N.W. main line from Manchester to London (via Buxton), will open up also the Beresford Dale water. The tickets for this length at 2s 6d per day are issued by Mr H Oliver host of the "Charles Cotton" Hotel; also an adjoining length may be fished by the guests at a boarding house viz., at Hartington Hall, Mr Wardle being the proprietor.'

Milldale's trout could be accessed by visitors to the *New Inn Hotel* on the Ashbourne-Buxton Road. The hotel is about a mile away, but a long mile back up a very steep hill. Day tickets were 1s 6d and were sold by Mr C Prince, the proprietor. The station was adjacent to the hotel. The Tissington Trail now follows the railway route. Most hotels had arrangements to meet trains with their 'omnibus' and deliver their guests in comfort. The *Dog and Partridge* at Thorpe also issued tickets for certain stretches of the Dove.

The lower Dove waters were served from Uttoxeter by the *White Hart* and *Talbot Inn*. The latter advertised itself as 'clean and old fashioned'. That would be an interesting stay!

The Manifold fishers who did not stay in the Dovedale inns put up at the *Crewe and Harpur* at Longnor or the *Watts Russell Arms* near Wetton. A hundred years ago the Manifold was, as now, a highly regarded river but at that time the access was limited. Much was in the remit of Sir Vauncey Crewe and very private water.

The upper Derwent waters were served by the *Snake Inn*. Near the inn, the two streams which made up the river Ashop joined, prior to the construction of the reservoirs. Up to August a number of rooms were to let but after the twelfth they were booked by grouse shooting parties. The *Snake Inn* offered six miles of fishing on a guinea season ticket or at 2s 6d per day. The river Ashop joined the Derwent near the now submerged village of Ashopton, located near the end of the Ladybower road bridge. A little further downstream the Ladybower Brook joined. The *Ashopton Inn*, now submerged, was described by Walter Gallichan as 'a model public house'. It was under the control of the People's Refreshment House Association, whose president was the Bishop of Chester. Here was good food, hot baths and three miles of trout water at 2s 6d per day with a reduction for guests. The manager would pick up guests at Bamford railway station. There is a telling remark from Gallichan, in *Fishing in Derbyshire and Around*, about the *Ashopton Inn*, '...there are occasions when a cup of tea is more enjoyable than a glass of ale...'

The *Ladybower Inn* provided accommodation for anglers along with a quarter mile

CHATSWORTH.

Edensor Hotel.

WILLIAM JEPSON,

THE Proprietor, begs to inform Visitors to Derbyshire that the Hotel is

BEAUTIFULLY SITUATED IN CHATSWORTH PARK,

and in the immediate vicinity of the princely residence of the Duke of Devonshire, a palace adorned with *chef d'œuvres* of art, and liberally embellished by nature. The Hotel offers every comfort and accommodation to Tourists, and is within easy distance of the Romantic Scenery of the Peak of Derbyshire, which has been justly pronounced by foreigners and other visitors to be unsurpassed by the most beautiful parts of Switzerland. The Midland Railway, intersecting England between London and York, has a branch from Ambergate Station to Rowsley Station, where an Omnibus from the Hotel meets every train; fare, 6d. This affords a delightful drive through Chatsworth Park. Parties staying at the Hotel can be accommodated with tickets for fly fishing in the river Derwent, which runs through the Park. A LADIE'S COFFEE ROOM for those parties not requiring private rooms.

THE

"DOG & PARTRIDGE" HOTEL,

DOVEDALE, ASHBOURNE,

DERBYSHIRE.

ACCOMMODATION FOR PICNIC PARTIES,

. . . GOOD STABLING.

Carriages meet Trains by Appointment, Ashbourne, N.S.R.

APARTMENTS.   FISHING.

GEORGE TOMLINSON, Proprietor.

stretch of fishing, and the *Yorkshire Bridge Inn*, now rebuilt above water level, had three quarters of a mile on the Derwent. The season cost one pound, a day cost two shillings.

There was good trout and grayling fishing on the Derwent a hundred years ago. The *Marquess of Granby* at Bamford had a well-known stretch available for 2s 6d per day to residents. Lower down the valley, other establishments had limited day tickets again for residents supplied by the Chatsworth Fishery. The *Chequers* had ten, *Baslow Hydro* and the *Wheatsheaf* fifteen, the *Rutland* at Baslow forty and unlimited numbers were allocated to the *Chatsworth Hotel* at Edensor and *Peacock* at Rowsley. This system led to 'misunderstandings' of the fishery rules by visiting anglers and the Chatsworth files contain numbers of warnings to both local and visiting fishers. In 1899, day tickets were three shillings a day when available. Day tickets priced at two shillings and sixpence were available at the *Square and Compass* for the Darley Dale Angling Club water.

Matlock, like Ashbourne, was an angling centre from the mid-nineteen hundreds and maybe earlier. The railway through the Derwent valley provided transport. Before that it would have been a stage coach over Starkholmes. In the Matlocks there was a wealth of hotels, hydros, inns and boarding houses. One of the latter was run by Alfred Smedley, who was a fly dresser and tackle maker. Part of the Derwent in Matlock was 'free water', an additional attraction to the less wealthy angler. The *Derwent Hotel* at Whatstandwell, the *Hurt Arms* at Ambergate and the *Red Lion* at Belper were further hostelries with available fishing and recommended accommodation for the lower reaches of the river.

Fishers of the Wye and its tributaries had a good choice of accommodation in Bakewell. Most popular was the *Rutland Arms*, which had four tickets available on a daily basis. The *Fashionable Visitors' List* and *High Peak Tourist Guide* of May 1871 has this to say about the River Wye. 'The Wye is equal to any river in the Kingdom.' This is followed with the information that the river is on the main line of the Midland Railway Company and well stocked with grayling and trout.

Today, some of these hotels and inns still offer angling on the Dove, Derwent and Wye. The *Izaak Walton* in Dovedale and the *Charles Cotton Hotel* in Hartington have water on the Dove. The *Cavendish* at Baslow has water on the Derwent and Wye. In Rowsley, the *Peacock* offers several miles of fishing on the Wye. Much of this fishing is available only to residents, and waterkeepers are available for advice and organisation.

'Away then, away,
We lose sport by delay,
But first leave all our sorrows behind us
If misfortune do come
We are all gone from home
And a fishing she never can find us.'

The Angler's Ballad Charles Cotton

Member or poacher? A fisher in Dovedale.

POSTSCRIPT

THE DERBYSHIRE ANGLER

Anne Watson

Off he goes with his rods and reels,
fly boxes and a landing net.
Plenty of food for nineteen meals
and a towel in case he gets wet.
He's taking a priest that can't baptise.
There's no washing on his lines.
He'll be by the Dove that never flies,
(but only while the sun shines).

But when he returns home on high
with very little to show,
his wife will insist on asking Wye?
The answer is 'I don't Noe'.
Too much water or not enough,
too cloudy or too bright.
It was too calm or else too rough,
the fish didn't want to bite.

He thinks he'll have more luck next time,
he'll tie some different flies.
She smiles, she isn't being weak,
as home's like Paradise!

GLOSSARY

Anger	Dropper or dropper fly (Aldam)
Armed, Arming	Whipping gut to hook or dressing on hook (Cotton)
Barbed	Trimming hackles on flies. (Cotton)
Barm	Brewer's yeast; pale yellow colour (Cotton)
Bloa	Flies hackled with blue grey or grey hackles
Blue dun	Various shades of smoke-grey hackle colour; Light, medium, dark
Braked hemp	Hemp crushed by an instrument called a brake, to soften the material. (Walton)
Brassy dun	Hackle with smoky-blue centre and brassy tips. Sometimes an all over brassy sheen.
Brended	Branded beast hair (Cotton)
Buzz	Fly with palmered or half palmered hackle. May be sparse or heavily dressed. (Ronalds *et al*)
Camlet	Cloth of camel hair (Cotton) Today, goat or wool
Cochin	Large breed of poultry with feathered legs (Aldam)
Coch-y-bonddu	Hackle with a black centre and red fibres tipped with black. Cock-y-bondhu. Coch-y-bondhu. Coch-y-bonndu.
Cock Wing, Cocked Wing	Upwing fly (Turton, Foster)
Cod-bait	Caddis or sedge larva (Cotton)
Copperas	Ferrous sulphate, also copper-sulphate (Foster *et al*)
Cree	Hackle with alternate bars of red and black
Creeled	Alternate light and dark bars on hackles (Aldam)
Creeper	Larval stage of stoneflies. Known in some parts as Water Cricket
Crewel	Fine worsted yarn.
Croggil	Blanket weed; *Spirogyra* (Turton)
Cuckoo	Grizzle hackle (Aldam)
Daping, Dapping	Fishing live flies with long rod usually on the surface (Ronalds *et al*)
Dark water	Peat stained or flood water (Turton)
Dibbing, Dibbling	As dapping, though at times the flies or baits are weighted and allowed to sink (Aldam)
Dotterel	Substitute starling under wing. Golden plover coverts (Ronalds *et al*)
Down	Underfur; Bear down; Fox down
Drop	Dropper or dropper fly
Dun	Sub-imago of *Ephemeridae*. Hackle of a grey-brown colour. Can also mean dirty yellow
Furnace, Furniss	A deep red hackle with a black centre (Ronalds)
Greenheart.	South American hardwood of laurel genus used to make rods.
Green Linnet	Greenfinch
Greenwell	Hackle with black centre and ginger edges
Grizzle	A hackle with black and white bars across the feather (Aldam)

311

Hackle fly	A fly dressed with a body and hackle but no wing
Heron herl	Substitute wood pigeon centre tail feathers
Honey Dun	A hackle with smoky-dun centre and honey or gold tips
Iron Blue Dun	Very dark blue dun hackle
Jack Hawk	Hobby. Merlin. Substitute moorhen blue breast feathers
Landrail	Corncrake. (Ronalds *et al*) Poultry or partridge feathers are good substitutes
Link	Horsehair cast tied directly to a fly prior to fishing
Lint	To rub up the knap of cloth to obtain dubbing
Longwing	Falcon
Marten	Yellow Marten; Pine Marten
Mohair	Goat hair, partially waterproofs a fly
Moor Game	Red Grouse (Turton)
Nankeen	Buff coloured cotton cloth (Turton)
Norwegian Crow	Hooded crow
Palmer	Fly with hackle wound from shoulder to tail
Pent	Wing of a fly tied forward over the eye (Bridgett)
Pewet	Peewit; Lapwing (Turton)
Poultry	A young grouse, sometimes the young of other game birds or poultry
Puddling	The use of clay to seal the base of a pond or lake
Russian leather	Colour – buff red (Aldam)
Sea Swallow	Tern. Substitute wood pigeon or herring gull
Shett, Shott	One year old grayling
Sneck hook	Hook with angular bend, often slightly offset
Stretcher.	The cast nearest the fly. At times the point fly on a cast (Shipley)
Tammy	Glazed cotton or wool (Cotton)
Umbra	Shadow - name for grayling
White Grouse	Ptarmigan (Turton)
White Owl	Barn Owl
Wood Owl	Tawny Owl
Yallow Carrited Stuff	Dubbing created by Aldam's '*Old Man*', substitute yellow seal fur fur on primrose silk

BIBLIOGRAPHY

Adam, W. D., *Scenery, Fishing Streams and Mines of Derbyshire and Surrounding Counties*, London and Wirksworth, 1861.

Aldam, W. H., ed. *A Quaint Treatise on Flies and Flymaking by an Old Fisherman*, John B. Day, Strand, 1876.

Amateur Angler, (Edward Marston), *An Amateur Angler's Days in Dovedale* and *Dovedale Revisited*, (1884; 1902), Phoenix edition, London, 1910.

Arundo, (John Beever), *Practical Fly Fishing*, London, 1849.

Atkinson, Rev. J. C., *British Birds' Eggs and Nests*, Routledge, London, 1899.

Bowlker, Richard and Charles, *The Art of Angling*, Birmingham 2nd, 1774.

Bromley, A. Nelson, *A Fly Fisher's Reflections 1860 – 1930*, The Fishing Gazette, 1930.

Broughton, R., ed. *The Complete Book of the Grayling*, Hale, London, 2000.

Bryant, Ashley, *Riverside Journey*, Lutterworth, Cambridge, 2001.

Bucknall, Geoffrey, *The Bright Stream of Memory*, Shrewsbury, 1997.

Cadman, Henry, *Harry Druidale*, 1898, Rep. 1990 Smith Settle.

Cholmondley-Pennel, H, *Fishing*, 1885.

Cotton, Charles, *The Compleat Angler, Part II, Being Instructions how to Angle for a Trout or Grayling in a Clear Stream*, 1676: John Major, London, 1823: Ingram Cooke, 1853.

Deindorfer, Robert D., *The Incompleat Angler*, NY 1977, U.K., 1978.

Dunne, J. W., *Sunshine and the Dry Fly*, A C Black, London (1924), 1950.

Ephemera – *The Handbook of Angling* (2nd Ed), 1848, Longman, Brown, Green.

Fogg, W. S. R., *The Art of the Wet Fly*, A. C. Black, London, 1979.

Foster, David, *The Scientific Angler*, London and Derby (1882), 7th 1898.

Foster, W. L., *Fishing Tackle Making and Repairing*, London, 1929.

Gallichan, W. M., *Fishing in Derbyshire and Around*, Robinson, London, 1905.

Goddard, J., *Waterside Guide*, Hyman, London, 1988.

Granby, Marquess of, *The Trout*, Longmans, London, 1898.

Grey, Sir Edward, *Fly Fishing*, 1899, 1907.

Halford, F. M., *Dry Fly Entomology*, 1897.

Harris, J. R., *An Angler's Entomology*, Collins, London (1952), Rep. 1977.

Hayter, Tony, *F. M. Halford and the Dry Fly Revolution*, Hale, London, 2002.

Heywood, G. G. P., *Charles Cotton and His River*, Sherratt and Hughes, Manchester, 1928.

Hill, Raymond., *Wings and Hackle*, Hutchinson & Co., London ,New Ed., c. 1933

Hills, J. W., *A History of Fly Fishing for Trout*, Waller, London, 1921.

Hofland, T. C., *The British Angler's Manual*, London (1841), 1847.

Kingsmill-Moore, T. C., *A Man May Fish*, 1960, Rep. 1985.

Lake, Richard, *The Grayling*, Shrewsbury, 2nd Edn., 1946.

Lawrie, W. H., *The Book of the Rough Stream Nymph*, Edinburgh and London, 1947.

Lawrie, W. H., *A Reference Book of English Trout Flies*, London, 1967.

Lawrie, W. H., *English and Welsh Trout Flies*, London, 1967.
Leverton, Wilshaw et al., *220 Favourite Flies*, EMAP, Peterborough, 1998.

Mackenzie, Gregor., *Memoirs of a Ghillie*, David and Charles, 1978.
Magee, Leslie, *Fly Fishing The North Country Tradition*, Smith Settle, Otley, 1994, Rep. 1996.
Marriot, Ernest, G., *Izaak Walton – A Short Study*, Staffs. B. Council, 1986.

Nemes, Sylvester, *Two Centuries of Soft Hackled Flies*, Stackpole Books, PA 17055, 2004.
Neville, John, *Trials and Triumphs of an Angler*, Sheffield, 1991.
Nooe, *The Angler's Notebook and Naturalist's Record*, 31/05/1880.

Ogden, James, *Ogden on Fly Tying*, John T Norman, Cheltenham, 1879.
Overfield, T. D., *Famous Flies and their Originators*, A. & C. Black, London, 1972.
Overfield, T. D., *Fifty Favourite Dry Flies*, Ernest Benn, London, 1980.
Overfield, T. D., *Fifty Favourite Wet Flies*, A. & C. Black, London, 1986.

Parton, Steve, *The Fly School Notes*, Sparton, 2000.
Platts, William Carter, *Modern Trout Fishing*, A. & C. Black, London (1938), 4th 1961.
Platts, William Carter, *Grayling Fishing*, London, 1939.
Pritt, T. E., *The Book of the Grayling*, Leeds, 1895.
Pritt, T. E., *An Angler's Basket*, Posth. Manchester and London, 1896.
Pritt, T. E., *North Country Flies*, 1885, Rep. Smith Settle, Otley, 1995.

Reid, John, *Clyde Style Flies*, Newton Abbott, 1971, Rep. 1988.
Righyni, R. V., *Grayling*, McDonald, London, 1968.
Roberts, John, *New Illustrated Dictionary of Trout Flies*, Harper Collins, London, 1995.
Roberts, John, *Fly Fishing for Grayling*, Excellent, Ludlow, 1999.
Robson, Kenneth, *Robson's Guide*, Worcester, 1985.
Ronalds, Alfred, *The Fly Fisher's Entomology*, 1836, 5th 1856, 1921, 1990.

Shipley, W. & Fitzgibbon, E., *A True Treatise on the Art of Fly Fishing*, London, 1838.
Smith, Geoffrey A., *Reflections of a Fisherman*, Souvenir, London, 1987.
Skues, G. E. M., *Minor Tactics of the Chalk Stream*, 1910, Rep. A. & C. Black, London, 1974.
Skues, G. E. M., *Silk, Fur and Feather*, 1950, Rep. Flyfisher's Classic Library, 1993.
Skues, G. E. M., *The Way of a Trout with a Fly*, 1921, Rep. 1950.
Skues, G. E. M., *Nymph Fishing for Chalk Stream Trout*, 1939, A. & C. Black, London, Rep. 1974.
Stewart, Tom, *Two Hundred Popular Flies*, Benn, London, 1979.
Stewart, W. C., *The Practical Angler*, Edinburgh, 1857, Rep. 1927.

Tagg, Bill, *The Art of Fly Dressing*, A. & C. Black, London, 1970.
Taverner, Eric, *Fly Tying for Trout*, London.
Taverner, Eric, *Trout Fishing from all Angles*, Lonsdale Lib., Seeley, Service & Co., 1950
Turton, John, *The Angler's Manual*, 1836, R. Groombridge, London; Geo. Ridge, Sheffield.

Veale, Michael, *Fishing Flies and their Plumage*, Sportsman's Press, 1989.
Veniard, J., *Fly Dressing Materials*, A. & C. Black, London, 1977.
Voss, Bark Conrad, *Fishing for Lake Trout*, Witherby, London, 1972.
Voss, Bark Conrad, *A History of Fly Fishing*, Ludlow, 1992.

Walton, Izaak, *The Compleat Angler*, John Major, London, 1823.
Walton, Izaak, *The Compleat Angler*, Ingram Cooke, 1853.
Walton, Izaak, *The Compleat Angler*, Folio Society, 4th imp. 1966.
Williams, A. C., *A Dictionary of Flies for Trout and Grayling*, 1949, 6th 1986.
Wilson, T. K., *Trout by all Means*, Angling Times, 1966.
Woolley, R., *Modern Trout Fly Dressings*, Fishing Gazette, 1932, 3rd 1950.
Woolley, R., *Fly-Fisher's Flies*, Fishing Gazette, 1938, 3rd 1950.

CATALOGUES

Allcock's Anglers Guide, 1937.
Cummins, W. J. Catalogue. 1881, and 19--, undated.
Foster Bros., List of Trout flies. Circa 1910- undated.
Foster Bros., Fishing Rods & Tackle, 1964.
Hardy's Anglers' Guide, 1934.
Mackenzie-Philps Catalogue, 1981, 1985.
Ogden-Smiths Catalogue.
Woolley, Roger., A List of Special Trout and Grayling Flies. Circa 1918 to 1950; also catalogues issued
    into the 1970's after Roger Woolley's death by Rosa Smith who acquired the business.

JOURNALS

Derby Evening Telegraph.
Derby Mercury.
Derbyshire Life.
Derbyshire Times.
Fishing Gazette.
Matlock Guardian and List of Visitors.
Matlock Mercury.
The Journal of the Grayling Society.
Trout and Salmon.

MANUSCRIPTS AND OTHER PUBLICATIONS

Bailey, Aubrey., *The Story of Flydressing*. 1975. Unpublished.
Classic Angling., '*Shedding a little light on Foster*.' John Knott. 22. 9. 2002.
Cromford Fly Fishers Club., Member's booklet.
The Devonshire Collection Manuscripts and Accounts (Chatsworth Estate).
Derby County Angling Club., Member's booklet.
Foster Bros., Bicentenary booklet. 1963.
Leek and District Fly Fishing Association Booklet.
Ordnance Survey Landranger Sheets 118 – 120, 127 – 129, 138, 139.
Peak Forest Angling Club., Member's booklet.
Roger Woolley's papers – Colleen Benson.
Waterlines 1 and 2 – Haddon Estate Fisheries Newsletters.
Wilson, T K., Unpublished, undated, manuscript, 'Oakden's Claret.'

INDEX

July 20th	Derwent, Willersle...
	effect at all. ...
4 grayling.	grayling on the ...
	lovely trout ...
3 Browns.	Found a King...
	dipper & wagtail...
	pleasant & enj...
	Sparton rod & ...
July 26th	Shelden House - Ma...
	one on a GRHE...
5 (4)	light red/ green w...
Browns Buzzard	12oz — 1lb. Pleas...
	angles fishing on...
	one grayling on...